VISIONS
OF
THE END OF DAYS

VISIONS
OF
THE END OF DAYS

*A Kabbalistic View of
the Book of Daniel
With a Guide to
Dream Interpretations*

R. Ariel B. Tzadok

Also by R. Ariel B. Tzadok:

WALKING IN THE FIRE

Classical Torah/Kabbalistic
Meditations, Practices & Prayers.
ISBN 978-0-9791601-0-3

PROTECTION FROM EVIL

Exposing & neutralizing
harmful spiritual forces.
ISBN 979-8-554-63579-3

ALIENS, ANGELS, & DEMONS

Extraterrestrial life in
Judaism & Kabbalah
ISBN 979-8-557-29557-4

Available on Amazon.com

Check out our courses in all areas of study

Available at **www.koshertorah.com**

YouTube: **KosherTorah School of Rabbi Ariel Bar Tzadok**

Visions of the End of Days

A Kabbalistic View of the Book of Daniel With a Guide to Dream Interpretations
Copyright © 1993-2020 by Ariel Bar Tzadok. All rights reserved.

The KosherTorah School
for Biblical, Judaic & Spiritual Studies
www.koshertorah.com
arieltzadok@gmail.com

ISBN: 979-8-554-64539-6

Layout, graphic and cover design by: Dovid S. Brandes
Kabbalistic artwork for sale at *www.brandesart.com*

PROUDLY PRINTED IN THE USA

וַיֹּאמֶר שִׁמְעוּ־נָא דְבָרָי
אִם־יִהְיֶה נְבִיאֲכֶם ה׳
בַּמַּרְאָה אֵלָיו אֶתְוַדָּע
בַּחֲלוֹם אֲדַבֶּר־בּוֹ׃

"He said, "Please listen to My words.
If there be prophets among you,
[I] the L-rd will make Myself known to him in a vision;
I will speak to him in a dream."

Numbers 12:6

"The dream is a little hidden door in the innermost and most secret recesses of the soul, opening into that cosmic night which was psyche long before there was any ego consciousness, and which will remain psyche no matter how far our ego-consciousness extends.

For all ego-consciousness is isolated; because it separates and discriminates, it knows only particulars, and it sees only those that can be related to the ego. Its essence is limitation, even though it reach to the farthest nebulae among the stars.

All consciousness separates; but in dreams we put on the likeness of that more universal, truer, more eternal man dwelling in the darkness of primordial night. There he is still the whole, and the whole is in him, indistinguishable from nature and bare of all egohood. It is from these all-uniting depths that the dream arises, be it never so childish, grotesque, and immoral."

Carl Jung
"The Meaning of Psychology for Modern Man" (1933)
In CW 10: Civilization in Transition. pg. 304

TABLE OF CONTENTS

SECTION THREE
JEWISH & KABBALISTIC MESSIANIC TEACHINGS

Dream & Hope

Dreams and hopes,
they are both great things,
they are both necessary things.
Dreams and hopes are what make
us human beings to be so very special.

I see things as they are today,
and I dream and hope
that there can be a better tomorrow.
If there is no hope for a better tomorrow,
then why tolerate the sad state of things today?

Evolution is real, because there is
a Law Giver, behind the laws of nature.
Evolution is nature's law,
therefore, it is the Creator's Law.
Evolution takes us from young to mature.
Evolution takes us from simple to complex.
Evolution takes us out of the dark, and into the light.
This is the Way and the Plan of the
Creator/Law Giver.

It is the Way and the Plan
for each of us to grow, to mature,
and to evolve spiritually,
from beings conceived in darkness,
into beings experienced in the light.

Evolution is a long road,
and walking its path takes a long time.
Evolution does not just happen randomly,
the Law is not random, it is very well fixed.
Yet, like life itself, we and the Law
flow with the tides of change.

Evolution is each individual's guided path.
The Creator guides, through the inner Voice,
heard within each heart.
When we listen, we hear.
When we listen, we know.
When we know, we do.
Doing the right things
is how the Path is walked.

We learn to listen, we learn to know,
we learn to do.
We evolve, from not knowing to knowing.
In this way, we follow the path of life
through the Valley of the Shadow of Death,
and into the wonderful light
of a successful, fulfilling,
and wonderful life.

Dreams and hopes guide this path.
Therefore, dream big!
Hope for the best of the best!
Maybe we will accomplish all,
then again, maybe we will accomplish less.
With dreams and hopes as our guide,
we can follow the path of spiritual evolution,
and transform ourselves into the
very best beings that our imagination can imagine.

When the rational mind (Binah)
merges with the intuitive heart (Hokhma),
we have the merging of the parents
of proper knowing,
and proper doing.

*There is no great mystical lesson
than this one.
There is no better practical lesson.*

*Do not seek G-d in Heaven.
On the contrary,
seek G-d down here on Earth.
As we grow up,
Heaven grows down.
We meet in the middle,
and that is where we will find our Paradise*

SECTION ONE

VISIONS IN THE BOOK OF DANIEL

Introduction

The Origins of Apocalyptic Literature

The Bible is full of prophetic proclamations for the future. The majority of such prophetic warnings, and proclamations were meant to be fulfilled in the historically not-too-distant future from the time that G-d spoke them to the individual prophets. However, there was another set of prophecies that dealt with the far-off future, when life on Earth as we know it would be drastically changed.

These prophecies are referred to as dealing with Messianic times. This is a time after a Messiah would come from G-d, and set the world straight. This Messiah would institute a comprehensive "new" world order of righteousness and holiness, where G-d is to be King over all humanity. The entire world is to be restored to the ways of peace, natural harmony, and brotherhood. Interestingly however, the majority of these same Messianic prophecies never refer to the coming of this Messiah specifically, nor do most of the prophecies relate specifically what it is that the Messiah is supposed to do, or whether it is he, or G-d that brings about the Messianic era.

Messianic prophecies relating to what life will be like after the coming of Messiah is not the topic of these lessons. Rather, our present investigation is to focus on the pre-Messianic times, which is the time period, or actually the process of how the world is to be transformed from its present course into something so profoundly different. Collectively, this period of pre-Messianic times have come to be known as the End of Days, Aharit HaYamim in the original Hebrew.

The Bible does not present one set, clear scenario as to how the End of Days are to unfold, all the more so as to when they will begin or end. Since Biblical times the End of Days has been a hot topic, with almost every generation believing that theirs was the End of Days. To this day, we see that each generation to have believed so was mistaken. Yet, what they believed, and why they believed it, needs to be understood.

The fear of the End of Days seems to be something deeply ingrained in the human psyche. Before we can ever understand why this is so, from a psychological point of view, we must first understand the concept of the End of Days, how it developed and how it has become the "fearsome monster" that it has become.

Here we are again in current times believing ourselves to be in the End of Days, with all the fear and terror this is bringing upon us. Whether or not our days are the actual End of Days, only time will tell. We may be right when everyone before us was wrong. Then again, we may be as wrong as they were, with the Biblical End of Days still to be at some unknown distant future date.

A full and comprehensive investigation of the concept of the Apocalypse, the destruction of the old world to make way for the new, which comes in the End of Days, is now appropriate. By understanding the origins of the concept of Apocalypse and its relationship to the End of Days, we can come to terms with elements in modern religious circles, Jewish, Christian and Muslim each of which has developed out of original and ancient apocalyptic, End of Days religious beliefs and expectations.

The actual genesis of Apocalyptic literature in the Biblical tradition, meaning both the Judaic and Christian schools, has its origins in the writings of the Biblical prophets, with specific emphasis on those who we call the later prophets, specifically those living in, or close to, (before or after) the Babylonian exile.

The exile and its aftermath seemed to have been a pivotal point in the history and destiny of the nation of Israel and, for that matter, the world. In order to place Apocalyptic literature in its place in the greater scope of Biblical studies, we must turn to the Bible to understand the Biblical plan for humanity. This is spelled out for us, specifically, in the Book of Daniel.

Daniel was a visionary, and a mystic sage, living in Babylon. But interestingly, however revelatory his visions were, never did Daniel receive a direct communication from G-d, as did the earlier prophets. Nor did any angel with whom Daniel ever interacts bring him the Word of G-d, as was brought to prophets both before him, and after him. At no time with regards to Daniel do we hear, (or see written), *"and the L-rd spoke to Daniel, saying, 'Speak to...'etc."*

Daniel was clearly connected spiritually, but nevertheless, he was not considered one of the Biblical prophets. As such, the Book of Daniel, while included in the Jewish canon, is still part of the third section, called the Writings (Ketuvim), and not part of the second section called the Prophets (Neviim). This difference is significant in that Daniel's revelations came from angels, but not from G-d directly. It is implied, therefore, that Daniel's visions, while being holy Writings, but not Prophecy, are not as clear and coherent as are the words of prophecy coming directly as they do from G-d.

Daniel's book, and his visions, therefore, are highly symbolic, and in need of not only interpretation, but outright decipherment. This skill was not lost to the members of his generation, or to those Sages of Israel who followed. It is from within Daniel that Apocalyptic literature has its origins. Granted, we can also turn to later prophets such as Zechariah, but Daniel came first, and has to be understood first.

As for earlier prophecies found in the other earlier prophets, most of these speak of the ultimate fall of specific nations, however at the time of their writings most of these prophecies were understood with regards to their immediate historicity and not as referring to the End of Days. Therefore, rather than start with them, we will return to them in other writings, and review them both in historical context as well as in light of growing Apocalyptic revelations.

While many later religious authorities and commentators point to specific verses in earlier scripture as having application to the End of Days and to messianic times, when we see the individual verses in context, we recognize that they are interpretations of a more moralistic and symbolic nature, rather than literal. Essentially, anything can be twisted and turned, and made into a Messianic prophecy. But just by doing so does not make the scripture verse any more authentic of a Messianic prophecy. We will deal with scriptural interpretations within the context of the later authorities who use these verses to somehow strengthen or to validate their points.

We must first begin with Daniel, and how Daniel is meant to be properly understood.

<u>Chapter 1</u>

Prophecy, Dreams & Interpreting Dream Symbols in Judaism & Christianity

Not only Daniel, but every other known case of actual revelation of original End Times/Apocalyptic content has come through visions, and dreams. Many authors have penned works quoting books they have read, or traditions they may have heard, but all such accounts have to be deemed second-hand, and viewed as hearsay. Only those individuals who have personally experienced Apocalyptic visions, and who can record them diligently can be accepted as first-hand direct information, the likes of which add to, and build the genre of authentic Apocalypticism. Therefore, throughout these lessons, I will be making reference to First-Degree Apocalyptic material, which is experiential in nature, and to Second-Degree Apocalyptic material, which is academic, philosophical, or anything other than a direct personal revelation.

Being that dreams and visions are the only true authentic vehicle through which authentic Apocalyptic content is received, we must understand the symbolic, archetypal nature of dream/vision language. Without such an understanding when we come to view Apocalyptic content, we completely and comprehensively misunderstand it. Something expressed in its original language has to be understood in that original language, or translated properly and accurately into another. Those who interpret dream symbols literally have no idea of what they are talking about. Let us shortly digress to discuss dream language, and symbolism.

It is presently a well-documented, scientific, psychological fact that dream content emanates from the unconscious, and is perceived and remembered as a series of images. These images, which may include dialogue, are completely symbolic, with no apparent literal reality to them whatsoever. The truth of this is clear from numerous Biblical examples, one of which is King Nebuchadnezzar's dream, recorded in Daniel, Chapter 2.

The King dreamed of a statue that Daniel clearly interprets as a symbol. In an earlier Biblical account, recorded in Genesis, Pharaoh dreams of seeing fat cows and skinny cows, plump grain and withering grain. Joseph interpreted his dream symbols, in similar fashion as Daniel interpreted Nebuchadnezzar's. Pharaoh's dream had no literal relationship or meaning to cows, fat or skinny or to grain, plump or parched.

Nebuchadnezzar's dream, likewise, had nothing to do with an actual statue, or an actual stone. Dream images are pictorial symbols, and they need to be interpreted, and understood correctly or their message is entirely lost.

When it comes to understanding Apocalyptic literature of the actual first-degree revelation kind, we must always apply this rule. Every individual dreamer or mystic who has a dream, or sees a vision of the future Apocalypse is seeing it through the same series of pictorial images, and symbolisms as are every other dreaming human being. All the perceived symbols, including and especially those written down in a book must be understood, and interpreted and never taken at face value. To understand dream or vision symbolism at face value can be considered a crime against the human psyche.

Thus we find in all later prophecies, Daniel and even Zechariah, when a vision is perceived, and there is an angelic entity involved, a symbol is shown, a question is asked whether or not the image is understood, and then an interpretation is given right there in the vision or dream as to what the symbols actually mean. Whenever we have such symbolic language, and no interpretation follows, we are left with a series of images with no key to unlocking them. They in turn remain a closed book.

Daniel 2:19 begins Daniel's narrative with the King, and is continued in verse 26. King Nebuchadnezzar dreamed his dream, and summarily forgot it. Realizing that his forgotten dream was somehow very important, he commanded his wise men to tell him what his dream was, and what it meant. Not one of the King's wise men was able to perform this apparently impossible feat. Daniel, as a normal human being, is also not able to delve into another person's unconscious, and extract from there forgotten dream content. Although he did exactly this, the text is clear that this revelation did not come about due to Daniel's abilities but rather through a direct intervention from what the text calls, "visions of the night." In other words, G-d spoke to Daniel in his dreams, and revealed to him the dream of the King. This interesting insight is very much related to Biblical prophecy, where G-d Himself states in Number 12:6, *"If there be prophets among you, [I] the L-rd will make Myself known to him in a vision; I will speak to him in a dream."* We will review King Nebuchadnezzar's dream, and Daniel's interpretation of it in the following lesson.

What we see from the Biblical record is that dreams are G-d's chosen form of communication with man. This is clear from the Biblical examples of Joseph, Pharaoh's cup-bearer, and baker, Pharaoh himself, Nebuchadnezzar, and later Daniel himself. In each and every one of these cases, the dreams experienced are expressed in what we now today recognize as normative, psychological, archetypal imagery. Each dream relates symbolic images, each in need of interpretation. Let us review the Biblical record of each account.

Genesis 37:5-10 - *"And Joseph dreamed a dream, and he told it to his brothers... And he said to them: 'Hear, I pray you, this dream which I have dreamed: for, behold, we were binding sheaves in the field, and my sheaf arose and also stood upright and behold, your sheaves came round about, and bowed down to my sheaf. And his brothers said to him: 'Shalt you indeed reign over us? Or shall you indeed have dominion over us?' ...And he dreamed yet another* *dream, and told it to his brothers, and said, 'I have dreamed a dream and behold, the sun, the moon and eleven stars bowed down to me.' And he told it to his father and to his brothers and his father rebuked him, and said to him: 'What is this dream that you have dreamed? Shall I, your mother and your brothers indeed come to bow down to you?"*

Gen 40:9-12 - *"So the chief cup-bearer related his dream to Joseph, and he said to him, 'In my dream, behold, a vine is before me. And on the vine are three tendrils and it seemed to be blossoming, and its buds came out; [then] its clusters ripened into grapes. And Pharaoh's cup was in my hand, and I took the grapes and squeezed them into Pharaoh's cup, and I placed the cup on Pharaoh's palm.' And Joseph said to him, 'This is its meaning.'"*

Gen. 40:16-18 - *"Now the chief baker saw that he had interpreted well. So he said to Joseph, 'Me too! In my dream, behold, there were three wicker baskets on my head. And in the topmost basket were all kinds of Pharaoh's food, the work of a baker, and the birds were eating them from the basket atop my head.' And Joseph replied and said, 'This is its meaning.'"*

Gen. 41:1-8 - *"It came to pass at the end of two full years that Pharaoh was dreaming, and behold; he was standing by the Nile. And behold, from the Nile were coming up seven cows, of handsome appearance and robust flesh, and they pastured in the marshland. And behold, seven other cows were coming up after them from the Nile, of ugly appearance and lean of flesh, and they stood beside the cows [which were] on the Nile bank. And the cows of ugly appearance and lean of flesh devoured the seven cows that were of handsome appearance and healthy; then Pharaoh awoke. And he fell asleep and dreamed again, and behold, seven ears of grain were growing on one stalk, healthy and good. And behold, seven ears of grain, thin and beaten by the east wind, were growing up after them. And the thin ears of grain swallowed up the seven healthy and full ears of grain; then Pharaoh awoke and behold, a dream."*

Judges 7:13-14 - *"And Gideon came and behold, a man was telling his fellow a dream. And he said, 'Behold, I dreamed a dream, and behold, a roasted cake of barley bread tumbled into the camp of*

Midian, and it came to the tent, and smote it, and it fell; and it turned it upside down, and the tent fell.' And his fellow answered and said, 'This is nothing else but the sword of Gideon the son of Joash, the man of Israel; G-d has given Midian, and all the camp into his hand.'"

As is now clear from the Biblical record, G-d speaks to man, and reveals to him things in his dreams, and never is the dream symbol ever understood to be literal, within the context of coherent conscious thought. There were no actual sheaves that bowed down before Joseph, neither did the actual sun, moon and stars change their physical orbits to bow to him either. Pharaoh's cup bearer was not actually standing before a vine, nor did he have an actual cup in his hand. Pharaoh did not see actual physical cows, nor did his dream have anything to do with cows. The Midianite soldier did not see real barley bread. These are all dream symbolism.

It is imperative to approach all first-degree Apocalyptic visions and dreams as we do all other dreams, and recognize the archetypal, symbolic nature of their contents. Apocalyptic archetypes are universal, and emanate from humanity's collective unconscious. They are not limited to one religion, or another.

Even in the Christian Bible, we have an account of a traditional Jewish dream vision. Long before Christianity spiraled out to become its own religion, its origins and original members were all Torah practicing Jews. As such, many if not most, of their beliefs, spiritual experiences, and dreams are most properly understood within the context of their native Jewish environment instead of by the superimposed later reinterpretation made by non-Jewish Christian authors, many of whom had a documented misunderstanding, and dislike of anything Jewish. Such points of view naturally skewer, and thus conceal much of Christianity's original Jewishness, and the original form and content of the message of Yeshu HaNotzri, later to be called Jesus. The following dream recorded in the Christian Bible, Book of Acts (10:9-16) is a clear example of a Jewish experience of first-degree dream vision, and how it was misunderstood by those taking its meaning out of context.

"Peter went up upon the housetop to pray, about the sixth hour [the traditional time of the afternoon Minha prayer, prayed by all righteous Jews] and he became hungry, and desired to eat: but while they made ready, he fell into a trance, and he beheld the heaven opened, and a certain vessel descending, as it were a great sheet, let down by four corners upon the earth: wherein were all manner of four-footed beasts and creeping things of the earth and birds of the heaven. And there came a voice to him, 'Rise, Peter; kill and eat.' But Peter said, 'Not so, L-rd; for I have never eaten anything that is common and unclean.' And a voice came unto him again the second time, 'What G-d hath cleansed, make not thou common.' And this was done thrice: and straightway the vessel was received up into heaven... And he said unto them, 'Ye yourselves know how it is an unlawful thing for a man that is a Jew to join himself or come unto one of another nation; and yet unto me hath G-d showed that I should not call any man common or unclean.'"

This dream vision, experienced by Peter again follows in the footsteps of earlier Biblical dream content in that it is symbolic, and not literal. This is even made clear by the continuation of the episode in verse 28. In the dream, Peter sees a vessel descending from Heaven with all kinds of permitted (kosher), and forbidden foods on it. He is told to partake in all. Peter refuses to eat of the unclean foods, wherein which a voice cries out, do not call unclean that which G-d has called clean.

Now, the interpretation of this dream is clear and obvious when we understand the nature of dream symbolism. This is again made clear later in the text itself (Acts 10:28). Peter is being told that the message of Yeshu's Torah was not to be limited just to the Jewish community, but outreach should be made to educate the non-Jewish community as well, drawing them close to the Ways of G-d. Walls of division dividing Jew and Gentile were to be broken down so as to include all righteous Gentiles alongside their brethren, righteous Jews. This revelation might indeed have been something startling to Peter, for I am sure he remembers Yeshu teaching him and the other disciples to go only to the lost sheep of Israel, and to avoid the Gentiles (ref. Matt. 10:5).

Gentile outreach was a point of controversy during the days of the Second Temple. The normative group of Rabbis, led by Hillel, always embraced righteous Gentiles, and encouraged their moral development in the service of G-d. However, not all Jews and Rabbis of the time were as accepting as was Hillel, and those who walked in his steed. To this day, one will find opinions from both sides of this argument recorded in numerous places throughout Talmudic literature.

Judging from Yeshu's own comments, as recorded in Matthew 10:5, he held to the stricter point of view (embraced by some Rabbis of his day) rejecting such outreach to Gentiles. Indeed, there is an episode recorded in Matthew 15:24-26 that when a Gentile woman approached Yeshu asking for his blessings, he clearly rejected her, referring to her as a dog. The Gentile woman responded not with scorn for such a rejection, but rather with humility and faith. Yeshu was impressed by her behavior and concludes by praising the woman for her faith. However, his initial reaction to her indicated his original non-interest.

Peter's dream, therefore, was for him an arbiter between these variant points of view. This new-found conviction of Peter's, I might add, is one that was practiced by sincere G-d fearing Jews from before Peter's time to our very own, by those who have embraced the path of the Sage Hillel. It has always been an honor and privilege for righteous G-d fearing Jews to embrace their righteous G-d fearing Gentile brethren. Together, we endeavor to serve G-d in righteousness, regardless of our theological or doctrinal differences.

Centuries later, with Christianity's complete detachment from Judaism, Peter's dream became a source of theological controversy, and found its way to become artillery in an anti-Semitic push to rip Jews away from their holy Torah. Some Christian leaders, who maybe were unaware of classical Biblical dream interpretation interpreted Peter's dream literally, (and obviously against scriptural precedent), and then proclaimed to the Jews that G-d had told Peter to rescind the Laws of clean and unclean foods that G-d Himself prescribe in Leviticus. Indeed, this dream of Peters has been misused as a weapon to try to force Jews to eat unclean foods, proclaiming to Jews that the Laws of Kosher foods have been nullified. Needless to say, this interpretation would contradict G-d own Word, as G-d Himself has stated through prophecy that He does not change (Malachi 3:6).

G-d would not command the Jewish people to observe His commandments throughout their generations, and then have someone come along, and based on a dream have His eternal Word nullified. This would make such a dreamer of dreams to be a false teacher, and subject to harsh punishment (ref. Deut. 13:2-4).

Yet, we do not ever see Peter himself interpreting his dream as did later Gentile Christians with an apparent anti-Semitic "ax to grind." Throughout his life Peter only ate clean foods. There is never any suggestion in the Christian Bible, or in any other historical record that he acted in any other way. Therefore, the dream of Peter the Jew should be embraced, and interpreted as are all other dreams in the Jewish Bible. This inclusion is important here to validate that symbolic dream interpretation is as much a part of the Christian tradition as it is of the Jewish. Without a proper understating of Christian Apocalyptic symbols, much of modern beliefs and myths are subject to misunderstanding and superstition.

Decades later with the recorded Revelation of John, who was another personal friend and student of Yeshu HaNotzri, we have another classic example of Jewish archetypal, symbolic Apocalyptic literature. Even though the Revelation of John, in its present form in translation, is part and parcel of Christianity and the Christian Bible, at the time of its writing there did not yet exist a separate Christianity per se, and most certainly there had not yet existed (if there ever did) an independent first-degree Christian apocalyptic experience.

Regardless of his beliefs and loyalty to Yeshu, like Peter, John was born and educated as a Jew. He most likely lived in accordance to Jewish Law to the day he died. Nothing about his faith in Yeshu ever changed that. Indeed, there was no Christian literature at the time for John to have perused. Therefore, all he ever knew and lived was Judaism. As such, his writings, especially his Apocalypse, have to be understood within the Jewish context of the author himself.

Although the writings of Paul were in circulation at the time, John was a first-degree, direct student of Yeshu. John had a life-long relationship with Yeshu's closest family and friends, like James and Peter. It is highly unlikely that John would have sided against his life-long friend Peter and adopt Paul's theology, something that I think is clear from both the Christian Bible itself, and history that the Church on Jerusalem, led by James, Peter and John, did not do.

As such, regardless of his allegiance to Yeshu, John was clearly still immersed in the ways of the Torah and Jewish prophets. His Revelation clearly follows in the genre of traditional Jewish apocalyptic literature. So, while the Revelation of John in its present format is clearly a Christian work, one should ponder the question, what the original text written by John himself, most likely in his native Aramaic might have looked like. Regardless of theological issues within the text, the symbols therein still follow the common pattern, and must be understood symbolically in the Jewish context and interpreted accordingly. It is important that we make mention of the Apocalypse of John because of the tremendous influence this work has had on Christianity and the development of western civilization. Due to this book's centrality, a proper understanding of it, within its original Jewish contexts is essential for our study. We will therefore return to the Revelation of John later in these lessons.

With these insights into the symbolic nature of dreams and its relevance to both Judaic and Christian Biblical traditions, let us turn to Nebuchadnezzar's dream of the great statue and understand its archetypal and Apocalyptic symbolisms.

Chapter 2

Nebuchadnezzar's Dream of the Course of Human History

Introduction
Comment on Secular Biblical Scholarship & Criticism

When it comes to the study of prophecy we must divide this study, and its commentaries, between those who believe in the reality and existence of prophecy, and those that do not. Those that believe in them are obviously the many members of numerous faiths. Those that do not believe in them are the secular scholars and academic theologians. There is a huge division in Biblical studies and commentaries between those who believe that it is possible to know the future, and those who deny the existence of this possibility. Needless to say, believers in religion accept the reality of prophecy, whereas, for the most part, secular scholars deny its existence.

For the secular scholar knowing the future is not a possibility that they are willing to accept. Therefore, in their eyes, any book, be it Daniel or any other, that claims to be predicting the future, be in through dreams or outright declaration by either an angel or G-d, simply cannot be true. For the secular scholar it is not possible to know the future. Therefore, in their so-called scholarly eyes, any book, Biblical or otherwise, that claims to predict the future, by definition, cannot be doing so. In their eyes, such a book can never have been written prior to the events prophesied. Such a book must have been written later by an author who wrote about past events in the form of predictions of the future.

The secular scholarly claim therefore is that, for example, the Book of Daniel could not have been written by Daniel, nor could it have been written at any time earlier than the period that they interpret the events described therein to have already happened. Essentially, in the eyes of secular scholarship, prophetic books by nature of their being, proclaiming the future, are all lies, and thus can never be accepted as having any real validity. The secular scholars then go to work trying to find answers as to who, in their eyes wrote such a book, and why they might have done so. Secular scholarship then comes up with all kinds of concocted ideas, theories and beliefs, which take them further and further away from the believers who look at the texts and accept them as true.

Needless to say, the secular scholars have little to absolutely no respect for the religious believers who accept prophecy at face value. Indeed, some secular scholars are often arrogant in the face of religious believers considering their embrace of prophecy rather primitive, and unscientific. In light of this very real schism in the domain of Biblical studies, I find it necessary to introduce the following material with these words.

I myself belong to the camp of the believers. I believe that there is such a thing as prophecy, that it is possible to know the future, and that the Biblical records do exactly this. As such, the views that I will express throughout this work will not take into account the various wild opinions, theories and conjectures of the numerous secular scholars.

Granted, there are those among said scholars who do indeed make valid points, and discoveries that are true. Nevertheless, such secular scholarship cannot be taken at face value as long as their underlying premise is the denial of prophecy, and the ability to prophesy. Such denials are tantamount to denials of G-d Himself.

While I do not wish to embark on any kind of nonsensical religious crusade, nevertheless, I must make my position known. I am "pro" prophecy and "anti" secular when it comes to the study of the Bible, and all the prophecies therein. With this being understood, my readers will now understand the nature of my orientation to the rest of this material, and why I do not include so-called Biblical criticism in any of my discussions.

Daniel, Chapter Two, Nebuchadnezzar's Dream

In the Book of Daniel, Chapter 2, we find recorded a most peculiar event. Nebuchadnezzar, King of Babylon has had a disturbing dream, which for the life of him, he cannot remember. He calls upon all his wise men, sages, and mystics to remind him of his dream, and to interpret it for him. However, in unison they all reply that none of them, and that no human being, could possibly reach into the depths of the human unconscious, and from there extract a dream that even the dreamer himself cannot consciously remember.

In a fit of rage, the King is ready to call for the execution of all his wise men. Then in comes Daniel, who the story implies is, at this time, still a youth, and not very close to the inner circle of the King. Nevertheless, as one of the King's wise men, Daniel offers to take up the task to extract from the King his dream, and to interpret it properly.

This dream of the King is most profound, because it is the first to reveal to us that there is a specific, pre-planned course of events for unfolding human history. Granted, we have always known that there is prophecy. We have always known that G-d ordains what is to be on the personal, national and even global scale. Yet, with all the prophecies of the Biblical prophets, none of them revealed that there was, what seems to be, a predestined planned for all humanity. Daniel seems to be the first to reveal this.

The fact that it is Daniel who is revealing this to us out of the dream of the King and that this predestined scenario did not appear in any of the earlier prophets is significant and profound. The reason why it is Daniel who brings us this revelation and not any earlier, and superior prophet, is because this predestined scenario of the four kingdoms did not exist prior to the Babylonian exile. Nebuchadnezzar was clearly sent by G-d to destroy

Jerusalem, and to exile Judea to Babylon. This was a Divine edict. Yet, it was an edict that did not have to be. The behavior of the nation so aroused Divine anger that the edict for punishment was decreed. Yet, what would have happened if the people of Judah had repented before G-d. Would there still have been need of an exile, or for that matter, four exiles under four kingdoms?

I believe that Heaven's plan for humanity takes different courses based upon the choices that both collective humanity and each individual take. Adam was not destined to eat of the forbidden fruit in Eden. Our exile from Eden was not preordained. The children of Israel were not destined to worship the Golden Calf, nor were they destined to cry over the report of the spies returning from touring the Land. It was not predestined for them to wander in the wilderness for 40 years. If only Solomon had stayed faithful to G-d, then maybe his son Rehoboam would not have provoked a civil war, leading to the northern tribes to abandon Judah, and form their own government and nation.

The history of Israel is full of "what ifs." Throughout the period from the Exodus to the destruction of the First Temple, G-d worked with Children of Israel with mercy. The prophets revealed the Divine word over and over again revealing how the nation could have peace and prosperity. Yet the nation, and the individuals therein, chose not to listen. Even when Nebuchadnezzar rose to power it was not destined for him to destroy Jerusalem. Yet, certain behaviors led to certain consequences. G-d worked with Israel through each and every one.

But now, the people were exiled from their homeland. The Ark of the Covenant, and the secret Urim & Tumim which kept the people in contact with G-d was now lost. Prophecy soon died out of Israel. While people were still able to talk to G-d, still, the only ones to talk back from Heaven were the angels, and they only revealed G-d's Will. They never revealed G-d's Word, and there is a big difference between the two.

Daniel was shown that with the Babylonian exile, the people had entered yet another phase of existence in their relationship with G-d. As the exile in Egypt seemed to be necessary for the sake of building Israel in the past, so now too, the four exiles would become necessary for the sake of building Israel in the future, the far future, the Messianic future.

This plan of exile, while non-existent prior to this time, had now become G-d's plan. This is what was revealed to Nebuchadnezzar, but the real message was for Daniel, and for him to share it with us. This is why Nebuchadnezzar could not remember the dream. This ominous dream was actually more for Daniel that for the King. Why then did it come to the King, and not directly to Daniel? Because G-d chose this way so that the eventual outcome would unravel as it did. As we all know, G-d works in strange ways.

One further point needs be mentioned. When it comes to commenting on the text of Daniel, or for that matter any other book of the Bible, we must remember that every classical commentary that we have, was written anywhere from 500 to 1500 years (or more), after the text of Daniel itself was written. The great classical Jewish commentaries were compilations of earlier materials, but those earlier materials themselves were also written long after the fact of the text itself, and from specific points of view.

In order to understand the text directly, we cannot immediately turn to the later commentaries. We must first look at the text, and see how it was interpreted by any earlier authorities. The earlier the insights into the text, the more authentic an understanding we will glean from it. Therefore, at this time, as we review the text of Daniel, we will not be following the later commentaries, but rather we will search for the earliest known sources that mention Daniel, and interpret his words. Only with the first strata of commentary, do I feel we are enabled to move on to the second. The way Daniel is understood today may not have been the way he was understood before the classics were written. We have to go back as far as possible to investigate, and bring to light the most original understanding that we can find.

Now let us turn to the dream of the King and understand it in its details.

"The king spoke up and said to Daniel, whose name was Belteshazzar, "Do you have the ability to tell me the dream that I have seen and its interpretation?"

An important cultural note to mention here is that King Nebuchadnezzar never referred to Daniel by his Hebrew name. Rather, Daniel is called Belteshazzar, his Babylonian/Aramaic name. While it is certainly in the King's power to discover or know that Daniel was a Jew, the text gives no overt revelation that this was on the King's mind. Mind you, Daniel did not hide his identity, but neither did he outwardly display it with any type of cultural garb. To the eye, Daniel was Belteshazzar, one of the many Babylonian wise men of the King's court. There was nothing significant about his appearance or demeanor to suggest that he was special and unique, and thus would have this dream catching and interpreting ability that was far beyond that of the other wise man of the kingdom.

"Daniel answered the king and said, "The secret that the king asks, no wise men, astrologers, magicians, or wizards can tell the king. But there is a G-d in Heaven Who reveals secrets."

In keeping with what appears to be his low profile, or maybe just being sensitive to the times, Daniel, when referring to G-d in Heaven, does not refer to Him ethnically as the G-d of Israel, or of Jerusalem. Belteshazzar is speaking of the universal G-d of gods, who is above ethnicity or identification with one single group of people. This is an identification that Nebuchadnezzar could understand. Had Belteshazzar corrected the King, insisting he be called Daniel, and that Daniel came speaking in the name of the G-d of Israel, Nebuchadnezzar might not have been so inclined to receive Daniel, or listen to what he had to say. Sensing, this, Belteshazzar acted as he did and the rest is, as they say, is history.

He lets King Nebuchadnezzar know what will be at the end of days; that is your dream and the visions of your head on your bed. You, O king, your thoughts came while on your bed, what will be after this, and the Revealer of secrets lets you know what will be.

G-d in Heaven is communicating directly with the King of Babylon. This is clear from the text. Nebuchadnezzar seems to have an interesting relationship with G-d. For scripture is clear that G-d sent him to destroy Jerusalem and the Temple therein (Jeremiah 25:8). Granted, Nebuchadnezzar might have acted the same even if not manipulated by G-d to do so. But we can never know this one way or another. In Jeremiah 25:8 and 27:6, G-d clearly calls Nebuchadnezzar, King of Babylon, his servant Clearly, Nebuchadnezzar did not worship the G-d of Israel, and his knowledge of such a G-d was possibly minimal at best. Although Nebuchadnezzar very well may not have even heard much about, (or care for), the G-d of Israel, nevertheless, G-d calls the King, his servant. G-d was moving Nebuchadnezzar like a pawn on the chessboard; all the while the King was most likely oblivious to the movement of the Divine Hand. At least, until now.

Biblical commentators learn from this episode, and the similar episode recorded in Genesis about the dreams of Pharaoh, that G-d does directly communicate with the world's political leaders. Indeed, sometimes these men can be outright evil, (which is what I am sure all of Judea thought of Nebuchadnezzar as he came to destroy their homeland). Nevertheless, G-d acts as He does, and communicates with whom He will. So, too this day, it is believed that somehow, and in some way, G-d still does communicate with modern world leaders, even as He has done so in the past. What are the dreams of modern world leaders, we may never know. Indeed, without a Joseph or Daniel on their staffs, they too may never realize how it is that G-d is communicating with them, and for that matter, manipulating them as pawns in G-d's Divine game of chess.

The End of Days is now mentioned. But, as we see from the dream, the term "End of Days" has to be understood figuratively. For while the dream, does speak of the End of Days, specifically of the One Stone to come, nevertheless, the dream also contains the course of human events, from the present moment of Nebuchadnezzar, through the ages, and culminating in the coming of the One Stone.

Daniel thus states that the dream is no small matter. This is not simply a message about some minor affair of state. No, this dream is something far bigger, something that a man, chosen by G-d for greatness would be "worthy" to receive. Nebuchadnezzar was a man bigger than life. His role in human history was far more than merely being a simple political leader of the day. No, this king, as his dream reveals, was the "head of gold" the beginning of G-d's plan for mankind, and the very best part of it, symbolized by the element gold. As being the head of all that was to come, it is only fitting that Nebuchadnezzar should see this dream/vision. For although he is but a man in time and history, his kingdom starts a series of interconnected world events, symbolized by the statue itself. It is only fitting that he should see the middle and end of that which he, the king, began.

The text (verse 29) then makes a very strange and enticing reference to the Galei Razaya, the "revealer of secrets." Although most will interpret this as being a reference to the G-d of whom Daniel/Belteshazzar speaks, the text does not make this connection, and actually leaves it open to conjecture that the "revealer of secrets" may indeed be some type of messenger or "angel" sent by the G-d of Heaven to reveal the Divine Will. This "revealer of secrets" in later literature has come to be identified with the Angel Gabriel, for reason we will discuss at another time. Yet, as said above, there is no indication that Gabriel is any less busy today speaking to modern day political leaders in their dreams as he very well may have done so in the past.

"And I, not with wisdom that I possess more than all living, did He reveal this secret to me, but in order that they should let the king know the interpretation, and you should know the thoughts of your heart."

Daniel/Belteshazzar, in keeping with his low profile does not want to take credit for his extraordinary feat. Rather, he wants to simply say that, like the King, he (Daniel/Belteshazzar) too can and does communicate with the "revealer of secrets." This is a very subtle statement on Daniel's part. For rather than boasting his superior wisdom over all the other wise men of Babylon, he ever so subtly says to the King, that he (Daniel) has a connection to Heaven that the others do not. This connection is the same as, or superior to, that connection which the King himself enjoys. Essentially, Daniel is ever so subtly implying that he too has royal blood within him, and thus merits the Divine communion. Although he is not smarter, he is definitely more connected. As we will see, this special ability to connect, earns Daniel, awe, tremendous respect and reward.

Now, we come to the dream itself.

"O King, you were watching, and behold, one great image, an image which had a large base and with unusual splendor, was standing opposite you, and its form was frightening."

As we know the great image represents the whole of the world's governments and civilizations. These are described as having unusual splendor and standing on a large base. The image is described as frightening. Indeed, when one looks at the power of government and the civilizations that arise, one can see within them that which is both splendid and frightening.

Human governments have always been a form of overwhelming repression over helpless populations. Nebuchadnezzar was certainly no exception to this rule; on the contrary he is the head of gold that establishes the rule. Nebuchadnezzar was a world-class dictator and ruthless oppressor. Stand in his way, and you pay the price. How many governments of both past and present can we point to that are exactly the same? We look upon government as being all powerful and indeed frightening. Yet, many go with the flow and see the splendor in the socialized system that governments, both past and present, have set up.

"That image had a head of fine gold, its breast and its arms were of silver, its belly and thighs were of copper. Its legs were of iron, and its feet were partly of iron and partly of clay."

This describes the kingdoms, again, which are bodies of world government, massive empires that apparently come in succession, one after the other. Mind you, notice that no time scale is even hinted to here. This progression could take place over a period of years, centuries or millennia. Regardless of the passage of time, one thing is clear and that is that the transition from one government to the next, is still being guided by G-d, and all the governments together, even if they span thousands of years are still considered to be part and parcel of the same human system, symbolized by the statue. There is no division, no anarchy, no haphazard or zig-zag progression. Everything that is to unfold (or from our point of view that has unfolded) is all part and parcel of the "the system," or what we can call, the "evil empire."

Essentially, world history has been one big predestined Divine plan, guided by Heaven in every respect. Yet, as predestined as things are, pay attention that there is no time reference with regards to the duration of the individual "kingdoms." The overall plan, one way or another, would be accomplished. Yet, would such a plan completely work itself out over the period of the existence of the Second Temple, or would there be a need for more time? This question was extremely important during Second Temple times because of the later "prophecy of the weeks" to be discussed in Daniel, Chapter 9. During Temple times, there was a sense of urgency then that gave rise to many apocalyptic movements, leaders and their literature.

From our present point of view, we know the answer that the End did not come with the destruction of the Temple. Yet, those who wrote Daniel, and the earlier generations who read it, certainly did not know this. The issue of when the End of Days will be upon us has become a revolving issue, concerning many in every generation. Judging from the disastrous effects apocalyptic speculations had on the generation that witnessed the destruction of the Temple, and the following generations thereafter, some of the Talmudic Sages (ref. T.B. San. 97b) expressed the opinion to actually curse those who try to calculate when the End of Days and the coming of Mashiah was to occur. They realized that absolutely everyone who has tried to make such a calculation has failed miserably, with such false predictions misleading many, disrupting and ruining the lives of many more. Nevertheless, the craving for redemption runs strong, and not just in the Jewish community. Such time speculations have literally shaped the course of world events. They provoked the hysteria that reigned in Israel prior to the destruction of the Second Temple, and centuries later provoked the hysteria that reigned in Christian Europe leading to the Crusades. Such messianic fervor pops up again and again, and even today is very popular and rising again to a feverish pitch, with all the dangers this implies.

"You were watching until One Stone was hewn without hands, and it struck the image on its feet of iron and clay and crumbled them. Then the iron, the clay, the copper, the silver, and the gold crumbled together, and they were like chaff from the threshing floors of the summer, and the wind carried them off, and no place was found for them, and the stone that struck the image became a huge mountain and filled the entire earth."

The One Stone, hewn without human hands, that strikes the figure and destroys it is interpreted later in the dream to be the coming Kingdom of G-d, the era of the Mashiah, prophesied by all the earlier prophets. Yet, the revelation made here is most profound. The Stone, representing the Kingdom is said not be hewn by human hands. In other words, the coming Kingdom of G-d is not one that will be established by mortal, normal means. The coming Kingdom of G-d will be established by the Hand of Heaven without the intervention, or intermediary of human involvement. G-d is to personally intervene in human history, from the outside, and remove human civilization, replacing it with one of Divine making.

The significance of this revelation cannot be underestimated. For if G-d Himself is to establish His Kingdom on Earth, then it is not for human beings to try to establish it for Him. It was this very mistake that led to the destruction of Jerusalem by the Romans many centuries after the Book of Daniel was written and disseminated. If the extremist zealots of Jerusalem did not try to create the Kingdom on Earth by themselves, maybe Jerusalem and the Temple would not have been destroyed. This is a major lesson and warning to modern day zealots who want to follow in the footsteps of the ancient zealots. G-d's plan will not be thwarted or rushed, not by the nations, and not even by his own people Israel.

"This is the dream, and its interpretation we shall recite before the king. You, O King, the King of kings, the G-d of Heaven gave you a strong, powerful, and prominent kingdom. And wherever people,

wild beasts, and birds of the sky dwell, He has given into your hand and has given you dominion over them all. You are the head of gold."

The first part of the image is the head of gold. Gold is the most precious of elements, and the head houses the mind, the domain of thought, the most precious of human commodities that separates us from the animal domain. This realm is Babylon. Babylon, we know, is the place of exile. It is the place of contamination and uncleanliness. Nevertheless, it is the place that G-d chose to send His people Israel. Of all the world powers to follow, Babylon was considered the closest to Israel, both in physical proximity as well as in culture and language. To this day, Judaism is under Babylonian influence. Although the Second Temple was built, and after the Babylonian exile Jewish life refocused on the Holy Land, nevertheless the communities in Babylon continued to exist. They ended up playing a central role in Judaism after the Second Temple and the Holy Land were decimated. To this day, modern Judaism follows in the footsteps of the Babylonian Talmud.

The historical Babylonian Empire came to an end long ago. However, the Babylonian influence continues to this day. This influence, while not as sublime as that of the Holy Land is still considered to be close to it spiritually. Symbolized by gold, the head and the ability to think, Babylon has become a symbol and an archetype for a way of living and thinking. It is the highest form of exile, closest to holiness in many ways, but nevertheless, not the "real deal."

The golden head of Babylon takes on archetypal proportions in later Jewish mystical literature. The head, which is Babylon, becomes transformed into the head of Esau, brother of Jacob. Scripture is clear that the relationship between the descendants of Esau and the Children of Israel was extremely hostile. Indeed, the fourth Kingdom to come, made of iron, said to refer to Rome, also is said to be that of the Children of Esau. Rome, as we know, destroyed Jerusalem and sent the Jewish people into the exile that lasts to this very day. Yet, as history documents, not all Romans, i.e., children of Esau were bad. Many of them were righteous Gentiles who were brothers (and sisters) with the Jewish people.

This relationship is reflected in an old Jewish legend that states that when Jacob died and his family ascended out of Egypt to bury him, they were confronted at Makhpelah Cave in Hebron, the family burial plot, by Esau and his minions. Esau claimed rights to the burial site and resisted having Jacob buried there. Legend has it that Husham, son of Dan, attacked Esau, decapitating him. Needless to say, war broke out between the children of Jacob and the children of Esau, a war that the children of Jacob won. Yet, a compromise was made, allowing the severed head of Esau to be buried in the lap of his father Isaac.

To this day, if one were to go to Hebron, to the Cave of the Patriarchs, one will find a room named for each of the Patriarchs and matriarchs buried there and one will actually find a small place entitled, "cave of the head of Esau." This legend, metaphorical or not, is used to describe how the best of Esau has a place next to Jacob himself. This is the inclusion of the righteous Gentiles, the likes of which Peter was shown in his dream (ref. Acts 10), as we discussed in the previous chapter.

The message is that the best of the Gentiles have a place with the righteous of Israel. These righteous Gentile souls are referred to as the "head" of the nations. Thus, here in the King's dream, he sees human civilization led, of course, by the Gentile nations to have a head of gold signifying the best of the human race. In Nebuchadnezzar's dream, they are called Babylon. In later Jewish literature, they are called the "head of Esau." Although the name has changed, the association with the head and being the best there is has stayed the same.

"And after you will arise another kingdom lower than you..."

Following the head of gold comes a second empire, symbolized by silver, the torso and the arms. The torso, as we know, houses the heart, instead of the head. The arms are the vessels through which action is materialized. While thought is paramount and thus symbolized by gold, the heart is considered secondary to the head and is thus symbolized by silver.

Now, the heart referenced here is not the same metaphor of heart that we find used in earlier Biblical literature. We must remember that this is Nebuchadnezzar's dream, not Daniel's. Nebuchadnezzar does not have the depth of spirit as does Daniel, so his vision of heart would refer more to human emotions than to deep-seated intuitive inner-knowledge. The heart empire of silver referred to here is not as sublime and enlightened as is the head empire of gold. While, it has its value, it still lacks in depth, just as human emotions lack the depth of insight that belongs to intellectual thought. Being that the symbol also includes the arms and joins them to the heart, this signifies that the silver empire is the period of pursuit of emotional pleasures.

This second empire in classical Jewish commentaries has always been identified with the Persians. Good insights into Persian culture can be gleamed from the Biblical Book of Esther. Apparently King Ahasuerus and Haman both were very emotional characters signifying their archetypal associations with the empire they ruled.

Interesting to note that in the Book of Esther, when the Jews were given permission to defend themselves against their enemies, many of those enemies converted to Judaism in order to avoid retribution for their planned assault on the Jews. Unlike the righteous Gentiles referred to above as Babylon or the head of Esau, these individual converts were not sincere. They associated with Israel only out of fear, and not out of a true conviction to serve G-d.

In the Middle Ages, one great mystical Rabbi, Yitzhak of Acco commented that he noticed there was always a stream of Jewish people who abandoned their faith, and joined the faiths of the surrounding nations. He commented and said that these individuals were the descendants of those who converted without sincerity in the days of Esther, and that in reality they were only returning to their original Gentile roots. Rather than pursue them to return, he bid them adieu.

"And another, a third kingdom, of copper, which will rule over the entire earth..."

The belly and thighs are the place where the life-force of the body resides, the guts and also includes the genitalia. This third empire represented by copper, indicates a driving, almost sexual urge to push out, conquer and expand. The nature of this third empire is represented by its position in the statue. It is not guided by either head or heart, but rather by pure base, gut libido energy. Everyone knows that raw sexual energy unharnessed is a very dangerous thing. Therefore, rather than associate this orientation towards intellect or emotion, this empire simply seeks raw, gut level sexual driven conquest. This level of the statue goes down to the thighs. This section has no arms attached for moving other things, nor does it have legs to move itself. This section is just raw power; it will rise in a flash, and almost as quickly burn itself out.

This third empire has been classically associated with the Greeks. Needless to say to anyone familiar with classical Grecian culture, the Greeks were a very sexually oriented people. Their nude performances in the gymnasiums in Jerusalem contributed greatly to the Maccabee revolt and civil war.

Started by Alexander, the Greek Empire in quick time conquered most of the known world, and then in almost as quick time fragmented and began to deteriorate after the sudden death of the young Alexander. It is interesting to note that the statue vision of Nebuchadnezzar is almost prophetic in not only describing the numbers of kingdoms to come, but also managed to archetypally manifest in the vision images, elements and aspects about each culture and civilization that each empire would become known by.

"And a fourth kingdom will be strong as iron, for iron crumbles and flattens everything, and like iron, which shatters all these, it will crumble and shatter."

The legs and the feet are the same, yet different. The legs are made of iron. Iron was a strong and crushing metal, used for utility instead of for an ornament, similar to gold, silver and copper. These feet of iron crush and smash everything that gets in their way. This fourth kingdom is said to represent Rome, the arch enemy of Israel, responsible for the destruction of Jerusalem, the Holy Temple and the deaths of about a million Jews.

The element iron is very interesting in that it is used for its utility. Indeed, the relationship between Rome and Israel was also one that had its benefits and demerits. The demerits we have already stated, yet, most do not realize that Rome never really conquered the land of Israel. Rather they were a force invited in, by none less than the heads of the Maccabee clan. Having Rome at their backs was the Maccabee way to make sure the northern Seleucid Greeks did not try to re-invade Israel. Like a tool of iron, the relationship with Rome was one of utility. It started out good and then became more and more oppressive. Needless to say, it was during the time of this great oppression that gave birth to a tremendous amount of original and authentic apocalyptic literature. These then will be discussed in later lessons.

"And what you saw, the feet and the toes, which were partly of potter's clay and partly of iron, so it will be a divided kingdom, and in it will be some of the strength of iron, in view of what you saw iron mixed with clay. And the toes of the feet were partly iron and partly clay, for part of the kingdom will be strong and part of it will be broken. And what you saw, iron mixed with clay, [connotes] that they will mingle with the seed of men, but they will not cleave one to the other, as iron does not mix with clay."

History records that the Roman Empire eventually split into two, with two heads, Rome and Constantinople respectively. The Western Roman Empire fell centuries before the Eastern Roman Empire did. But these two cannot be the divided kingdom spoken of here by Daniel. Simply, the description as portrayed here in the text does not coincide with the history.

There is, however, another dual empire, born out of Grecian-Roman philosophy and following in its footsteps of ruthless repression of all opposition. The two great powers that have struggled with one another for the last one thousand five hundred years have been the Christian west, and the Muslim east. The Christian west is clearly the continuation of Kingdom of Iron that dominated the domain of the shins of the statue. Yet, now, in the feet, at the very bottom of the stature, signifying the very end of time before the coming of the One Stone, it is mixed with another element, one more pliant, yet impossible to be mixed with. The clay is therefore interpreted to be the Caliphate of world Islam.

Islam plays a great role in later Jewish eschatology and it will be discussed when we review the literature that mentions it by name, but this material did not come into existence for maybe a thousand years after the Book of Daniel. Therefore, although we may recognize the Islamic world within the statue vision, detailed discussion on this matter will be addressed only when we arrive at our discussion of the later material of the later time period.

"And in the days of these kings, the G-d of Heaven will set up a kingdom forever, it will not be destroyed, and the kingdom will not be left to another people; it will crumble and destroy all these kingdoms, and it will stand forever. Just as you saw that from the mountain a stone was hewn without hands, and it crumbled the iron, the copper, the clay, the silver, and the gold. The great G-d has let the king know what will be after this, and the dream is true, and its interpretation is reliable." (Daniel 2:26-45)

The G-d of Heaven, Himself, will set up a Kingdom, not mankind, not even the children of Israel acting on behalf of G-d. G-d Himself is to intervene in human history in, what for us, will be a most supernatural way. G-d's Kingdom comes as it may, and it immediately strikes the statue, and brings down the entire edifice, the clay, iron, copper, silver and gold.

What we must recognize here is that the entire statue is toppled and it falls all at once. Although the initial interpretation of this dream is that the statue is referring to successive historical governments and empires, nevertheless, all four are still in existence and are toppled together with the coming of the One Stone. Therefore, we are required to extrapolate from this vision two things. One, is that the lands these ancient civilizations inhabited will continue to be and two, that there will be some remainder of their influence and civilization that will exist simultaneously and side-by-side with the other later empires.

We clearly see this to be true. Today modern civilization is modeled upon the European model. Europe was built upon Roman Christianity and thus continues in its own way the legacy and name of the fourth empire Rome. Grecian influence in the world today is broadly visible, especially in our architecture, the likes of which can be seen in almost any modern western city. Also, we should remember that the chosen form of western government is a democracy, a concept that originated in ancient Greece. Persian influence, in the world body politic is ever growing. And as for Babylon, it is today's Iraq, still a place of contention and unrest. And metaphorically, Babylon is considered to be the best of all Gentile cultures and people, the closest thing to Biblical holiness.

Yet, once the One Stone comes, however it does, all these influences, cultures and civilizations are all blown away, apparently in an instant.

"The great G-d has let the king know what will be after this, and the dream is true, and its interpretation is reliable."

Again, Daniel reiterates that G-d in Heaven reveals His plans and secrets to world leaders and somehow, like Pharaoh in Egypt and now Nebuchadnezzar in Babylon, (and like all other future rulers), makes them fulfill the Divine purpose for which G-d allowed them to rise to power in the first place.

While Nebuchadnezzar's dream is an outline of world history, there is actually only one small part of it that is actually apocalyptic. This part is the reference to the coming of the One Stone, and how it smashes into the statue destroying it, and making room for the coming Kingdom of G-d. Therefore, Daniel is here presenting to us that the end of human civilization, as we know it, will occur with a colossal, destructive collision between human forces, and a power not of this Earth. While I would be amused to interpret the coming One Stone not hewn by human hands as a reference to an alien invasion from Outer Space, with all the flying saucers and little green men included, I can only do so jokingly. While it is clear from this vision (and later Jewish apocalyptic literature) that only Divine intervention will introduce the Kingdom of G-d to Earth, what exactly this means, and how it will occur is not described in this vision. Therefore, we cannot address such issues here.

King Nebuchadnezzar's vision was the first to outline to us G-d's plan for human history. Nowhere does the vision imply over how long a period the lives of the four kingdoms was to last. They could have lasted only for the period of the Second Temple or (as we see) they can last to this very day. As for when the End will come, this vision of King Nebuchadnezzar did not reveal to us any dates, times or other signs. Next for us to explore will be Daniel's own vision of the great beast to come. Daniel's vision contains within it much more detail than does the dream of the King. In our next lesson we will thus proceed to examine Daniel, Chapter 7.

Chapter 3

Daniel's Dream of the Four Beasts

Introduction
The Revealed & Concealed In Revelations

In Daniel, Chapter 7, we have recorded a dream/vision the likes of which is unique to all Biblical literature. While we are able to shed considerable light on to the interpretation of this dream/vision, nevertheless, there are significant portions of it that to this day defy explanation. When it comes to interpreting the dream/vision, part of it is interpreted in the dream itself by an angel present therein. We might then conclude that everything the angel describes is to be understood literally, just as the angel describes. But we forget that dream language is symbolic, and that even the communication of angels has to be understood within this symbolic context.

As we shall see, when the angel refers to the beasts described in the dream as kings, he is not exactly referring to any individual king, monarch, or political ruler personally and in particular. When the angel refers to a kingdom, he is not referring to any specific government in particular. The psychological realities of archetypal dream symbols requires of us to understand Daniel's dreamed images, and the angel's interpretation of these images within the metaphorical, symbolic context that they deserve. Therefore, rather than interpret this Chapter 7 of Daniel in an almost literal sense as has been done by almost every commentator, Jewish and

Christian alike, we must delve into the archetypal imagery, and try to understand the dream vision in the way it must have been meant to be understood.

As for how this vision was understood by the members of Daniel's generation, and those closest to it, this is an entirely another story, a story, mind you, that most likely had many "chapters" to it. For as with all prophecy, there was that which was publicly revealed, and that which was kept concealed within the closed circle of the prophets.

As we see from Ezekiel's famous chariot vision in Chapter 1 of his book, prophets had experiences and visions that they understood, but that outsiders did not, and would not, unless they were given the keys to unlock the prophetic system. Daniel, in this respect, was no different. Although he was not technically a prophet, he nevertheless experienced similar things that were experienced by every other prophet. Therefore, Daniel follows the rule that while he obviously revealed things to the members of his generation, (thus we have his book written), there was still a body of information that remained safely concealed. This is even referred to later in Daniel, when the angel tells Daniel specifically to conceal specific matters. Therefore, what is concealed is not meant for public consumption, at least not way back then.

In modern times, however, we can gain insights into Daniel's revelation using the terms and concepts of mystics and Sages who lived many centuries after the Book of Daniel was written. And even with these modern insights and concepts, there is still much in Daniel that remains hidden, as we shall soon see. In order to enable us to understand Daniel 7, I will introduce in this lesson some terminologies and concepts of the later Jewish mystical Sages. Their vocabulary is familiar to many in Orthodox Jewish communities, and thus by making these terms and concepts accessible to a greater reading audience, we can reveal much that cannot be done otherwise.

If the Book of Daniel is historically chronological, then the intervening Chapters 3 - 6 show us that a good deal of time has transpired between Daniel's dream vision here in Chapter 7, and his interpretation of Nebuchadnezzar's dream back in Chapter 2. I am not sure that such a time gap is actual, or for that matter, if it is in any way significant. The stories in the life of Daniel only prove to us how righteous he was and indeed blessed by G-d. His dream visions, therefore, are separate from the narrative of his life's story.

While the great image of Nebuchadnezzar was rather simple in describing the four "kingdoms," Daniel's experience in his dream offers much greater details and revelations. Yet, we must remember what we have already learned in Chapter 2. Although the four kingdoms are referring to historical periods to come, they are also identifying four specific archetypes, styles and forms of human government that exist simultaneously in the minds of men, and thus therefore in the world body politic. We remember that when the Stone, mentioned in Daniel 2, comes it breaks down all four kingdoms together, and thus we learned that all four exist simultaneously until the very end.

What these four kingdoms are we have already begun to describe in the previous section of this work. Now, let us turn to Daniel 7 and look at the details.

Before we delve into Daniel 7, let me here reiterate to you a very important concept. As we know by reading this, and other prophetic/apocalyptic material, the symbols used to describe future events are mysterious, baffling and often indiscernible. Unlike Pharaoh and Nebuchadnezzar, we do not have at our disposal a Joseph or Daniel to interpret for us apocalyptic imagery by the power of Divine inspiration. Therefore, what we have are the records of the visions, and literally centuries and centuries of interpretations, most often every one contradicting the ones before them.

Essentially, what we are left with is a record without a definitive understanding as to exactly what the record is saying. As such, all I can do, and will do, is to review the original source material, comment on it as simply and directly as I can, and then proceed to discuss how others have interpreted this material in later literature. What we will be left with in the end will be a variety of different opinions and insights. As for which of these will be the truth, only time will tell. This is the essential lesson we must understand with regards to all eschatological material. We very well know what it says, but we very well do not always know what it means.

Daniel, Chapter 7
The Four Beasts, The Horn, The Saints & The Son of Man.

"I saw in my vision by night, and, behold, the four winds of the heaven broke forth upon the great sea."

Needless to say, at least I hope it is needless to say, that Daniel's vision of winds and water here are archetypal images that express the depths of his own unconscious, and how the images to follow are all coming up out of those depths. In Ezekiel's Merkava vision (Chapter 1), Ezekiel was also in a day-time trance of prophecy. What he saw was also not physical or actual but symbolic. We see that Ezekiel himself confirms this when he says that he saw "what appeared to be" an image of something. He never said that what he saw was exactly that, but rather "similar to," or "in the image of."

Daniel here is having a similar experience. The winds and the sea are psychological symbols showing that what Daniel was then "seeing" was not coming from the depths of his personal unconscious, expressing his own subconscious beliefs, desires or fears. Rather, what Daniel was to experience in this dream/vision arose from out of his trans-personal self, a level of the unconscious known in Jungian psychology as the collective unconscious, or the objective psyche. This is important to emphasize here because what follows is not Daniel's own personal thoughts, but rather something that is coming into him from the root source of all collective human thought. This is itself the secret of prophecy, although what we have here is different from prophecy by only a technicality of definition.

Notice the repetition of the number four. There are four winds, and four kingdoms. This number is no coincidence. The relationship signifies to us that the four kingdoms themselves are a reflection of individual aspects within the natural order created by G-d, whose Name is not coincidentally spelled with four letters, Yod Hey Vav and Hey.

The four winds are, of course, the directions, north, south east and west. Yet, in every ancient religious and philosophical system these four also represented certain character traits. The four world empires, therefore, aside from their historicity also represent psychological elements in human society throughout the ages. Even G-d's four letter Name is said to be a coded symbol for what is called in psychology a quaternity, the symbol of balance represented by the number 4. This is also the significance of Daniel's revelation to King Nebuchadnezzar in Chapter 2.

The significance of the number 4 is that the 4 beasts come to represent the wholeness of human civilization. The number 4, therefore, does not have to be literal; it can be metaphorical to symbolize this wholeness. The four beasts also represent the symbolic parts of the whole. This orientation of looking at this is important because, since the Book of Daniel has been written, those not trained in understanding the prophetic arts have interpreted these symbols in some way literally, and tried to make predictions based upon their literal interpretations. Needless to say, all such predictions have been proven wrong. This is because the literal approach here is not valid with regards to dream vision symbols, even with something as simple as a number.

"And four great beasts came up from the sea, diverse one from another."

The four great beasts come up out of the sea. The sea always represents the depths of the mind of man, the unconscious. Yet, as we said, this "sea" represents the collective unconscious of all humanity. The beasts signify not only political bodies of power, but also the specific political philosophies that are invented out of the minds of men.

Today's political philosophies are mostly economically defined. The three modern forms of government and economics are capitalism, socialism and communism. Aside from being actual forms of government, they are also philosophical outlooks on life. The relevance of these modern three, we shall shortly see.

The text says that the beasts are diverse from one another. This means that they are different, but not necessarily entirely separate.

This reflects back to Daniel, Chapter 2 with there being four diverse elements in the one statue. Four diverse beasts, representing four philosophical orientations to the world, arise out of the minds of men that then take over great portions of the world, causing many to submit to their edicts. Not only is this a revelation of ruthless government, but also equally ruthless philosophies intent upon first twisting the minds of men, and only then to rule over them.

"The first was like a lion, and had eagle's wings, I beheld till the wings thereof were plucked off, and it was lifted up from the earth, and made stand upon two feet as a man, and a man's heart was given to it."

The first beast, representing the first empire, Babylon, as we already know. It is represented by a lion, which also is one of the Faces on the Divine Chariot (Merkava), as seen my Ezekiel. This lion had eagles wings, another animal whose Face was represented on the Divine Chariot. It was made to stand like a man, and had a man's heart, but it did not receive a man's face, similar to yet another Face on the Divine Chariot. Yet, in order to receive a heart of man, it had first to lose its eagles wings. Nowhere does it say it lost its lions body, just its eagle's wings.

The wings represent movement and ability to conquer with speed, similar to an eagle catching is prey. Babylon, as a political force, lost its power to the Persian Empire that conquered it, but nevertheless Babylonian culture survived even under Persian rule. Portions of Babylonian culture are still with us to this very day. The body of the lion still exists, but now without wings, standing upright, and with a human heart.

The worst of Babylon was removed, whereas its inner guts were transformed and made human. This was reflected in Nebuchadnezzar's stature as the golden head, the level of world government closest to the reign of G-d. The way we measure time today, broken up into 24 hour days, and 60 minute hours, had its origins first in ancient Egypt, and later in ancient Babylon. These two cultures although separate in time and space were spiritually, or as we have been saying here, psychologically/philosophically actually one, and the same.

It is no coincidence that Israel was first held in exile in Egypt, and then later in Babylon. Also, it is no coincidence that both Pharaoh of Egypt, and later Nebuchadnezzar of Babylon had their dreams, and that each had their interpreters, Joseph and Daniel respectively. This Egyptian/Babylonian connection indicates to us how, while an empire might fall from political power, its inner spirit lives on and takes on different cultural forms as time marches on. This point is vital to understanding our present world situation, as will be discussed in a later section.

"And behold another beast, a second, like to a bear, and it raised itself up on one side, and it had three ribs in its mouth between its teeth and it was said thus unto it, 'Arise, devour much flesh."

Beast number 2 is the bear. The appearance of this bear is not altered in any way from physical reality. It does what bears do, it eats. It has three ribs in its mouth, and it is commanded from Heaven to eat. That's it. That is all that is revealed about the bear, said to symbolize the Persian Empire. This is most fitting. For although the Persian Empire ruled over 127 individual nations from India to Ethiopia (ref. Esther 1), nevertheless, once the Persian Empire was conquered by the Greeks, we do not find much indigenous Persian culture left behind. Instead, we find more of the Babylonian cultural influence over the Greeks and Persian. Nevertheless, much of Persian mysticism and mythology blended with the earlier Babylonian, and these together became absorbed into the later Greek culture, giving rise to many of the foundational beliefs still embraced by many of the western world's religions.

There are three ribs in this bear's mouth. Ribs are an interesting archetype that we recognize from Genesis 2:21, with regards to the place next to the heart of Adam, from where Eve was taken. Here the bear is munching on three ribs. Classical commentaries refer to these three as symbolizing the three Kingdoms that the Persians assimilated, the Assyrian, the Babylonian and the Median. Others refer to the three as the three great Kings, Cyrus, Ahasuerus and Darius.

Regardless of whether or not either of these interpretations is correct, the interesting thing to note is the metaphor itself. Why is the image one of ribs, and not another sign? Daniel understood this metaphor. Certainly he knew and understood the Genesis story. For him, the sign of the ribs had an emotional content, similar to Eve having an emotional content with regards to Adam. Ribs always indicate something next to the heart and here, what was next to the heart, was in the mouth of the bear. The ribs, therefore, must have signified something much more dear than previous kingdoms or individual rulers. Yet, just what these ribs meant to Daniel, what the Persian Empire was meant to devour is something of great interest, but it is a revelation that at present remains unrevealed.

"After this I beheld, and lo another, like a leopard, which had upon the sides of it four wings of a fowl, the beast had also four heads and dominion was given to it."

The Greek Empire is symbolized as a devouring leopard, with four heads and four bird's wings. The word for bird used here is "Off," and indicates a domestic bird, possibly even a chicken. Chicken wings, needless to say, are nowhere near as impressive as eagle wings. As such, the image indicates that although this empire will devour like a leopard, still it is not as ferocious as the lion, nor will it move with the speed and stealth of an eagle. While historians can argue the merits and demerits of the Babylonian versus the Grecian empire, comparing one to another, in Heaven's eyes, the Grecian Empire is not considered as fierce as the Babylonian.

The four heads are classically understood to be the four kingdoms that would result with the break-up of Alexander's empire. However, with a careful review of history, we find that the Diadochi, the rival generals, friends and family of Alexander never broke up Alexander's empire into four separate kingdoms. Therefore, the four heads of the leopard, although classically referred to as such kingdoms does not match the historical record.

In light of our understanding of the symbolic archetypal nature of dream vision language we recognize that this number four again plays a role similar to the role it played when referring to the four winds of the world. The four comes to mean the inclusive whole that is subdivided into a specific collective pattern. This pattern is discussed in great detail by the later Kabbalists from the 16th century and onwards. While I do believe that Daniel's image here does reflect the reality expressed in that mystical language of later Jewish philosophy, I am not going to delve into it here so as not to lose focus of our present intent. What we can conclude here is that the image of the quaternity is powerful and complete and potent with numerous meanings and insight and is worthy of a study on its own.

"After this I saw in the night visions and behold a fourth beast, dreadful and terrible and strong exceedingly and it had great iron teeth, it devoured and broke in pieces and stamped the residue with its feet and it was diverse from all the beasts that were before it and it had ten horns."

Now, we get to the crux of the matter, the evil fourth empire that conquers and destroys the world, and is even able to overcome the saints. Here we have a source of mystery that is well worth our time to investigate.

The fourth beast is not here described as looking like any animal. No lion, bear or leopard is mentioned here. Yet, this beast is described as dreadful and terrible, a description not used to describe the others. Great iron teeth are an unnatural metaphor, not associated with the animal kingdom. Eagle's wings, or bird's wings or four heads are still images within the animal domain, but not iron teeth. Teeth, as we know, are used to grind, and to eat. The image here is that this terrible fourth beast devours and destroys, very much unlike those previous to it. Not only did it eat, it broke everything else into pieces, and then trampled it under foot in a show of complete disdain and lack of caring or concern. In this ferocity it was different from anything before it. And its difference is expressed in that this beast has ten horns.

Now again, here is where we have to be cautious in interpreting archetypal symbols. Like the number 4, the number 10 is potent with meaning far beyond its literal value. So, while most classical commentaries, identifying this fourth beast as Rome and want to refer to the ten horns as the ten emperors who ruled the empire, there is no reason for us to consider that such an interpretation is all there is to it. On the contrary, noting the significance of the ten horns, and the later horn to come, the symbols would indicate a much more archetypal meaning than a mere historical one.

"I considered the horns and, behold, there came up among them another horn, a little one, before which three of the first horns were plucked up by the roots and, behold, in this horn were eyes like the eyes of a man, and a mouth speaking great things."

The ten horns of the fourth beast symbolize not ten individual leaders, but rather specific nuances, or forms of government. Therefore, to try to apply these ten, and the little horn that follows them, to specific individuals is way too simplistic and misguided. The little horn, that is to come, is the final form of government before the coming of the kingdom of G-d. As such, we must question whether or not this form of government has, as yet, manifested itself in our world body politic. This little horn is also more a form of government than a specific individual.

In later Jewish literature, this little horn becomes synonymous with the character of Armilus, who is known in Christian literature as the Anti-Christ. Yet, while most commentaries seek to define this character as a personal individual, his identity might not be so specific or precise. The Armilus/Anti-Christ may indeed be a specific individual, but it is the system of government that he institutes and represents that prophecy speaks of.

The system, therefore, creates the man, and not the other way around. The man at the head is a figure-head. He can be anyone because he represents something bigger than himself. He is the little horn, with eyes like a man and a big mouth speaking arrogant words. Yet the key to his (or its) identity is that the little horn only emerges by destroying three other previous horns that exist in "his space."

These three horns are, like the others, interpreted to be systems or forms of government. In later Jewish apocalyptic literature, these three horns are referred to as three Kings.

Therefore, these three should be properly identified as three forms of government. If we are to apply this vision to modern times then the dominant three forms of government ruling the planet today are those mentioned earlier, capitalism, socialism and communism. Mind you, none of these three are limited to any one nation. On the contrary, all nations on Earth today subscribe to one of these three "horns" or "kings" in one way or another.

Daniel's vision, therefore, is revealing to us that somehow and in some way a new form of world government will soon arise, and "pluck up by the roots" these three forms of modern governmental systems. Therefore, some new form of government is destined to arise that "sees with the eyes of man," and is by nature extremely arrogant in the eyes of Heaven. This new form of government will so overwhelmingly impose itself that the previous structures will be, as it is written, plucked up by their roots. Therefore, the government of the Armilus/anti-Christ to come will not be communist, socialist or capitalist, rather it will be something else much more ruthless and vicious, may Heaven help us. Maybe this is what many modern conspiracy theorists have been referring to with the term "New World Order."

"I beheld 'til thrones were placed and one that was Ancient of Days did sit, his raiment was as white snow and the hair of his head like pure wool, his throne was fiery flames and the wheels thereof burning fire."

In Daniel's vision, the thrones were not originally or immediately set up. Daniel had to wait "'til thrones were placed." Again, in Heaven's eyes, there is no time, as we measure it. What this symbolizes is that G-d's judgment comes in its time, when Heaven is ready to judge. This is similar to the time that the Children of Israel spent in Egypt. They were under a decree from Heaven to be in servitude until a precise moment (ref. Genesis 15:13-14).

Then the scripture in Exodus (2:23-25) states that, *"G-d heard their groaning, and G-d remembered His covenant. And G-d saw the children of Israel, and G-d took cognizance of them."* Of course, G-d heard them before this and at all times. Yet the time was not yet right to intervene. As to why this is so, who among us can question or challenge G-d? We do not know why this is so. Some things just are the way they are, and beyond our understanding to grasp.

So, whether it was the suffering of the Children of Israel during the Egyptian exile or the suffering to be experienced by the saints in the End of Days, in both cases, both are directed by Heaven to last for a time (or in this case, a time, two-times and half-a-time). When the moment is right as decreed by G-d, then Heaven intervenes via the many ways Heaven has open at its disposal.

Then comes the Ancient of Days. This is a symbol greatly expounded upon in later Jewish mystical philosophy, called the theoretical Kabbalah. Rather than get into hair-splitting details as to what level of G-d this metaphor is referring to, it is best that we remain simple and recognize the simplicity that it is He who ordains the ways and course of the world, and of human history. He will send His angels to finally intervene, and bring about the Divine plan for proper order (ref. Daniel 4:14, Zechariah 14:5).

The description here of the Ancient of Days is completely metaphorical and symbolic. Although I do believe that this image is exactly what Daniel saw in his dream, nevertheless, it was his own mind that cognized this image corresponding to Daniel's own conscious and unconscious thoughts and projections of what an encounter with the Creator might be. Daniel's vision is most true, but we face the danger of creating mythology out of the dream symbols. We must endeavor to understand these symbols in the dream-like metaphorical context that they are intended.

Needless to say when we compare this vision of G-d to others found elsewhere in scripture we find alternative descriptions of G-d's appearance (ref. Ezekiel 1:26-28). This is not because G-d changes, but rather because the individual prophet is viewing the non-corporeal spiritual reality through the visage of his own human mind. Therefore, the individual makes a mental image in his personal mind that enables him to personally grasp the non-corporeal spiritual experience that he is witnessing in his mind's eye.

This is how the human psyche works throughout all humanity. Being that there is no physical element to spiritual reality, any experience of spiritual reality is siphoned through the imaginative faculty of the human mind. This explains the great rule of prophecy as we see from every example in scripture that no two prophets see the exact same vision of G-d. There are always subtle details of difference between the individual minds of the individual seers, and these are responsible for their minds filtering non-corporeal reality in subjective symbolic ways.

This also explains how individuals of each religion always seem to have visions that coincide with the subjective truths of their personally chosen cherished beliefs. For example, Christian Catholics, who believe in the sanctity of their Virgin Mary, will often have a vision of her. However, Born Again Christians, being of the Protestant persuasion, never have visions of Mary, but might have a vision of Jesus. Mormons will have visions of those that are special and sacred according to their traditions. Jews, on the other hand, never have visions of Mary or Jesus, but might very well have a vision of Elijah the Prophet.

Who can tell a sincere believer that their visions are false or wrong, just because one's theology is different? We do not endeavor to reject or condemn one's visions of one's sacred beliefs. On the contrary, we endeavor to understand it and get to its essence, by removing its dream image metaphorical packaging.

"A fiery stream issued and came forth from before him, thousand thousands ministered unto him and ten thousand times ten thousand stood before him, the judgment was set, and the books were opened."

"Fiery streams and thousands upon thousands of ministers." These ministers are also called G-d's messengers, better known as angels. Angelology is a very involved course of study, not immediately relevant to our present topic. However, in later literature, we will see a tremendous amount of angelic activity involved in the End of Days, in bringing about G-d's judgment upon the wicked, and to equally bring about the protection of the saints.

Indeed, Daniel earlier revealed to King Nebuchadnezzar that the angels of G-d are in charge of all the affairs of man. G-d acts through His infinite number of agent to execute and manifest the Divine Will. Daniel 4:14 states, *"The matter is by the decree of the Watchers, and the sentence by the word of the holy ones; to the intent that the living may know that the Most High rules in the kingdom of men."*

"I beheld at that time because of the voice of the great words which the horn spoke, I beheld even till the beast was slain, and its body destroyed, and it was given to be burned with fire."

Here we have a profound secret with regards to the coming of the End. The arrogant little horn which removes three forms of government in order to rule in their stead is destroyed in fire. Maybe this can be compared to the famous verses in the Book of Joel (3:3-4) that says, *"And I will show wonders in the Heavens and in the earth, blood, and fire, and pillars of smoke. The sun shall be turned into darkness, and the moon into blood, before the great and terrible day of the L-rd come."*

Fire is placed in conjunction with the pillars of smoke. The original Hebrew term for "pillars of smoke" is *Timrat Ashan*, which literally can be translated as "palm trees" of smoke. The classical commentators comment that the reason why this term *Timrat Ashan* was used to describe the pillars of smoke is because they will be shaped like palm trees. They will billow up narrow and then expand at the top, similar today to what we would call a mushroom cloud. The implication here is ominous. Yet, juxtaposing Daniel with Joel, one can interpret these verses as predicting that the little horn to come, who is to destroy three forms of world government in order to make room for himself to rule, will himself be destroyed in a nuclear holocaust. Yet, even this, is not the end of the world, or of human governments as the next verse clearly states.

"And as for the rest of the beasts, their dominion was taken away, yet their lives were prolonged for a time and a season."

The remaining beasts lose their dominion, yet as the text says, although they no longer rule, they nevertheless do survive the nuclear holocaust. In blunt terms, even after the dreaded nuclear war, and the death of the arrogant final horn, human civilization continues. In what form and for how long, this remain a secret. For here the secret of the times is introduced. The length of time of the horrible period following the slaying of the beast and its horn, wherein the other three beasts remain alive but not dominant is made known to us.

The original Hebrew term for "a time and a season" is *Zman V'Idan*. The word *Zman*, a time, can be any amount of time, however short or long. However the word *Idan*, a season, can also mean in Hebrew an epoch (Alcalay Hebrew-English Dictionary, page 1858). As such, "a time and a season" does not in any way indicate a short period of time. What is curious here, as we shall see is that this verse 12 does not seem to be mentioned later with the angel's interpretation of the fall of the fourth beast. Although the time period after its fall is not mentioned, neither is it contradicted. Therefore, we must conclude its accuracy and wonder why the angel, as we shall see below does not seem to mention it.

"I saw in the night visions and, behold, there came with the clouds of Heaven one like unto a son of man, and he came even to the Ancient of Days, and he was brought near before Him. And there was given him dominion, and glory and a kingdom, that all the peoples, nations, and languages should serve him, his dominion is an everlasting dominion, which shall not pass away, and his kingdom that which shall not be destroyed."

Here we have one of the first scriptural references to what we can interpret as a supernatural Messiah. He is said to have the likeness of a son of man. Although this term "son of man" takes on a special messianic character in later Jewish and Christian literature, here its indication simply seems to be that of a mortal human being. The original Hebrew does not say that he is a son of man, but rather one "like" a son of man.

In later literature, this individual identified as the Messiah to come, is also identified by his angelic character. In later apocalyptic literature this "son of man" is identified as the archangel Metatron, who is said to be translated Enoch. This then becomes the foundation of Enochian, and later Merkava literature. This association of the coming Messiah with the archangel Metatron is important because it was believed by many in Second Temple times that the coming Messiah would indeed be the incarnation of this special "angel of the LORD."

This association became the central belief of the original Nazarene/Ebionite Jewish community of Jerusalem, that their "Rebbe" Yeshu was indeed this long expected angel, now come in the flesh. The character of a special "supernatural" Son of Man/Messiah plays a pivotal role in a sizable portion of apocalyptic literature that came after Daniel. It is the source and foundation of what almost all later Christianity came to believe about Yeshu. So important is this issue we will have to devote an entire lesson to it in a later chapter.

"As for me Daniel, my spirit was pained in the midst of my body, and the visions of my head frightened me."

The nature of disturbing dreams and visions is common to the Biblical prophets.

"I came near unto one of them that stood by, and asked him the truth concerning all this. So he told me, and made me know the interpretation of the things."

The one whom Daniel approached is interpreted to be the angel Gabriel, the "revealer of secrets."

"These great beasts, which are four, are four kings that shall arise out of the earth. But the saints of the Most High shall receive the kingdom, and possess the kingdom forever, even for ever and ever.'

The natural sequence of human history is here outlined. We have already known that the four beasts represent four systems of government here referred to as Kings. The symbol of Kings become highly relevant in later Jewish mystical literature, when the term in used to describe a system of Divine manifestations that was ordained by G-d and came to become the source of evil in the world (ref. Isaiah 45:7), *"I form the light, and create darkness; I make peace, and create evil; I am the LORD, that does all these things."*

These Divine manifestations were later elevated (rectified) becoming the source of holiness and Divine revelation. They are called in the later mystical literature, Sefirot. The Kings are also called the "husks" or "shells" (klipot), and the "broken vessels." Although the usage of these terms in later Jewish mystical literature is highly apocalyptic, it is of the second-degree, philosophical kind, and not due to direct revelation. We will engage this topic in a later lesson. Again, I mention this here to emphasize that we must not consider the Kings to be literal human individuals. Remember, this is a dream, and regardless of how literal it seems, it still follows the spiritual/psychological pattern set by all other Biblical dreams, and the proper ways of understanding them.

In the end, it is the saints of the Most High who receive the kingdom and possess it forever. Now, here is a very interesting subtlety. Who are these saints? The Hebrew/Aramaic term here translated as saints is Kadishei Elyonim, which literally means the holy supernal ones.

Now just who are they? We assume that they are Israel. Yet, if this is so, why then does Daniel not come right out, and say so. This is his dream now, not Nebuchadnezzar's. The identities of the saints are surely safe in Daniel's mind, and in his writings. Why then does he use such a nebulous term and not something more outright, ethnic and nationalistic?

In numerous Biblical verses, too many to quote, both the earlier and later prophets speak about G-d's promises to restore the Jewish people to the Holy Land, with a renewed covenant, and a rebuilt Temple. Granted, these are messianic prophecies, and not the topic of our present concern. However, being that Israel is so identified by the earlier prophets of Israel, why now does Daniel not follow outright in their footsteps to speak clearly as do they?

The answer to this may have to do with the fact that Daniel is not in Israel, but rather in Babylon. Then again, Ezekiel is also in Babylon, and he had no problem speaking clearly about the redemption of the entire House of Israel (ref. Ezekiel, Chap 37 and the vision of the valley of dry bones). Daniel's generality here is indicative of something deeper. This is not merely a simple omission on his part. The language is clear, and at the same time the meaning of the language is not.

This unusual reference to the Kadishei Elyonim, instead of to the Children of Israel, is significant, and I believe it is prophetic in a way to reveal that not all of the saints of G-d will be exclusive to the Jewish people, and the nation of Israel. This was clear to the last of the prophets Malakhi (1:11), who prophesied after returning to Israel, saying, *"From the rising of the sun even unto the going down of the same My name is great among the nations; and in every place offerings are presented unto My name, even pure oblations; for My name is great among the nations, sayeth the LORD of hosts."*

The classical commentators ask how is it that the name of the G-d of Israel is great amongst the nations that do not know Him? They respond in brief by commenting that even if an idolater approaches Heaven, believing in his heart that he is worshiping the true Creator, G-d accepts the devotion of that one's heart, regardless of the idolatrous thoughts that have confused that one's mind.

While today it is difficult to ascertain who really is steeped in idolatry, we do nevertheless see many who call on G-d, the Creator in different ways, in accordance to the many different faiths. Regardless of these differences, G-d always judges by what is in a man's heart, and not by the thoughts that are in his head. In this way, the Jewish understanding of righteousness is open to include anyone from everywhere.

We see today in our times that there are millions of righteous Gentiles from all walks of life, and from every religious path on Earth. Although we may all disagree theologically, doctrinally, and live differently, culturally and sociologically, there is still a code that binds us all. This is the code of righteous behavior. Those who live honestly and do the right things, seeking always to honor Heaven and serve their fellow human beings, these are the righteous.

In later Jewish literature, these are called the Hasidei Umot HaOlam, the righteous of the nations. It is indicated in other prophecies (ref Isaiah 66:20-21), that when G-d gathers in Israel from amongst the nations he will also take in many from the nations, placing them in positions of service in the future Temple. *"And they shall bring all your brethren out of all the nations for an offering to the LORD, upon horses, and in chariots, and in litters, and upon mules, and upon swift beasts, to My holy mountain Jerusalem, says the LORD, as the children of Israel bring their offering in a clean vessel into the house of the LORD. And of them also will I take for the priests and for the Levites, says the LORD."*

Later Jewish literature, (Tana Dvei Eliyahu, Eliyahu Rabbah, Chapter 9), speaks of the accomplishment of the righteous Gentiles as even being enabled to receive Ruah HaKodesh (Divine inspiration), based upon the nature and level of their righteous deeds. Needless to say, the same holds true for Israel. Not all who are born Jewish merit to ascend to the spiritual level referred to as Israel. Certainly, just because one is born a Jew does not, by any stretch of the imagination, entitle such a one to be termed Kadishei Elyon, a supernal holy one. This title is not one that is given; it is one that is earned.

"Then I desired to know the truth concerning the fourth beast, which was diverse from all of them, exceeding terrible, whose teeth were of iron, and its nails of brass, which devoured, brake in pieces, and stamped the residue with its feet. And concerning the ten horns that were on its head, and the other horn which came up, and before which three fell, even that horn that had eyes, and a mouth that spoke great things, whose appearance was greater than that of its fellows."

These verses are a mere repetition of the description above. This style of symmetrical writing was common in the ancient Middle East, and was done for poetic symmetry. This is called a ring structure or chiastic pattern. There is little revealed here that was not already previously revealed. Here the beast has nails of brass, this was not previously mentioned. Brass is a hard metal, but not as hard as iron. The teeth are thus harder than the nails. Nails are used to scratch and rip. Teeth are used to chew and devour. Nails are parts of the hand, which is controlled by the will; this indicates an intention of thought. Teeth indicate an intention of hunger. Thus the two indicate one is an act of thought and intent, whereas the other is an act of nature and instinct. The instinct of the fourth beast to devour is greater than its intellectual prowess. Therefore, while the beast may be wild and unstoppable, nevertheless, its tearing power of brass nails symbolize that although his intellectual intent is almost as bad as his voracious appetite, it still weaker and could possibly be analyzed for a weakness to be exploited against it.

"I beheld, and the same horn made war with the saints, and prevailed against them. Until the Ancient of Days came, and judgment was given for the saints of the Most High and the time came, and the saints possessed the kingdom."

Now, in spite of however close to G-d the saints are, and no matter how divided they are on the surface, separated by doctrine, theology, culture and ethnicity, the evil horn is allowed by Heaven to prevail against them. Many secular scholars want to interpret this verse in light of either Roman, or earlier Grecian oppression against the Jews. This idea may have some merit, but the meaning of the verse cannot be limited in scope to such a limited time period. For although there is no definite time line constructed here, the prophecy is open ended, and although the saints are destined to win in the end, the time of that end is not stated, or even suggested.

"Thus he said, the fourth beast shall be a fourth kingdom upon earth, which shall be diverse from all the kingdoms, and shall devour the whole earth, and shall tread it down, and break it in pieces. And as for the ten horns, out of this kingdom shall ten kings arise and another shall arise after them and he shall be diverse from the former, and he shall put down three kings."

The fourth beast/kingdom, not its eleventh horn alone, is diverse from all the other kingdoms previous to it. It shall devour the entire earth, a level of conquest not ordained for the previous kingdoms. Ten kings rise out of the fourth beast, which again is a sign of its complete state of manifestation, from beginning to end; as the later mystics would say, from the sefirah Keter to Malkut.

Again, I interpret the kings spoken of here in light of later Jewish mystical literature that uses the term "kings" to identify specific elements of psychological expression, from the initial thought of being (Keter), until the final deeds in action (Malkhut/kingdom). This fourth kingdom will have the time, and the ability to fully materialize itself, its wishes and its program for humanity. None will hinder its growth or its progress. Yet, in the end an eleventh horn rises, cutting off the last three, leaving only seven, (and itself). The three removed, as stated above, may be forms of government that this world system has adopted.

"And he shall speak words against the Most High and shall wear out the saints of the Most High and he shall think to change the seasons and the law and they shall be given into his hand until a time and double-time and half-time."

The eleventh horn speaks words against the Most High. He is arrogant and challenges G-d for dominion over the Earth. Now, no man can fight a G-d in Heaven, therefore, the horn turns to fight those who shine G-d's light in this world, the saints. Remove their torch, and it is tantamount to removing G-d. This was the same sin perpetuated by the ancient King Nimrod as he pursued the building of the Tower of Babel.

Now, we see here that the horn does something so evil that no one before him ever attempted to do. He endeavors to change the fundamental reality of times and seasons. He will change the fabric of how we perceive reality, here called Dat, translated as law, but today translated as religion. The horn will try to change the fundamental understanding of man's relationship to G-d, to G-d's creation, the natural world, and even that of man's understanding of religion itself.

We see attacks of this nature prevalent today. Instead on outright assaults against traditional religion, the minions of the horn are seeking to rip out the meaning of religion, and its moral codes from inside out. In the name of righteousness, the modern minions of the horn work effortlessly to confuse the public mind into believing, accepting and acting upon their perverted vision. The modern horn seeks to teach that good is evil, and evil is good.

In many ways, the modern horn has become most successful in this endeavor.

Classical Jewish mystical literature describes how this evil horn takes full advantage of the mental confusion infused collectively within us by Adam and Eve's partaking of the forbidden fruit of the Tree of Knowledge Good and Evil. The horn is destined by Heaven to succeed even in confusing many of the saints, bringing them down. His domain is to last for a mysterious period of a time, double-time and half-time. To this day, no human being has ever understood this term, or has been able to measure just how much time this is, or when it would begin or end. We cannot even be sure whether or not this is a measure of time as defined by human standards, or Heavenly standards. Human time is measured in days, weeks and years. Heavenly time is measured by the morals, and deeds of men.

"But the judgment shall sit and his dominions shall be taken away, to be consumed and to be destroyed unto the end."

It is only after Divine judgment decrees an end to the dominion of the horn that he is cast down, just like it says in Daniel 4:14. We can provide all kinds of philosophical answers why we think G-d does what He does, but in the end, we are as much in the dark as Heaven desires for us to be. Isaiah 55:8-9 states, *"For My thoughts are not your thoughts, neither are your ways My ways, says G-d. For as the Heavens are higher than the earth, so are My ways higher than your ways, and My thoughts than your thoughts."*

Why must the saints be worn out? Why is the horn allowed to rise in the first place? There is very important reason for this! As I mentioned above, mystical Judaism considers all humanity to be blemished by the proverbial forbidden fruit of the Tree of Knowledge Good and Evil. As such, all human knowledge is considered blemished, unclear and in many ways limited and incorrect. As such, there is only so much that we human beings can know and understand.

G-d is very well aware of our blemish, and human history is not directed for the sake of refining our blemished intellect. On the contrary, our minds are so limited that they are incapable of experiencing Divine truths, the mere symbolic nature of apocalyptic revelations are clear proof of this. After all, if G-d wanted to tell us something, why does He not do so directly? Why do we have need of all this dream symbol stuff that is nothing other than confusing?

The answer here is that it is not G-d who is doing this, but us! This is the way our minds work, even at the unconscious level, because the domain of blemish is not just the intellect, but also that area the Bible refers to as the human heart. This is why G-d has commanded us to love Him with all our hearts and to place His Words upon our hearts (ref. Det. 6:5-6). Never is our heads mentioned. Our thoughts are blemished, and it is they that cloud our hearts.

So G-d's plan for humanity throughout all human history is to test and try our hearts. G-d does not want us to rely upon our heads, and our intellects. We use them, true, but G-d desires of us to purify our hearts, and to know Him intuitively and naturally. Only this heart-based inner knowledge and moral conscience connects us to G-d, and enables us to gaze upon the true Divine wisdom.

This is why we have so much disagreement in doctrine and theology between Jews, Christians, and different subgroups within each. These divisions are not from G-d. These divisions are from the blemished minds of men, who again and again relish the taste of the forbidden fruit of the Tree of Knowledge Good and Evil.

The saints are united by their heart-felt desire to serve G-d, and to bond with Him. Doctrine and theology never divide them. The saints know well the old saying, "united we stand, divided we fall." The evil horn seeks to redirect the saints from their hearts and to be like him, head oriented. As such the way of the evil horn is to crush and divide. This is how he conquers.

The saints fight the evil horn by throwing down the walls of separation, and stand united with all G-d fearing men and women, who are brother and sister saints in this good fight. The heart knows this to be true. This is why the term saints, referred to here, also echo the words of Isaiah and Malakhi that the term saints

69

include "greater" Israel, which includes the souls of the righteous Gentiles of all nations who through their devoted efforts to serve Heaven in heart-felt truth merit this inclusion in Messianic times.

"And the kingdom and the dominion, and the greatness of the kingdoms under the whole heaven, shall be given to the people of the saints of the Most High, their kingdom is an everlasting kingdom, and all dominions shall serve and obey them."

Unlike verse 13 above, notice here that the kingdom is given not to the son of man mentioned previously, but rather to the saints of the Most High. It clearly speaks in the plural here, referring to "their" kingdom, and how all dominions shall serve "them." This is clearly a veiled reference to restored Israel referenced by all the earlier prophets.

"Here is the end of the matter. As for me Daniel, my thoughts much frightened me, and my countenance was changed in me; but I kept the matter in my heart."

The visions that Daniel saw within his mind affected him so much that his face actually contorted with the revelations. This shows that Daniel took these matters to heart, and did not just place them in the back of his mind. Again, the heart is mentioned here as the seat of thought, not the mind; for a thought that is not tempered by the heart, can and is used as an instrument of death and evil. We see this around us all too much today, with so many people perpetuating so much evil, all of it justified in their minds because as they say, "it makes sense to them." These are the tentacles of the evil horn. May Heaven protect us.

Daniel's visions continue in the next few chapters. We will deal only with that material which is directly relevant to our ongoing discussions about the growth, and development of our understandings about the apocalypse.

Chapter 4

Daniel's Vision of the War Between the Two-Horned Ram & the Unicorn Goat

The Quantum Nature of Prophecy

The rational human mind always seeks to look at the surface of things, and accept such a perception as the literal truth of a thing. This unfortunate superficiality always seems to become a stumbling block when it comes to Biblical prophecy. If Biblical prophecy was mere predictions of the future, then when the future event would come about, we would see that the prophecy was true, and that it was fulfilled. We could then relegate that prophecy to the footnotes of history, with nothing left in it for the future. However, prophecy is never so monolithic.

Prophecy is not made out of stone, on the contrary it is made out of spirit. Prophecy emanates from that place where the human unconscious merges into something greater than the individual self. It is far from superficial, it is far from rational, and like the human mind itself, it is far from being monolithic. As such, the inherent nature of prophecy is fluid and alive. Prophecy expresses archetypes of humanity's collective unconscious.

Religiously speaking, we believe that the prophetic message is emanating from outside humanity, coming from the source of all, G-d. Divine communication is not a superficial thing applicable only once in space, time, and in the human mind. All Divine communication, be it the written Torah, Bible, and especially the prophecies therein all have multiple contexts and applications. A prophecy can be literally "fulfilled" in one context, and at one time can also have many other multiple meanings and applications that are "fulfilled" over centuries, in numerous instances, and even in personal aspects of an individual's life.

Prophecy is the living word of the living G-d. As such, unless one can come to know the living and understand the true spiritual nature of life itself, one will consider the living to be dead. In other words, a mere intellectual, academic approach to prophecy, trying to ascertain its exact meaning for one time and one place and no more, by definition contradicts the very nature of the prophecy itself. One cannot understand prophecy, and contradict it at the same time. However, one can indeed understand some aspects of a prophecy and at the same time misunderstand, or totally miss, other aspects of the same prophecy.

Academic, intellectual vision and insight, by themselves, are rather limited. Without an internal, psychological, psychic connection that connects the individual to his/her own personal doorway into humanity's collective unconscious, then all emanations arising from that deepest level of human thought, wisdom and revelation will be closed, and concealed to the individual. Without the inner connection to shine depth, wisdom and insight, all one has at one's disposal to understand the outside world is one's limited conscious intellect.

The conscious intellect was designed by G-d to enable us to experience, explore and understand the outside world. It is vital for such a connection. However, when it comes to connecting to "inner-space," which is our own personal unconscious, and from it to the great beyond, the method of external embrace does not work when applied internally. Internal, psychological and spiritual explorations and revelations come about in an entirely different manner, using a different mode of human thinking.

What I am describing here is the basic fundamental differences between aspects of personality known psychologically as extroversion and introversion. It is not enough that we come to the study of prophecy. We might mistakenly approach prophecy as a science, and try to analyze it. Indeed, this is why Biblical research has become such a convoluted area. So-called scholars go round and round in circles, each one hypothesizing a theory, and then jump through hoops of stretched imagination to try to prove their concocted beliefs. All, needless to say, to no avail.

Prophecy is not a science; it does not emanate from the outside world, and therefore cannot be subject to extroverted scientific methods of study. Prophecy is an art. Its flow is the beauty of the paint brush, or the musician's quill as he writes a symphony. Prophecy is quantum in nature, in that it has multiple meanings and multiples applications. Prophetic words move, flow, and breath, and thus can be understood in many different ways. Needless to say, with regards to the prophecies dealing with the End of Days, trying to figure out just what the prophecies are saying is a daunting task.

Prophecy will never be properly understood when examined exclusively in accordance to an intellectual or historical orientation. In order to understand prophecy, one must spend time in long and hard contemplative meditation, seeking one's own revelations, and insights into the written word. Without this living vibrancy of the living word, understanding prophecy remains an elusive goal.

In Second Temple times, the members of the Qumran community were led by a Teacher of Righteousness. It was the responsibility of this leader, to delve into prophecy in just this way, and to extract from it its meaning and application for the day and times at hand. The Teacher understood quantum prophecy, and was considered by the members of his group uniquely qualified to extract the subjective prophecy from its objective form.

This method of Biblical interpretation came to be called the Pesher Method. It is not the analytical method used by scholars. The Pesher is not an intellectual or rational process. It is spiritual and insightful. It is psychic Torah at its best. Pesher is the closest thing to actual prophecy that we have in our days.

Pesher is the body, form and structure of the moment embraced by the Living Torah. So vital is Torah's fluidity that for centuries it was prohibited to ever give a written form to this style. Therefore, it was always called Oral Torah in the language of the Sages. Not for naught were the Sages, after the destruction of the Second Temple, deeply concerned to permit the writing down of segments of the Oral Law, fearing that the written form would lead to a loss of its fluid vitality. Their fears proved legitimate.

Centuries later, the editor of the Babylonian Talmud, Rav Ashi tried to address this very issue when weaving together the texts that we now know as the Babylonian Talmud. Every student of Talmud knows that the texts are a curious combination of both rational analysis, and intuitive, speculative imagination. Halakha alongside agadata weaved together in an intricate and very precise web. Rav Ashi edited the Talmud in such a way that when it is studied properly, in the spirit in which it was designed, it could lead its students into a pesher mode of thinking, leading to fluid, living insights into the texts.

For the most part, later Talmudic students (to this day) have lost sight of the compilers original intent.

Although the Qumran community and the Teachers of Righteousness are long gone, the Pesher method of delving into prophecy, and revealing its relevant applications have never ceased from Israel. There are those who have mastered this art to this day. But alas, these modern day masters must maintain their anonymity due to the rash response that their revelations would receive in a world today dominated by religious intellectualism and academia, a religious society that goes to almost all extents to discount, dismiss and disregard psychic intuitive awareness.

Yet, without psychic intuitive awareness, attaining this vital goal of proper insights into prophecy cannot be achieved. Without a properly trained mind, enabled to delve into the unconscious, and to extract from there both archetype and meaning, no prophecy can be opened up for the here and now, and made understandable and applicable for modern times.

The Book of Daniel is the most excellent example of all this. In our past lessons, covering Chapters 2 and 7, we delved into psychological archetypes and dream vision symbolisms. We interpreted them as having specific meanings for specific times. We even went beyond this to describe the psychological elements of empires and kingdoms that transcend their historical realities. However, here in Daniel, Chapter 8, we are faced with a different type of vision. This vision is one of quantum nature. It has more than one application, and more than one interpretation. In other words, it is destined to come true at more than one time, and in more than one way. Let us now turn to the text and endeavor to understand a portion of its depth.

Daniel 8,
Rams & Goats, Persians & Greeks, Muslims & Christians?

The Book of Daniel is our only true apocalypse in the entire Jewish Bible. While other books reveal other specific elements in the End Times scenario, none of them match the mystery, elusiveness and generality that we find in Daniel. We have already addressed Daniel's revelations about the four world kingdoms, in both his dream and the early dream of King Nebuchadnezzar. Each description of each dream revealed important, significant details of the future, not necessarily found anywhere else in scripture.

In Daniel, Chapter 8, we come to, what for me, is a very disturbing section. The chapter deals in detail with a great war described as being between a Two Horned Ram and a Unicorn Goat. Verses 20 & 21 make it clear that the identities of these two animals are Persia and Greece respectively. However, without any further consideration, numerous commentators in both Jewish and Christian circles express in confidence that this chapter and the war in question is to be understood to be exclusively about the great battle between the Persians, symbolized by the Two Horned Ram, coming out of the east and the Greeks, symbolized by the Unicorn Goat, coming out of the west.

While this application of the prophecy certainly seems true, we are still left however, with an outstanding concern. Verses 17 & 26, spoken by the angel of G-d, identified as Gabriel, reveals to Daniel that this is a vision for the End (*L'et Ketz*, "for the End" in verse 17 and *L'yamim Rabbim*, "after many days" in verse 26). If this is indeed so, as the angel so reveals, then the Greeks and Persians spoken of in this chapter have to be much more than the actual historical characters of an ancient time.

There must be an aspect of the Greeks and the Persian that will be still be around at the time of the End, after many days. Therefore, we again see quantum prophecy here. For it would be difficult to dismiss the valid application of these events to the time period of the Second Temple. At the same time, the angel Gabriel must know what he is talking about and, therefore, there must be a complete second application of this prophecy to modern times as we approach the End of Days. This dual nature of quantum prophecy is overlooked by almost every Biblical commentator.

Therefore, we must include Daniel, Chapter 8 as another apocalyptic vision of the future, speaking of a yet future war. The details in Chapter 8 are most ominous, and we must delve into them here.

"I saw in the vision and I was by the stream Ulai. And I lifted up my eyes, and saw, and, and, behold, there stood before the stream a ram which had two horns and the two horns were high, but one was higher than the other, and the higher came up last."

The details of this vision that are not applicable to its apocalyptic nature I will not be addressing here. However, we will notice that Daniel's vision occurred by the stream Ulai. Ezekiel's chariot vision occurred while he too was alongside water, a river. There is clearly a connection between receiving prophetic visions, and outdoor locations of natural water.

"I saw the ram pushing westward, and northward, and southward and no beasts could stand before him, neither was there any that could deliver out of his hand; but he did according to his will, and magnified himself.

And as I was considering, behold, a he-goat came from the west over the face of the whole earth, not touching the ground and the goat had a conspicuous [lit. a seeing or a looking] horn between his eyes.

And he came to the ram that had the two horns, which I saw standing before the stream, and ran at him in the fury of his power.

And I saw him come close to the ram, and he was moved with embitterment against him, and smote the ram, and broke his two horns and there was no power in the ram to stand before him, but he cast him down to the ground, and trampled on him and there was none that could deliver the ram out of his hand.

And the he-goat magnified himself exceedingly and when he was strong, the great horn was broken and instead of it there came up the appearance of four horns toward the four winds of heaven."

Here again we have mention of the four inheriting the one towards the four winds of heaven. While we cannot accurately apply this dream vision metaphor literally, we recognize its archetypal nature, even as we have discussed in the previous lessons.

"And out of one of them came forth a little horn, which waxed exceeding great, toward the south, and toward the east, and toward the beauteous land.

And it waxed great, even to the armies of heaven and some of the armies and some of the stars it cast down to the ground, and trampled upon them."

This would take a great stretch of the imagination to consider that the conquering Greek Empire, even if it were under Alexander himself, would have the ability to also conquer the armies of Heaven and the stars, casting them down to Earth, trampling them. Therefore, most classical commentaries consider all these references to the armies of the heavens, the stars and even the Sar Tzava (prince of the army) to all be referring to the faithful of the Jewish people, and the High Priest.

In my opinion, it take an equal stretch of the imagination to apply this most mundane of meanings to this most profound of texts. We see in other literature of the time, preserved in the Merkava, Hekhalot and Apocalyptic traditions that indeed, human affairs are very much influenced by the angelic realm, and that human behavior can in turn affect the angelic realms. Therefore, to understand these verses in light of their implied spiritual meaning seems to be the more correct way. Somehow, and in some way, the evil affairs of men influence, affect, and blemish the Heavenly domains.

The one having such influence is the "Little Horn." We should question here the identity of the "Little Horn," for we had revealed to us in the previous Chapter 7, another "Little Horn" emanating from the fourth beast. Yet, Greece is only the third beast. Is this "Little Horn, spoken of here in Chapter 8, a different "Little Horn" than the one spoken of in Chapter 7? Do we have two separate "Little Horns," or have the two Empires, Greece and Rome, somehow managed to become one, similar to how they were portrayed in Nebuchadnezzar's dream, being two parts of the same whole?

How this Horn is described here in Chapter 8 makes it sound awfully familiar and similar to the one described in Chapter 7, which also had the power to conquer the Kadishei Elyon, the supernal holy ones. This term, Kadishei Elyon, which we understood in Chapter 7 to refer to the righteous on Earth, might indicate the same identification here in Daniel 8. Indeed, the classical commentaries do think so. However, as I said above, judging from other literature of the period, which now may include certain Dead Sea Scroll material, the references here might very well be applied to the angels in Heaven. Indeed, that term is used more often to describe the angels than to describe mortal men.

This "Little Horn" then has the ability to topple angels, and to cast stars out of the sky. Stars have always been a symbol for spiritual beings. What this verse is saying should be terrifying to anyone. Not only can this "Little Horn" conquer men, he also has what it takes to conquer portions of Heaven itself. This description is far beyond anything that could be ascribed to any historical ancient Greek leader, even the Seleucid Antiochus IV Epiphanes, the famous villain of the Hanuka story. While he did try to outlaw the Jewish religion, and punish with death all those who defied him, it could never be said about him that he conquered Heaven, and cast angels down to Earth.

Throughout history many have tried to identify the "Little Horn" as Antiochus, but as we can see from the details of the scripture itself, this identification does not exactly match. We are left with a conundrum, for how can we interpret the "Little Horn" described here in Chapter 8 as a historical reference to Antiochus, when the facts just do not match the prophetic revelations. Whereas at the same time, up until mention of the "Little Horn" everything may indeed have been able to be interpreted, and understood within the context of that historical time period.

Welcome to the wild world of prophetic interpretation, where quantum multiple realities reign supreme, wreaking havoc on the rational mind. Prophecy is quantum in nature. The "Little Horn" can be describing a spiritual reality that is created in Heaven, and it might very well be a spirit, or an archetype, that incarnates in one man after another, in past history and the future.

Why G-d in Heaven has made this to be so is surely a mystery to us mortal men. Nevertheless, we need to be aware of its reality. For we shall find that we have amongst us many fallen angels cast to Earth, and other fallen angels who have, since their fall, turned to the proverbial dark side, under the domain of the "Little Horn."

"It magnified itself, even to the prince of the armies (Sar haTzava); and from him the continual burnt-offering was taken away, and the place of his sanctuary was cast down."

This "Little Horn" has some power! Not only can he challenge angels in Heaven. He can also confront the angelic leader, himself. The Sar HaTzava spoken of here might very well be the angel Metatron, who is alternatively identified as Mikhael, the great price spoken of in Chapter 12. In Joshua 5:14, we also find an encounter with the Sar Tzavah of G-d. It is written, *"I am captain of the army (Sar Tzavah) of G-d, I am now come.' And Joshua fell on his face to the earth, and bowed down, and said to him: 'What says my lord to his servant?"* We have already made reference to this most important apocalyptic figure, identifying his presence and role in both Jewish and Christian circles. Again, we will address this issue in full in a future lesson.

In the apocalyptic scenario, the Little Horn is considered to be the final evil king prior to the destruction of the world empires, and the coming of the true kingdom of Heaven. He is referred to as

Armilus in the Jewish tradition. His name is a reference to Romulus, founder of Rome. In the Christian tradition, this individual is called the "Anti-Christ." The Horn is said to have the power of evil, similar to the power of good to be found in the Messiah. Therefore, the Horn is said to be able to challenge the Heavenly host, and even its Prince.

The text then continues to state that the continual burnt offering is taken away, but from whom? Who is the offering taken away from? The grammar in the text is clear. The continual offering is taken away from "him," and the only "him" that can be referenced here is the "him" mentioned previously. This has to refer to the Sar Tzavah himself. So, we must now ask ourselves. How is it that the chief angel in Heaven is said to have continual burnt offerings? The text does not say that the angel receives the offerings as if they were offered to him. Rather the text implies that it is the angel himself who is performing the sacrifice. It is as if the angel is performing a Heavenly counterpart of Temple sacrifice corresponding to that which occurs in the human Temple here on Earth.

Indeed, this concept is not foreign at all to Judaism. We find numerous indications of this in Qumranic/Essenic literature of the period and we even find a reference to this in later Rabbinic tradition (Hagigah 12b). *"Zevul is [the level of Heaven] in which is the heavenly Jerusalem and the [Heavenly] Temple, and the altar is built there, and Michael the great prince stands and offers upon it an offering."* The same reference is expounded upon in the Merkava literature of the Second Temple period, and expanded beyond that in later Kabbalistic literature. There is even significant reference to this concept found in Christianity, in the Book of Hebrews, where Yeshu is aggrandized, and given the place of Metatron/Mikhael as the Heavenly High Priest. This association of a man to the chief of angels is not unique to this source, for it is also found in earlier Enochian literature.

We should note that although Malakhi (2:7) does refer to the Earthly High Priest as an angel of G-d, no Earthly High Priest is ever referred to as the Sar Tzava. This is a unique term. Therefore, with all due respect to many of the classical commentaries, to identify the Sar Tzava as a historical human High Priest during the Second Temple period, this does not seem to fit the specific wording of the text. Granted, it is documented that the legitimate priesthood was kicked out of the Temple in Jerusalem, and that there existed a group that considered themselves faithful to what they believed to be authentic Temple service, and not the type that had usurped Jerusalem. It is possible to refer to the taking away of the continual offering to this event, but we are stuck with the troubling identity of the Sar Tzava, which as I said, shows no precedent of being identified with any human High Priest.

The reference to the "place of his sanctuary" being cast down can indeed be a historical reference to the casting out of the authentic Priesthood from Jerusalem. However, in light of identifying the Sar Tzava above, we are again split as to how to understand this entire verse. Is it speaking historically about the past or is it speaking prophetically about the future? Granted from Daniel's personal point of view, both time periods were in his future. But we are no longer in Daniel's time, and we must learn how to approach this most peculiar section of scripture from our personal perspectives. While the rational mind, and the many commentaries interpreting things in that light, will see this all as applying to our past, there is something, deep within the psyche, and validated by the words of the text themselves, that indicate that we have not yet seen the fulfillment of this prophecy, and indeed it must be relegated to our insights about the End of Days.

"And the host was given over to it together with the continual burnt-offering through transgression; and it cast down truth to the ground, and it wrought, and prospered."

The reason why all this seems to happen is because of the sins of the people. In other words, it is not enough that human sin causes problems in our society. Apparently, human behavior can have a trans-dimensional affect, and can even cause damage in parallel domains, even influencing that realm which we call Heaven. One has only to read the other literature of the time period to recognize that the Children of Israel, while in Babylon, Persia and even later with the return of many to the Holy Land, still never seemed to get themselves completely right and balanced before G-d. The Biblical record on this is clear.

One of the unfortunate results of religious hypocrisy is the loss of religious truth. The verse here says that truth is cast to the ground. Mind you, it does not say that truth is destroyed, or even concealed. Rather, it simply says that truth is cast to the ground. The ground is a lowly place, a place of insignificance and low respect. The prophecy thus indicates that as a result of human religious hypocrisy, here called sin, actual true spiritual teachings will be disregarded, disrespected and dismissed. That which should be great will be considered small, that which is valuable beyond measure will be considered worthless. When true spirituality is treated such, we should consider it to be a sign that the End is near.

"Then I heard one holy one speaking, and one holy one said to the anonymous one who was speaking, 'How long will be the vision of the daily sacrifice and the mute abomination, permitting the Sanctuary and the host to be trampled?'

And he said to me, 'Until evening and morning, two thousand and three hundred, and the holy ones shall be exonerated.'"

Here we have more proof that the times in question cannot be referring to the historical period of Greek dominance over Israel. Granted, while the Temple was invaded and defiled by the forces of Antiochus, we have a full record of these events recorded in the Book of Maccabees. According to substantiated historical record, recorded in Maccabees and reconfirmed in Josephus, the period of the Temple's defilement was only three years. There is no mathematical way, however inventive many commentaries have become, to fit the three year period into the predicted time of two thousand three hundred. Most classical commentaries have used this prediction as a base to make their own messianic predictions, yet as one commentator says about the other, that the other predictions has already come and gone and has not been fulfilled. Those fluent in Hebrew should see the original texts in the Rashi and Malbim commentaries on this section.

"And it came to pass, when I, even I Daniel, had seen the vision, that I sought to understand it and, behold, there stood before me as the appearance of a man.

And I heard the voice of a man between the banks of Ulai, who called, and said, 'Gabriel, make this man to understand the vision.'

So he came near where I stood and when he came, I was terrified, and fell upon my face, but he said to me: 'Understand, son of man, for the vision belong to the time of the end.'"

The word used here for the appearance of a man is *Gever*, and is related to the root of the word Gabriel. Although the name specifically means, G-d (*El*) is my strength (*gavar* being the root), nevertheless, *gavar* (strength) and *gever* (man) are spelled alike. Although the text does not clearly state it, there is a definite connection here.

Remember that even this interpretation is part and parcel of Daniel's dream vision and is equally in need of interpretation as the first part. Daniel is visualizing the angel, similar to how angels were perceived in the past by some, but radically different as perceived by others. Ezekiel (chap. 1), and before him Isaiah (chap. 6), both have visions of the Heavenly throne, and their vision of angels can only be described as something totally extraterrestrial, whereas Manoah, father of Sampson, sees an angel clearly in the image of man (Judges 13:6-11). This was an experience shared earlier by Lot in Sodom (Genesis 19), and Abraham in his tent (Genesis 18:2). Commentators also say the man who pointed Joseph in the direction of his brothers was none other than Gabriel the angel (Genesis 37:15). We learn from this that there is an entire race of angels that have a strong humanoid resemblance. These angels are called *Ishim* (men) Reference here Maimonides, Foundations of Torah, Chapter 2. They are said to have been the type of angel that came to Earth, as described in Genesis 6 taking for themselves the daughters of men.

Daniel is still communicating with Gabriel, who appears to be similar to a man, when he is told here clearly that this vision, which most commentators apply to Second Temple times, belongs to "the time of the end." Needless to say, these words are pivotal and require of us to interpret Daniel's vision in this light.

"Now as he was speaking with me, I fell into a deep sleep with my face toward the ground, but he touched me, and set me upright."

Somehow Daniel fell into a deeper trance in his vision. The angel touches him and sets him on his feet. We see a similar experience with Ezekiel (2:1), who after witnessing his profound vision of the Merkava, falls on face, but does not receive his prophecy until G-d says to him, *"Stand upon your feet and I will speak to you."* Apparently, both of these experiences are happening within the dream trance, and have a specific meaning within the context of the level of prophetic acuity.

"And he said, 'Behold, I will make you know what shall be in the latter time of the indignation, for it belongs to the appointed time of the end (Mo'ed Ketz).'"

Here we have again a reference to this being not only in the latter time, but also "the appointed time of the end" (*Mo'ed Ketz*). Some commentators wish to propose that maybe the term *Ketz*, End of Days, is itself a metaphor, with numerous applications in many generations. However, upon examination this understanding is a stretch of the imagination, without any real clear foundation. It is presented by these commentators as a philosophical point, as a means to explain the variants in prophetic language. The concept marginalizes the clear teaching here in Daniel, that G-d has a definitive plan for humanity, and a Divinely ordained time schedule for us. While we may not know or understand when G-d's plan for the End is, He certainly does.

"The ram which you saw having the two horns, they are the kings of Media and Persia.

And the rough he-goat is the king of Greece and the great horn that is between his eyes is the first king.

And as for that which was broken, in the place whereof four stood up, four kingdoms shall stand up out of the nation, but not with his power."

Again, we have here a clear identification for application in Daniel's not too distant future (if we consider a few hundred years, not that distant). Again, most commentators interpret this to refer to Alexander, and his generals who followed him. The secular scholars use this as their "proof" that this prophecy must have been written after the fact (thus hundreds of years after the historical Daniel). For the secular scholars say how else could Daniel have known the future? I have already addressed this issue in a previous lesson.

"And in the latter time of their kingdom, when the transgressors have completed their transgression, there shall stand up a king of fierce countenance, and understanding stratagems."

Notice the text says here, *"the latter time of their kingdom."* This is not a term for the End of Days, and thus can clearly be taken out of the later apocalyptic scenario. This King spoken of here is often interpreted to be Antiochus, and most likely is. But, at the same time, as quantum prophecy shows us, this interpretation does not have to be monolithic. This can be referring to many others who share a common spirit of evil, both past, present and future.

"And his power shall be mighty, but not by his own power, and he shall destroy wonderfully, and shall prosper and do, and he shall destroy them that are mighty, and the people of the saints."

Antiochus clearly declared war on the religion of Judaism, and the Jewish people faithful to it. He did destroy many of the mighty, in both body and spirit. Many others have arisen throughout the centuries in the spirit of Antiochus, with the intent to harm the Jewish people, and to destroy the Jewish religion. All such efforts clearly emanate from the singular evil spirit spoken of here.

"And through his cunning he shall cause craft to prosper in his hand, and he shall magnify himself in his heart, and in time of security shall he destroy many, he shall also stand up against the prince of princes; but he shall be broken without hand."

He shall stand up against the price of princes. The classical commentators associate this with the Sar haTzava mentioned above. They also state how this evil Little Horn will actually be able to dominate over parts of the Heavenly realm. Being that Heaven is not an actual physical place anywhere above us, or in outer space, it is proper to identify it with domains accessible only through travel in inner-space. As such, the evil Little Horn, knowing the secret of spiritual connection, will confuse the minds of the righteous, filling them with lies and falsehoods. Once so confused, the righteous will be placed in a psychological form of bondage and exile.

Without the spiritual flow from below to above, the flow from above to below also ceases. This has as much a negative effect on the powers above as it does on the powers below. This is exactly the intent of the Little Horn, and what he will plan and succeed in doing. When the flow between the worlds cease, then even the Prince of angels is effectually weakened. This is the true meaning of being in exile. Exile and bondage first begin in the mind before they ever manifests in the flesh.

"And the vision of the evenings and mornings which has been told is true; but you, shut up the vision; because it is for many days [to come]."

Shut up the vision? Gee, thanks! That is a real help! Why is this said? Because the vision belongs to the many days to come. This indicates that confusing quantum level in prophecy. Does this vision speak of the historical period of Persian-Greek conflict followed by the Seleucid occupation of Israel? Does it speak metaphorically entirely about a time in the far, far future? It is speaking about both simultaneously in a unique way that only quantum prophecy can do? Of course, the later appears to be correct.

Some of the classical commentators state that the reason why the vision was ordered concealed was because it reveals the extreme length of the exile, which we are still in, after almost two thousand years. It was believed that if at that time, the nation of Israel knew that such a future awaited them, there would be an explosion of collective despair, and a massive falling away from the paths of G-d. So as to avoid all the negative repercussions, the vision was sealed.

"And I Daniel fainted, and was sick certain days, then I rose up and did the king's business and I was appalled at the vision, but understood it not."

Even after Gabriel talked to him in his vision, Daniel confesses that he does not understand fully what it is that he saw. The question to ask is that when the command to shut up the vision was given, who was it given to? Was it spoken to Daniel to conceal what he had seen, or was it spoken to Gabriel that he should not reveal all the details to Daniel? Judging from this confession that Daniel says he did not understand the vision, maybe Gabriel was not totally forthcoming in revealing to him everything.

While Gabriel showed Daniel many things about the far, far future, possibly into our present days, how could Daniel possibly conceive who the players would be, and what details would ensue. Consider what we would understand if we were shown a vision about the far future 2500 years from now. What will life on Earth be like in 4511 AD? We cannot conceive. Who will be the warring parties then? What nations will exist then? What languages will they speak, how will they dress, and with what weapons will they fight? We would have almost no frame of relevant reference for a vision of a future so far, far away from us. Why would we think Daniel in this respect to be any different? He very well may have been shown actual things, but without a modern context, these things, identities and the like, would have not been comprehensible to him. Thus, Daniel himself was perplexed. But, as we see in later chapters, he did not end his prophetic career here. As we shall see in future lessons, Daniel has much more to reveal about times closer to him.

The vision in Daniel 8 clearly states that it is referring to the conflict between Greece and Persia. This is why most interpret this chapter literally as referring to those two political bodies in a historical time frame. Yet again, we must remember the symbolic nature of this type of vision. While Persia and Greece may be literally referred to, at the same time, they must mean very much more. How else could this vision be declared by the angel to be of the End of Days?

Who then are the Grecian and Persian Empires today that can fit the role of being the two-horned ram, and the unicorn goat spoken of herein? Needless to say, Daniel himself could not be expected to recognize and thus identify modern nations in modern times. We should never expect this of any Biblical text. Yet, applying our understanding of archetypes, we may very well be able to penetrate into Daniel 8, and consider how we might apply its mysterious message for events soon to unfold in our immediate future.

An interesting understanding of Daniel 8 can be found in the Babylonian Talmud. The Sages quoted in the following Talmudic teaching are located in the Holy Land, and date to a time over one hundred years after the destruction of the Second Temple. It can, therefore, be understood that their insights would have been passed down from an earlier generation. Just how early and from what point of origin may very well be lost in history. Nevertheless, the following section, without overtly saying it, identifies the future ram and goat, and even "predicts" their inevitable conflict, and its outcome. After reading the following Talmudic passage, pause a moment before you continue and see if you can recognize the modern significance of this material before we proceed to comment on it. The following section is from T.B. Yoma 10a:

"R. Joshua b. Levi in the name of Rabbi said: Rome is designed to fall into the hand of Persia... Rabbah b. Bar Hana in the name of R. Johanan, on the authority of R. Judah b. Ila'i, said: Rome is designed to fall into the hands of Persia may be concluded by inference from a rational argument: If in the case of the First Temple, which the sons of Shem [Solomon] built and the Babylonians destroyed and the Babylonians fell into the hands of the Persians, then how much more should this be so with the Second Temple, which the Persians built and the Romans destroyed, that the Romans should fall into the hands of the Persians.

Rab said: Persia will fall into the hands of Rome. Thereupon R. Kahana and R. Assi asked of Rab: [Shall] the builders fall into the hands of the destroyers — He said to them: Yes, it is the decree of the King.

Others say: He replied to them: They too are guilty for they destroyed the synagogues. It has also been taught in accord with the above, Persia will fall into the hands of Rome, first because they destroyed the synagogues, and then because it is the King's decree that the builders fall into the hands of the destroyers.

Rab also said: The son of David will not come until the wicked kingdom of Rome will have spread [its sway] over the whole world for nine months, as it is said: Therefore will He give them up, until the time that she who travails hath brought forth; then the residue of his brethren shall return with the children of Israel."

Let us begin our review of this section by remembering Daniel's revelation in Chapter 7, that after the fall of the Horn of the fourth beast, the other kingdoms have their dominion overturned but, nevertheless, their lives extended. All four beasts are alive simultaneously. This was also understood from Daniel, Chapter 2. The four kingdoms again have been identified as Babylon, Persia, Greece and Rome.

Now, historically and politically speaking, none of these ancient governments still exist today. However, the lands are still inhabited and they have modern governments, called by modern names that, with rare exception, are as powerful as was their ancient predecessors. Greece and Rome are the foundations of Christian Europe. Babylon and Persia are the foundations of the Muslim Middle East. Therefore, the Talmud is passing down to us an ancient tradition from a yet unknown source that the coming war between Rome and Persia would be understood today as a conflict between the Christian west, and the Muslim east.

The Christian west would most likely also include Russia, which is clearly to the north of the Middle East. Therefore, we can identify Daniel's king of the north (referred to later in Chapter 11) as the Christian world, and the king of the south as the Muslim world. If we want to understand Daniel 8 as referring to the End of Days, even as the angel says it does, now the mystery of who the End Times players are, can be understood. Indeed, in light of current events, the prophecy in Daniel 8, and the association understood from Yoma 10 makes our immediate political future ever more frightening.

As can be seen, Daniel most likely received the revelation that an extended period of exile, lasting centuries was awaiting the Jewish people. Yet, what becomes clear in Chapter 9 is equally profound. The centuries long exile does not necessarily have to occur. As we shall see in our next lesson, if the people truly repented, and returned to G-d, G-d could alter and arrange His time-line differently.

Many things need to occur before the coming of the Kingdom of G-d, but there is no definitive period of time over which these events need to occur. G-d can speed things up, and He can draw them out. Heaven is, after all, in charge, not us. As we proceed into our next lesson, discussing Daniel 9, we shall introduce some concepts that truly had a major impact on the generations of the Second Temple period.

Chapter 5

Daniel, Chapter 9: The Prophecy of Weeks The Secret of the Lost Years, The Secret of the Zadokite Anointed Prince, Pharisees or Essenes & Correcting a Small but Significant Grammatical Error

Time References in Prophecy

When it comes to understanding the reference to specific times in prophetic visions, we often run into practical problems. Although a prophecy may be clear that such a thing is to happen in such and such a time, we can often examine the historical facts, and find that the events and times do not exactly match, at least not from any point of view that we can envision, or measure.

This incongruity should come as no surprise to us, especially about specific times, and their durations as revealed by angelic beings from an un-earthly realm. Although G-d in Heaven knows well the flow and movement of time on Earth and in Heaven, it is possible that the angelic hosts do not have this same level of clarity as does our mutual LORD and Creator. We see throughout Daniel's vision a number of references to periods of time that seem to defy human logic to accurately interpret. Well here in Daniel 9, we have yet another mention of times, this time in the form of weeks, a seven week period, followed by a sixty-two week period.

While most commentators agree as to how to define this metaphor, and thus determine its duration, nevertheless, we must continue to keep in mind that this is a prophetic vision, and that nothing is as literal and exact as we may like it to be. Therefore, as we review these time periods let us keep in mind that from Heaven's point of view these times are more archetypal, and speak more about the passage and flow of spiritual energy. From our human, Earthly perspective these times should be viewed as approximations, and not as exact structures as measured by us.

Here, in Daniel 9:20-27 we find the Prophecy of Weeks. A specific amount of time is mentioned in which certain specific things are prophesied to occur. Granted certain things did occur, however not necessarily within the context of the time frame stated in the prophecy, and understood as it is commonly interpreted.

Now, personally speaking, I do not challenge or question prophecy. However, I most certainly do challenge and question the standard, classical interpretations of prophecy. When certain facts do not align with historical realities, then instead of questioning the validity of the prophecy itself, I instead question our understanding and interpretations of it. I am compelled to redefine prophecy, as it has been traditionally understood, in a rational, intellectual format. If we accept as a given that the prophecy is correct and that somehow it does not properly coincide with historical events, then it is our understanding that has fallen short, not the prophecy itself. We must therefore again, delve into prophecy from a quantum point of view, applying Pesher insights instead of rational academic interpretations.

The Prophecy of Weeks

Daniel (9:20-27) records the Prophecy of Weeks. This prophecy says many things, and has been used to say many more that the language of the text does not seem to properly support. Let us review the prophecy in total, and then we can return to contemplate it section by section.

"And while I was speaking, and praying, and confessing my sin and the sin of my people Israel, and presenting my supplication

before the LORD my G-d for the holy mountain of my G-d. While I was still speaking in prayer, the man Gabriel, whom I saw in the vision at first, approached me in swift flight about the time of the evening offering.

And he made me to understand, and talked with me, and said: 'Daniel, now I have come to make you skillful in understanding. In the beginning of your supplications, a word came forth, and I have come to tell it, for you have desirable qualities, now contemplate the word and understand the vision.

Seventy weeks have been decreed upon your people and upon the city of your Sanctuary to terminate the transgression and to end sin, and to expiate iniquity, and to bring eternal righteousness, and to seal up vision and prophet, and to anoint the Holy of Holies.

And you shall know and understand that from the emergence of the word to restore and to rebuild Jerusalem until the Anointed Prince [Mashiah Nagid] [shall be] seven weeks, and sixty-two weeks it will return and be built street and moat, but in troubled times.

And after the sixty-two weeks, the Anointed one will be cut off, and he will be no more, the city and the holy place will be destroyed, [by?] the nation of the Prince that comes, and his end will come about by inundation, and until the end of the war, it will be cut off into desolation.

And he will strengthen a covenant for the many for one week, and half the week he will abolish sacrifice and meal-offering, and on high, among abominations, will be the dumb one, and until destruction and extermination befall the dumb one."

The text opens with Daniel's narration how he was in the middle of prayer when suddenly he has a vision of the angel Gabriel, the revealer of secrets, approaching him. Gabriel reveals to Daniel the purpose of his coming is to answer Daniel's prayer. Daniel was praying about Jeremiah's prophecy about the return of the Children of Israel to the Holy land, asking Heaven when this was going to transpire. Gabriel informs Daniel that because he is a man of good character (desirable qualities), Heaven has decided to forthwith answer his supplication. The immediacy of this response is curious in light of what occurs later on in Chapter (10:12-13) when Gabriel attempts to reach Daniel but is hindered by the angelic Prince of Persia. That confrontation will have to be examined at another time.

Gabriel now tells Daniel that he must contemplate the word, and understand the vision. In other words, Daniel will need to apply psychic intuitive insight into understanding both what he is about to hear, and what he is about to see. Yet, we only have recorded the words of the vision; no actual pictorial image is recorded. The angel Gabriel does not throw around words haphazardly. If he says there is a vision then there must have been a vision, and if we do not have a record of that vision then something is either missing, or concealed, from this narrative. Being that Daniel himself writes later that he was commanded to conceal the truth of these matters, we must conclude that whatever vision came accompanying these words must have been concealed. And now Gabriel speaks to Daniel the words of the Prophecy of Weeks.

The "weeks" referred to throughout this prophecy are classically interpreted to be years. Therefore, the understanding of this prophecy is as follows. From the time the call goes forth, as it did from Cyrus, King of Persia to rebuild Jerusalem until the coming of an "Anointed Prince" shall be seven weeks, 7 x 7 = 49 years. It, meaning the Anointed Prince, is destined to stand for sixty-two weeks, 62 x 7 =434 years. This accounts for 69 out of the 70 weeks.

The prophecy says that the city of Jerusalem will be rebuilt with both street and moat. We must pause to ask, what is the meaning of this reference to street and moat? Jerusalem never was surrounded by a moat! There is more to this than meets the eye, but this is not the time or place to delve into it. These years of the Second Temple period were indeed times of great trouble of Israel, both politically and spiritually.

The political problems are well documented in historical record. The spiritual problems, however, were even greater. Due to the tremendous loss of direct spiritual insight and communion with G-d over the centuries, the significance of the spiritual loss has for the most part been forgotten. This is the greatest shame of the entire exile. However, according to some, this too was prophesied.

Although the Temple was rebuilt, the Ark of the Covenant was never rebuilt. Apparently only the original Ark could suffice for service in the Temple, and its location was (and still is to this day) a closely guarded secret. There was no Ark in the Second Temple. There was no Breastplate of Judgment, no Urim and Tumim, thus no way for the High Priest to make direct contact with G-d. Maybe because of this, prophecy soon came to an end in Israel. Malakhi was the last of the prophets.

Prophecy is direct communication with G-d. When it ceased, no one anymore could say, "Thus says the LORD, speak to the children of Israel saying." There were no more prophetic collective messages for the nation at large. Nevertheless, during this time, the Children of the Prophets survived and continued the practice of prophetic ascent, the likes of which we have described in the first chapter of the Book of Ezekiel.

During this period when direct communication with G-d was no more, direct communication with the Heavenly hosts, the numerous angels did continue. During this time, there arose an entire body of literature about these angelic communications. They became the foundation of Hekhalot and Merkava literature, and thus the beginnings of the recorded mystical traditions of Judaism.

These were the passed-down teachings of the Biblical Prophets and were thus called the Reception, known more popularly today by the Hebrew name, *Kabbalah*. This is the original and authentic Biblical Kabbalah, as opposed to that which developed centuries later in Spain, and elsewhere. The vast majority of these authentic, first-degree angelic interactions not only described events about the ancient past, they also were full of revelations about the near and far future. This is the cradle of all Apocalyptic literature.

After 420 years, the "Anointed Prince" is "cut off." It does not say that he is killed; therefore, the indication here is rather that he is concealed. "And he will be no more" is additional proof of the cessation of his function, but not necessarily of his being, similar to the existence of the Ark. It too is "cut off," and "no more," but legend has it that it has never been destroyed, and that it is destined to make a comeback.

Does anyone bother to ask, where is the Ark really? And with whom? And with whom will the Ark return, and what else will "they" be bringing with them? There are many teachings associated with all these questions that provide some interesting and profound answers. I hope to address these questions in the future, for the return of the Ark and its carriers play an important part in Apocalyptic lore.

After 420 years, the Anointed One is concealed, and with his concealment comes a "people of the coming Prince." This is usually interpreted to be a reference to Rome. These people destroy both city, and Sanctuary. The Roman destruction of Jerusalem in 68 CE, is well documented in both the Babylonian Talmud (Gittin), and Josephus.

Let us turn to the identity of the "Anointed Prince" (*Mashiah Nagid*). The title *Mashiah* is a very precise term when used in Scripture. It refers to only one of two types of individual. It refers to either a properly ordained King, or to a properly consecrated Priest. There are absolutely no other references to the word *Mashiah* (anointed one) throughout the Bible other than in one of these two contexts. Although a prophet can be anointed (ref. 1 Kings 19:16), he is still never called a *Mashiah*. We have no evidence, or even reason to suggest, that Daniel would have used the term *Mashiah* here in any manner other than what is consistent throughout all other Jewish Scripture. Therefore, we must conclude that the "Anointed Prince" must refer to either a king or priest.

Now, the text is clear, this Anointed Prince comes on the scene seven "weeks" after the call to rebuild the Temple goes forth. The Anointed Prince then stays for sixty-two weeks, and is cut off. Now, the term *Mashiah* has to be applied to either king or priest, as is consistent with Biblical precedent, and we know for a historical fact that there were no anointed kings of the House of David throughout the Second Temple period. The only ones anointed during the entire Second Temple period were the priests of the Temple.

The first priest to return from exile in Babylon was Yehoshua Ben Yotzadak (Ezra 2:2), but as Scripture records, his own sons did not follow in his footsteps in piety and righteousness. Although the Scripture refers to an Anointed Prince, and we have no one to apply this term to other than to a priest, we do have another candidate, who also was a priest, but not necessarily the High Priest in Jerusalem. I refer to Ezra the Scribe, who was also a priest (Ezra 7:1-5).

Ezra was a pivotal man in Jewish history. He single-handed rebuilt what today we call Torah and Judaism. He established what became known as the Great Assembly, a body of 120 men which served as a parliamentary body for the growing Jewish community in the Holy Land. More than this, the Babylonian Talmud (Megilah 15a) records an ancient teaching, backed by scriptural evidence that Ezra was actually the secret identity of the final Biblical prophet Malakhi. As a priest, Ezra would follow a long line of priest/prophets which included Isaiah, Jeremiah and Ezekiel.

It is possible that he down-played or even concealed his prophetic side so as to not have it come into conflict with his political office. Ezra, although a priest and prophet, was foremost a religious reformer and governor. His spiritual connection certainly enabled him to accomplish the great tasks ahead of him. Ezra, as reformer, priest and prophet was central to Israel in his day as was Moses in his day. In light of Ezra's central role in rebuilding both Judaism and the Jewish community in the Holy Land, more than anyone else he would be the right prime candidate to identity as the *Mashiah Nagid*. As a priest, we would have been a Mashiah, and as a governor, but not a king, he would have been a Nagid (prince).

If this identification is true, then Ezra, as the Anointed Prince, started a movement that lasted 420 years. This movement established by Ezra is considered to be that which is referred to in Malakhi 3:16, *"Then they that feared the LORD spoke one with another and the LORD hearkened, and heard, and a book of remembrance was written before Him, for them that feared the LORD, and that thought upon His name.*" This movement would have been either the Great Assembly itself or something else. Some even consider this verse to be the initial establishment of the band of Hasidim (pious ones) who many years later came to be the militant supporters of the Maccabees. Some believe this verse to be referring to the origins of what later became the Qumran community.

Maybe this is why the next verse speaks about the cutting off of the Anointed, but not specifically to the Anointed Prince. The reference to the first, the Anointed Prince, *Mashiah Nagid* and then to *Mashiah* in general shows a relationship of identity that the two are one. Yet, the two do not have to be speaking about an individual, for we have no record of any individual living for 420 years. However, the Torah faithful priesthood that existed during Second Temple times did meet such a fate of being established in holiness, existing in holiness for a very long time, and only then becoming corrupted by outside forces, causing the true priests to abandon Jerusalem.

The true priests headed for the wilderness there to maintain the purity of the priesthood, and the prophetic traditions that the priesthood have always guarded. Historical record shows that the righteous, faithful, anointed priests fled Jerusalem and set up camp in many places, but one is specifically known to us today. This is Qumran. The community of the Dead Sea Scrolls was clearly the remnant of righteous priests dedicated to safeguarding the holiness of their anointment. When they were cast out of Jerusalem, they were indeed cut off, and made as if they were not.

The Qumran community always referred to themselves as the Sons of Tzadok. This is a reference taken from the Book of Ezekiel (44:15) that speak of the faithful sons of the Biblical High Priest Zadok who maintain faithfulness to G-d and Torah throughout the days of exile, when the rest of Israel went astray. Another interesting point to mention is found in Ezekiel 45:7. We find reference to one who serves in the rebuilt Temple envisioned by Ezekiel. He is called there a Nasi, which means prince, the same meaning and usage of the word Nagid. The two are interchangeable. In order to enter into the Temple in the fashion described in Ezekiel, this Nasi would have to be a priest. He could not be of the bloodline of anyone else, including the bloodline of the House of David. Therefore, Ezekiel's Nasi cannot be the Messiah, son of David.

Now, here we have an interesting issue. Many of the classic commentators do refer to the Nasi described in Ezekiel as a reference to the King Messiah, Son of David. However, this cannot be so, for the office and the functions described belong to a priest and not to a king. Therefore, the Nasi spoken of in Ezekiel 45 must be the High Priest who is to serve in the rebuilt Third Temple, that is yet to come. Indeed, this is exactly how the Qumran community interpreted this passage in Ezekiel. They even gave this High Priest a very special name. They refer to him and the Messiah, Son of Aaron.

So, we have an association between the *Mashiah Nagid* (prince) in Daniel, and the Nasi (prince) in Ezekiel. Both are given a subordinate title of prince (Nagid, Nasi) which indicates a role and position second to a king. No priest is called a king, but he is called a prince. Thus, we can now identify the *Mashiah Nagid* as being the priestly line of faithful Zadokite priests who served undisturbed for 420 years only to eventually be deposed by an illegitimate priesthood. The Biblical record does record that Ezra was of the Zadokite priestly line (Ezra 7:2).

One quick note to mention here, one that will have to be expanded on in an essay of its own, is that although the Essenes and Qumran are today not considered part of mainstream Torah Judaism, they should be. There has long existed, what in my opinion, has been a historical misidentification between the Second Temple period religious groups known as the Pharisees, and the Essenes.

Although described by the historian Josephus as being two distinct and separate groups, it is unusual that there is absolutely no mention of the Essenes in any Talmudic literature, even a negative mention. This is most peculiar because the Talmud, as a compilation of Jewish life covering over a one thousand year period certainly would have mentioned a group as large and influential as the Essenes. The Talmud must make mention of the Essenes, but maybe the Essenes were not called Essenes. After all, the title Essene is of modern origins. What then were the Essenes known as during Second Temple times?

The pieces of the historical puzzle can be put together, and it is rather easy to identify the Essenes as the group known in Talmudic times as the Hasidim (ref. T.B. Berakot). And references about the Hasidim are found throughout the Talmud and Talmudic literature. They were known by various names, including the *Edah Kadisha d'Yerushalayim* (Holy Community of Jerusalem), and the *Watikin* (the Ancient Ones).

Indeed, in the 16th century, Rabbi Hayim Vital wrote in the introduction to his book, the Gates of Holiness (Sha'arei Kedusha), a description of the spirituality of the Talmudic Sages. Although he calls them there Pharisees, the actual Hebrew term is Perushim, and means the Separate Ones. This name, in and of itself, literally describes the attitude and lifestyle of the Essenes. What Rabbi Vital describes has now come to be the description of the Essenes, even though he calls them by another name. The line between these two groups is not as clear as some might think.

Granted, not all Pharisees were holy and pious. The Talmud itself (Sotah 22b) clearly states that there were "seven" types of Pharisees, six of whom were hypocrites. It seems that religious superficiality and hypocrisy existed back in those days, even as it does today. Like King Solomon said (Ecc.1:9), there is nothing new under the sun. Therefore, just because history has painted us one picture of who and what the Pharisees were, we should never accept such a monolithic view of representing the whole.

The Hasidim/Essenes were not a fringe cult or, for that matter, a group separate from the Sages. Although the Talmudic Sages have been traditionally considered to be Pharisees, this identification can surely be questioned. For there were many Talmudic Sages who lived like, studied like, taught like and were in every other way, like what we know about Essenes. Indeed, the difference between Pharisee and Essene in Second Temple times might be no more different than the differences between modern day Hasidic and Litvak Orthodox communities.

Granted the Essene documents sometimes express Torah Law legal opinions different from the dominant Pharisee view of the day. But in those days, prior to the codification of the Oral Law hundreds of years later, there were many variant opinions and practices of Torah Law. Such variants did not not make those who practiced such variants to be fringe groups or outcasts. Indeed, such differences of opinion and practice in Torah Law are even to be found today in Orthodox Jewish circles.

In my opinion, the Talmudic Sages included in their number as many Essenes as Pharisees. So rather than consider the Essenes and Qumran to be outside the framework of modern Torah Judaism, we should instead recognize that they are a part and parcel of it. Indeed, the Essenic influence is what gave rise to today what we call Jewish mysticism, *Kabbalah.*

The Scripture here in Daniel 9 then continues, and says that once the priesthood had been disposed the "nation of the [other] prince" would come and bring destruction. This has always been interpreted as being a reference to the coming of the Romans. Yet, the Romans did not come to the Holy Land in 68 CE. That is the year they destroyed Jerusalem. The Romans had entered into Israel over 100 years before this. Therefore, if we look to the date of the Roman entry into Israel, we can place the deposing of the priesthood to a time before that. Therefore, the 420 years does not speak about the length of time that the Second Temple stood as many have suggested. Rather the 420 year period is a reference to the time period of the righteous, faithful priesthood serving undisturbed.

And once the righteous Anointed Prince was deposed, then a dark evil prince comes to punish the land and the people. The first prince was the Anointed Prince. The Anointed is cut off and no more. Then comes another "people of a prince," but this one is never called anointed, but he is a ruler, although he is not a king. The ruler, Caesar, "king" of Rome, never personally came to conquer Israel. This was accomplished through his subordinates, thus they were princes, and not kings. They came with their armies, and are thus properly referred to as his people.

So now let's turn to some dates. In 586 BCE, the First Temple was destroyed by King Nebuchadnezzar of Babylon. Seventy years later in 516 BCE, the order went forth under Cyrus, King of Persia, to rebuild the Temple. Seven "weeks" after this, or 49 years, the Anointed Prince (*Mashiah Nagid*) comes, who is now clearly identified as Ezra. The year is 467 BCE. Ezra established the restored, Torah faithful priesthood that is to last for 420 years. This would take us to the year 47 BCE. By this time, the true priesthood is long gone out of Jerusalem and has relocated in exile to Qumran and elsewhere. Rome was already present in the Holy Land. By the year 6 CE, Rome had annexed Israel totally.

What we must pay attention to is that the calculation of the weeks was not a prediction that specific things had to happen at specific times. Rather the prophecy is clear that the weeks were a probation period, during which the Children of Israel had to get their behavior straight before G-d. Lacking this would set into motion a sequence of events that would lead to this long exile from which we have as yet to be redeemed.

For the 420 year period, Heaven watched, waited and judged. Heaven witnessed the corruption of the priesthood in Jerusalem (as is evident from the Book of Malakhi). Heaven watched as the true priesthood fled to the desert. Heaven watched as anarchy reigned supreme. And then Heaven paused, and allowed nature to take its course with the Romans entering the scene.

Prophetic dates never match exactly to calendar dates, however we do see that this time-line, and these associations do match completely and, therefore, should be considered the proper understanding of the Prophecy of Weeks, found here in Daniel 9.

"And he will strengthen a covenant for the many for one week, and half the week he will abolish sacrifice and meal-offering, and on high, among abominations, will be the dumb one, and until destruction and extermination befall the dumb one."

Most classical commentators interpret this to be a reference to Roman emperors, and their relationship to Israel.

In its day, the Qumran community interpreted this to be a reference to the compromised non-Zadokite priesthood that they viewed had usurped the Temple. Judging from Talmudic records from the period, the Sages were well aware of the compromised nature of the Second Temple priesthood, and made extra efforts to secure that the person serving as High Priest would at least follow their directions how to properly perform the sacred Yom Kippur ceremonies.

Indeed, in the prayers recited to this day on Yom Kippur, in the section called the Avodah Service, which enumerates in precise details all the events in the Temple on Yom Kippur and its sacrifices, there is, in the beginning section, mention how the Sages would, before the day, approach the High Priest, and make him swear that he would follow all the instructions that they would give him. Then it says they would turn and cry because, as a High Priest in the Temple and that time, he was subject to suspicion of not being true. To be fair, the text continues and says that the High Priest would also turn and cry because, being a High Priest in those days, made him subject to such suspicions. In conclusion, we again see that the Sages were very well aware of the problems with Temple Service in those later days of the Second Temple.

There is also an opinion that these words expressed in this verse are not about the Second Temple period at all, but rather a prophecy about the Armilus/Anti-Christ that is to come in the End of Days. Therefore, while this entire chapter seems to be a prophecy about Second Temple times, all of a sudden, a later interpretation of this "covenant" seems to be thrown in here. This would be inconsistent with the straightforward reading of the text and would therefore seem to exclude it. However, in light of the quantum nature of prophecy, I am not sure that we can exclude anything. Therefore, I believe that the interpretation of this verse needs to wait, and to be viewed in light of other similar verse that we find later in the conclusion of the Book of Daniel (12:11).

When Was The First Temple Destroyed?

What we see in this prophecy in Daniel 9 seems simple enough; however, there are a great number of problems that need to be addressed. The first of these issues is the numbering system. We see, and understand the metaphor of the seven weeks, and then the sixty-two weeks, but when did these "weeks" start, and when did they end? This question leads into into a controversial area of sharp disagreement as to what year was the First Temple destroyed in Jerusalem. The standard dating of the destruction was 586 BCE. However according to classical Jewish chronology the date of the destruction of the First Temple was 422 BCE. There is here a period of some 164 missing years. This is, needless to say, very important, for how can we properly date things, when the authenticity of the dates themselves are in question.

Here now lies the problem. The Prophecy of Weeks is used by classical Jewish sources to date the times of the Temples. Being that we know the Second Temple was destroyed in 68 CE. We can use that as a starting point to count backwards. Subtracting 420 years of the Second Temple and 70 years of the Babylonian exile, we arrive at the date 422 BCE. Now, the problems with this are overwhelming and contradict every known historical record.

It is documented that Nebuchadnezzar destroyed Jerusalem and the First Temple. The controversy revolves around whether this happened in 586 BCE or 422 BCE. We also know for a fact that Alexander the Great marched on Jerusalem in 332 BCE. Therefore, if we accept the standard Jewish dating for the destruction of the First Temple to have occurred in 422 BCE, then from there we begin the count of the 70 years of the Babylonian exile. Thus, the Second Temple would have begun to have been built in the year 352 BCE.

This would have been the year that Yehoshua Ben Yotzadak and Zerubabel, referred to in the Book of Zechariah, returned with the original exiles out of Babylon. Yet, this would have been only 20 years before the historically documented coming of Alexander. This is impossible, for such timing would totally contradict the Biblical record itself. For we know from the Books of Ezra and

Nehemiah that it was not until an entire generation after Yehoshua and Zerubabel that Ezra and Nehemiah themselves returned to the Holy Land. Thus, according to the classical Jewish dating, Ezra and Nehemiah would have returned to the Land of Israel decades AFTER the arrival of Alexander the Great, and this contradicts absolutely everything.

Therefore, this dating cannot possibly be correct. Nevertheless, it is the dating of the Sages of the Talmud. They knew the Biblical record as good as anyone today. Certainly they could not have made a mistake like this which is so glaring and obvious. If therefore, their dating system is no mistake, then what is it?

I suspect that the Sages knew very well what they were doing, and like Daniel before them, they were intentionally trying to cover up, and conceal both the secret of the long exile that awaited the Jewish people, and the secret as to when it was expected to end. Such a conspiracy of silence should not be quickly dismissed.

Many of the Talmudic Sages were first-degree experiencers of Merkava visions. We see this clearly with Rabbis Yohanan Ben Zakkai and Akiva. We even see Akiva's association to Qumran, being that he must have been there with Bar Kokhba when Qumran served as the rebel headquarters. If Qumran was a place of ill repute then the great Sage Akiva would have never agreed to associate himself with a potential messiah who would choose such a place as his stronghold and headquarters. Clearly the dating system of the Sages on its surface is factually incorrect, but this was not by accident. They were of the children of the prophets, of those who knew the secrets of prophetic ascent, and they were directed by Heaven, like Daniel before them to conceal matters, and that is exactly what they did.

The Book of Daniel is not what it seems. Neither is most of Talmudic literature. The great Sages of old concealed many secrets, only some of which can now be revealed. There are also many secrets left to reveal within the Book of Daniel, and their connection to the End of Days. We will thus continue our lessons in Daniel in the upcoming lesson.

Christian Understanding of Verse 9

The Anointed Prince referred to in Daniel 9:25 has always been interpreted in Christianity to be a reference to Yeshu. To Christians, the mere mention of the word Mashiah in prophecy has to be a reference to their cherished beliefs. My intent here is not to challenge the faith or cherished beliefs of anyone. However, the association of this verse with Yeshu is built upon a grammatical misreading of the text.

Jewish version - *"And you shall know and understand that from the emergence of the word to restore and to rebuild Jerusalem until the Anointed Prince [Mashiah Nagid]*

וְתֵדַע וְתַשְׂכֵּל מִן־מֹצָא דָבָר לְהָשִׁיב
וְלִבְנוֹת יְרוּשָׁלַם עַד־מָשִׁיחַ נָגִיד שָׁבֻעִים
שִׁבְעָה וְשָׁבֻעִים שִׁשִּׁים וּשְׁנַיִם תָּשׁוּב
וְנִבְנְתָה רְחוֹב וְחָרוּץ וּבְצוֹק הָעִתִּים׃

The Original Text of Daniel 9:25

*[shall be] seven weeks, and sixty-two weeks it will return **and** be built street and moat, but in troubled times."*

Christian version - *"Know and understand this: From the time the word goes out to restore and rebuild Jerusalem until the Anointed One, the ruler, comes, there will be seven 'sevens,' and sixty-two 'sevens.' It will be rebuilt with streets and a trench, but in times of trouble."*

Most likely, early Christian scholars perusing Hebrew Scriptures looking for any proof texts to validate their faith came upon this section. What they read was most likely in Greek, and not the original Hebrew. Thus, they interpreted the verse as they did, not knowing that they erred in not knowing Hebrew grammar well enough to translate the verse properly. I would like to believe that this grammatical error crept in by accident. Maybe, I am naïve, but I do not wish to accuse anyone of outright intentional misrepresentation or fraud.

The error in reading the verse this way is a curious and subtle shift in reading the original Hebrew text. The text states, *"...from the going forth of the word to restore and to build Jerusalem unto the Anointed (Mashiah) Prince, shall be seven weeks and sixty-two weeks it will return and be built street and moat."*

The verse says, *"from the going forth... unto the Anointed Prince shall be seven weeks."* Then the verse continues, with the Hebrew letter Vav introducing the next phrase, *"and for sixty-two weeks it shall be built again."* The Christians have broken up this phrase into two by inserting a break (period or comma) after the words *"sixty-two weeks"* and before *"it shall be built again."*

So, they read the verse as *"from the going forth... unto the anointed prince shall be seven weeks and sixty-two weeks. It will return and be built street and moat."* The Christians thus merge together the seven week period alongside the sixty-two week period claiming them to be one.

Now, why would the verse break down the measure of time, and separate them into two periods, one for seven week and one for sixty-two weeks? There is clearly a reason for each space of time to be separate and unique as we defined above, yet, the Christian interpretation clearly ignores this.

Also, their interpretation is not true to the rules of proper Hebrew grammar. When introducing the words, *"And sixty two weeks"* the following word in Hebrew is *Tashuv* (it will return). This word is not introduced with the letter Vav (meaning "and") and, therefore, indicates its association with the word before it that does begin with the letter Vav, indicating the proper flow of words in a Hebrew language sentence. The word *Tashuv* (it will return) is the continuation of a sentence, not the start of a new one, as the Christian version of the translation is rendered.

I know these subtleties of Hebrew grammar are not part and parcel of this book. Nevertheless, because the Christian faith in Yeshu is so important to them, and they attach so much meaning to this verse, it would not be proper to avoid mention of their beliefs, and an explanation of how such an association came about.

For Christianity, the Anointed One mentioned here in Daniel 9 is a clear reference to Yeshu. As we see, the foundations of this association cannot be supported by a proper grammatical rendering of the text. Yet, regardless of how the text is to be read, properly or improperly, the years themselves, however divided or undivided still do not add up to place this prophecy into the generation of Yeshu. In other words, the dates do not add up. Let us see.

Following the Christian rendition of Daniel 9:25, we would merge the seven week period, and sixty two week period together. This would only give us a total of 69 weeks for a sum of 483 years (69x7). The verse is clear that the time of counting the years begins, *"from the going forth of the word to rebuild Jerusalem."* This occurred in the year 516 BCE, (although some claim the date is earlier). The entire 483 year period would then have concluded, like we mentioned above, in about the year 47 BCE, a full generation or more before Yeshu was born.

The next verse (26) specifically states that, *"And after the sixty-two weeks, the Anointed one will be cut off, and he will be no more."* This would mean that Yeshu would have to come to his end, more than a generation before he was ever born. The contradiction in this is self-evident.

Needless to say those of the Christian faith will be unmoved by these revelations of the proper reading and translations of Hebrew scripture, and their correct historical applications. Faith does not require proofs and many times ignores them. I, for one, most certainly do not wish to challenge anyone's faith. However, when there is an inaccuracy proven by clear evidence, it becomes our moral obligation to correct such a mistake, and to expose it. How the individual of faith will chose to deal with this is a choice between the individual and their conscience.

Daniel, Chapter 9 clearly gives us warning that G-d is to place the nation of Israel on spiritual probation, to give them the opportunity to properly repent before G-d and to live righteous and holy lives under the direction of the proper holy priesthood, the Sons of Tzadok. Failure to accomplish this most sacred of task would be punished with the removal of the holy priesthood, even as the Ark was previously removed. Then would ensue a period of spiritual blindness and loss, leading to a difficult and prolonged exile.

Indeed, if the Sages did not arise to confront this terrible spiritual gap, the Jewish people would have ceased to exist. But being that this is not now or ever G-d's plan, Heaven enabled the Sages, specifically those trained in the spiritual and mystical arts, to take the positions of leadership over the nation, and to work effortlessly to ensure that the Nation of Israel would survive, and somehow remain faithful to G-d's Torah throughout the long and painful exile that the Sages foresaw in their prophetic wisdom.

Here we are today, almost two thousand years after the fact, and we see the results of their wisdom and efforts. The fact that we are here today reading these words is proof that the Sages were indeed correct, and indeed did succeed in their endeavors of safeguarding the Jewish people and G-d's Torah.

With all this said done, Daniel's revelations about the End of Days are far from done.

Chapter 6

Daniel, Chapters 10-12:
The Heavenly Sanhedrin & The Angelic Wars, Prophecy & Angelic Time Continuums, The Final Battles, The End & The Transformations

The Heavenly Sanhedrin & The Angelic Wars

Before we delve into the prophecies of the End found in Daniel 11, we must first review some profound revelations revealed in Chapter 10. While this chapter itself does not discuss the prophecies, it narrates the events that led up to them. These events reveal to us profound secrets about the nature of dream/vision revelations, and we also discover another very disturbing spiritual reality. Angels conduct warfare with one another in manners not to different than those conducted by human beings. In order for us to understand the true nature of human conflict we are obligated to delve into the angelic wars, to understand them, and thus to better understand ourselves.

Daniel, Chapter 10:5-6 states, *"I lifted my eyes and saw, and behold a man clad in linen, and his loins were girded with a girdle of gold studded with jewels. And his body was like Tarshish, and his face was like the appearance of lightning, and his eyes were like firebrands, and his arms and his legs were like the appearance of* *brandished copper, and the sound of his words was like the voice of a multitude.... (12-13) And he said to me, 'Fear not, Daniel, for since the first day that you set your heart to contemplate and to fast before your G-d, your words were heard, and I have come because of your words. <u>And the prince of the kingdom of Persia has been standing against me</u> for twenty-one days, and behold Michael, one of the first princes, has come to help, and I remained there beside the kings of Persia.' (20-21) And he said, 'Do you know why I have come to you? And <u>now I shall return to battle with the prince of Persia</u>; then I shall leave, and behold the prince of Greece is coming. Indeed, I shall tell you what is inscribed in a true script, but no one strengthens himself concerning these matters except Michael, your prince.'"*

The angel has been sent to answer Daniel's prayer. Yet, as the angel descends to Earth to somehow make actual contact with the mind of Daniel, he is hindered by another angel, blocking his access. Remember, this angel only came into Daniel's mind. This is clear from the verse 7, *"And I, Daniel, alone saw the vision, but the men who were with me did not see the vision, but a great quaking fell upon them, and they fled into hiding."* The others with Daniel were psychically and intuitively aware that something was happening inside Daniel. Although they could not comprehend it, they were still able to feel it and such feelings caused them to panic and to flee. Daniel was thus left alone to experience an inner vision, which could not be seen or shared with others.

What makes this episode unusual and unique is that there have been numerous times, previously recorded in scripture, where angels are present and invisible, yet do not provoke fear in those around (ref. 2 Kings 6:17). In this episode, here in Daniel, we have a clear description of a clearly "extraterrestrial" being. Yet, this close encounter of the third kind is still happening only in Daniel's mind. This makes the encounter with the Prince of Persia even more revealing.

Apparently, the Prince of Persia is no mere psychological archetype. He is a very real, actual entity. His existence and influence is quite real, existing far beyond the limits of the minds and imaginations of mortal men. This angelic Prince, does not exist alone. He is one of a race of such angelic beings, whose Divinely ordained job it is to watch over the fate of nations, and the individual subjects therein. These angels are called the Watchers.

These are the ones referred to earlier in Daniel 4:14, who by Divine authority serve as G-d's agents through which all activity on Earth is monitored and controlled. *"By the decree of the Watchers is the matter and by the word of the holy ones is the edict, in order that the living should know that the Most High rules over the kingdom of man, and to whom He wishes He gives it, and the lowest of men He sets upon it."*

We learn from this that every nation has its "guardian" angel. What is curious is that these heavenly princes do not seem to get along any better than their human counterparts. Angelic Princes struggle with one another, and when angels in Heaven above fight, so too do their corresponding nations below go to war.

How is it that there is conflict amongst the angels in Heaven? How is it that G-d allows such conflict to exist? How is it that G-d, who is over all, enables such a system to be maintained? Who is this Prince of Persia and how dare he stand against an angel sent by G-d to answer Daniel's prayer? How is it that this angel cannot resist the Prince of Persia, whereas another angel, Mikhael, can? The answers to these questions are not enumerated in Biblical literature. Indeed, other than the Book of Daniel, we would have no Biblical foundation to support this concept that there are actually warring angels. Although Biblical literature does not expand of these topics, other literature, written in close time proximity to Daniel does elaborate. One of the greatest sources of Torah revelations on these subjects is the Book of Enoch.

The Book of Enoch was written sometime during the period of the Greek occupation of the Holy Land. Its author is unknown, and is purported to be the Biblical Enoch himself. The book was written at a time, when original Torah literature, especially first-degree apocalyptic material was outlawed on punishment of death. Nevertheless, the righteous souls who practiced the spiritual ascents of the Ma'aseh Merkava continued to receive revelations and to record them, but under assumed names of Biblical characters. In this way, they could claim their books were of ancient antiquity and not of modern origins. We do not know if this idea actually fooled anyone. Nevertheless, it did keep the identities of the true authors safely concealed.

The Book of Enoch is a major work of apocalyptic literature. Much of modern day Torah *Midrashim* (legends) have their origins here. Although unknown to most today in religious Jewish circles, in its day, the Book of Enoch was most likely read as widely as were the books of the Bible themselves. What Daniel introduces, the book of Enoch elaborates in great detail. The revelations about the Watchers are startling.

The existence of the Watchers plays a significant role in all Apocalyptic literature, from both the early Second Temple times, all the way through later Zoharic literature, and materials of later dates. In later material of Talmudic influence, the Watchers are referred to as the Heavenly Court. They are said to correspond to the Court of Elders that existed during Second Temple times, and are thus called by their name, the Sanhedrin. Yet, this is the Heavenly Sanhedrin, the Court of the Watchers. While we might think this body to contain angels high and sublime, we see from literature, both old and more recent, that the Heavenly Sanhedrin of the Princes of the Nations are not exactly sympathetic towards G-d's people Israel. Recognizing the source of these Watchers helps us shine light on their struggles, and their motivations.

The Book of Enoch teaches that a group of Watchers rebelled against Heaven, and actually came to Earth, and procreated with human wives. These are the "sons of G-d" spoken of in Genesis 6, who fathered the Nefilim. Enoch's revelations expand on Daniel in many ways, yet the pertinent information regarding the source of these fallen Watchers has their source in the following selections.

"In those days when the children of man had multiplied, it happened that there were born to them handsome and beautiful daughters. And the angels, the sons of Heaven saw them and desired them and said to one another, come, let us choose wives for ourselves from among the daughters of men and beget us children."
Enoch 6:1-2

"And I, Enoch began to bless the LORD of the Mighty Ones and the King of the Universe. At that moment, the Watchers were calling me. And they said to me, Enoch, scribe of righteousness, go and make known to the Watchers of Heaven who have abandoned the High Heaven, the holy eternal place and have defiled themselves with women, as their deeds move the children of the world and have taken for themselves wives." Enoch 12:4

"Indeed you formerly were called spiritual (having) eternal life and immortal in all the generations of the world. That is why (formerly) I did not make wives for you, for the dwelling of the spiritual beings of Heaven is Heaven. But now, the giants who are born from the (union of) the spirits and flesh shall be called evil spirits upon the earth, because their dwelling shall be upon the Earth and <u>inside the Earth</u>." Enoch 15:6-8

This startling revelation of the location of the Watchers in Inner Earth plays a great role in many modern day apocalyptic scenarios and conspiracy theories. Judging from this quote from Enoch, maybe there is something to some of this.

"The spirits of the giants oppress each other, they will corrupt, fall, be excited and fall upon the Earth and cause sorrow. They eat no food, nor become thirsty, nor find obstacles. And these spirits shall rise up against the children of the people and against women, because they proceed forth (from them)." Enoch 15:11-12

"They will corrupt until the day of the great conclusion, until the great age is consummated, until everything is concluded (upon) the Watchers and the wicked ones." Enoch 16:1

Somehow it is these very same fallen Watchers that are placed by G-d to watch over the individual nations after the flood. These Watchers both serve G-d, and serve to further the unraveling of human history. In a way these Watchers both serve G-d, and fight G-d at the same time. There is mention of this Heavenly Sanhedrin, angelic Princes over the nations in both Qumranic and Talmudic literature. Most refer to these angels as the "other gods" spoken of in scripture (ref. Deut. 11:16).

Indeed, it is very possible that many of the legends of the nations, be they those of Olympus or Asgard, might very well have some foundation in truth, based on the escapades of these angelic entities and their mixed-race offspring.

In the early 1600's, Rabbi Avraham Azulai wrote a section about these entities in his work entitled *Hesed L'Avraham*. His words neatly sum up the insights and teachings of this subject that have, by his day, been passed down for centuries. It is appropriate to translate a portion of his words here. This selection is from Section (Me'ayin) 6, Chapter (Nahar) 1.

"Each and every nation below has above a corresponding Prince for his land. Each one stands facing his land and he receives from the external ten crowns and seven palaces. From there he nourishes his nation, be it energy (shefa) for the people's souls or be it for their sustenance. All the spiritual energy that nourishes his land comes to it through the Prince that sustains it. For he has a portion in the upper firmament, thus all physical armies are like his spiritual armies and the physical land and forces are just as much his as are the spiritual. No earthly king can defeat another earthly king before there is a prior war between their two heavenly Princes and their armies above."

The angelic Prince of Persia has sole rule over his domain. He has the authority, and the right to bar entry to any other angelic entity seeking entry. The Prince can delay him or deny him access at will. Apparently this is exactly what happened. The Prince of Persia did not care that the angel seeking entry was on a mission from G-d. As far has he was concerned the Prince of Persia was also on a mission from G-d, that being to maintain and direct the welfare of the Persian nation. In such a position of authority, he has the right to allow or deny spiritual entry to anyone approaching his land.

Daniel, however, was not a Persian, although he did live in the land of the Persian Prince. Daniel, as a Jew, is under the dominion of the angelic Prince of Israel, who is identified here as Mikhael, and who we have identified earlier as being Metatron, the Prince of Princes (Sar haPanim).

When the angelic envoy is barred from entering Persia, rather than return to G-d's throne to complain, the angel merely goes through the proper angelic diplomatic channels. He approaches Israel's angel, Mikhael, and informs him that he (the envoy angel) has a "special delivery" for Daniel in Persia. Mikhael, apparently has jurisdiction over the souls of Jews wherever they are. Needless to say, this does not sit well with the Prince of Persia (or for that matter, with all the other angelic Princes). Regardless of their resentment of not having control and dominion over a population residing in their territories, the angelic Princes are subject to Mikhael/Metatron and are forced to submit to his will and authority. In this way the angelic envoy was able to bypass the Prince of Persia, and contact Daniel. But, mind you, this argument amongst the angels still took up time as measured here in the physical world. These conflicts are by no means metaphorical or symbolic. We are talking here about real entities that exist in real time.

Angelic Princes to this day, do not always like the Jews, simply because they are a nation within their domain not subject to their authority. When Jews act for the betterment of their host nation, then the angelic Prince over that nation welcomes them with open arms. When, however, Jewish people abuse their welcome and act sinfully in their host nation, the angelic Prince of that nation, fearing Divine retribution for the sins of the Jews in his territory seeks to have them removed, and cast out from his domain. This is why since the days of the Babylonian exile Jews have wandered from nation to nation. Some nations welcome them with open arms and embrace, others reject them. This is all due to the behavior of the people, and the prerogatives of the angelic Princes.

The great apocalyptic wars in the End of Days is considered to be G-d's final judgment upon the fallen Watchers for their original betrayal of their heavenly source and for the way they have mistreated Israel throughout the centuries. Isaiah (24:19), *"On that day, G-d will punish the hosts of Heaven in Heaven and the kings of the Earth on the Earth."* It is G-d who arouses the Watchers to war, and it is they who arouse the nations beneath them to battle. In this way, both man and fallen angel are punished for their sins, evil is removed from Earth, and rebirth can then occur. All this is discussed in numerous places throughout all apocalyptic literature written over many centuries.

Prophecy & Angelic Time Continuums

As we begin our discussion of Daniel, Chapter 11, we are at first confronted with a dilemma. Is this chapter speaking about the immediate days after the Grecian take-over of the Middle East? Do we identify the warring kings of the North and South as the Seleucid and Ptolemy? If this is so, then why does the prophecy state that these are visions for the time of the end, *"And at the end of years" (verse 6)* and *"And at the time of the end" (verse 40)?*

Here again we have another example of the quantum nature of prophetic revelations. The quantum nature of prophecy places together future events that, from our point of time reference, might be separated from one another by centuries or even millennium. As we review the final revelations in the Book of Daniel, Chapters 11 & 12, we have such an occurrence. Chapter 10 explains the preamble of the vision that is then fully revealed in these final two chapters. Yet, as we read Chapter 11, we get the impression, as almost every classical commentator did, that the chapter is discussing events that occurred during the times of the Grecian occupation of the Middle East. To interpret this material in this light sounds so right. Yet, we are bothered by two simple phrases, which take our nice comfortable understanding, and stand it on its head.

Ul'ketz Shanim "And at the end of years" (verse 6) and *Uv'et Ketz "And at the time of the end" (verse 40),* takes us out of a scenario in the Grecian period. This period in Second Temple history was by no definition "at the end of years," or "at the time of the end" of anything. Therefore, Daniel Chapter 11 could not be talking about the time of the Greeks, or could it? And, if indeed, it is speaking about events in our future, "at the end of years" and "at the time of the end," then what exactly is the entire prophecy actually saying?

Here is where, I believe, our understanding of quantum prophecy needs to slip in. It appears to me that both periods of time are being prophetically discussed simultaneously. And it is very possible that the prophecy is not being expressed in a monolithic, straightforward time sequential. This means that the events in later verses could very well happen before, or after, the events in previous verses.

It is very possible that we are here addressing a prophecy that, to a point, makes sense by applying it to the past, and at the same time will only make full sense once it has been completely fulfilled in the future. Without skipping a beat, the text just makes this jump, seemingly out of nowhere. Yet, the text continues to discuss the same cast of characters and what appear to be the same events.

How is it that this is possible? How can we be discussing a military conflict, and then jump forward in time thousands of years, and continue the battle without even mentioning a break in time, hostilities or anything?

How, and why, angelic revelations are the way they are is a matter known to the angels, and unknown to humanity. From this we must conclude: angels experience time and reality, be it their own reality or ours, radically differently that do we here on Earth. What for us seems to be confusing and mysterious, in the eyes of the angelic races is rational, logical, straightforward, and clear as a bell.

I might add that the reverse is also true. Angels looks upon human beings with bewilderment, and disrespect. They wonder how we can live and exist the way that we do. Indeed, there is an entire genre of Torah mystical literature that teaches one how to prepare to commune with angels. Among the requirements to be able to tune into angelic communion is the full detachment from human desires and physical pleasures. Angels look upon such associations with disgust.

Aside from the ardent disciplines necessary to detach from the things of this world, the adept must also develop a mindset that, judging from normal psychological standards, would be considered insane. Prophets were taught to become, what we today call, "right-brain" dominant, and to live in a psychic reality, where that which is invisible, unseen to others, is as real to the prophet as anything that can be seen and touched by others.

The prophets, and the later children of the prophets, who communed with angels, looked at life and the world from a point of view almost as radically different from us as that of the angels themselves. Indeed, throughout First Temple times, the prophets were often called insane (*Meshugah*), see 2 Kings 9:11. From a standard human point of view, maybe they were, but from a Heavenly/angelic point of view, their perceptions of reality were far more correct than those considered by us to be normal.

It is very evident that our two races, human and angelic, have radically different perceptions of the time space continuum that surrounds us. It may very well be that time in the angelic realms flows in the exact opposite direction than time flows here in our universe.

Our time flows according to our perception flow, in a straight and single line, from past, to present, to future. Angelic time, from their perceptions flows the same way, however, when viewed from our point of view the flow is opposite. In other words, angels live in a time space continuum wherein which their time flows backwards, by our standards. For them, our future is their past. Thus their time flows from (for example) right to left, whereas our time (for example) flows from left to right. Eventually the two opposite time lines are destined to meet, And what will happen then? Will they converge and blend into one, going off into a yet unknown third direction? We do not have any answers for this.

What we do know is that prophecy clearly shows that the general course of human history is predetermined. The prophets, seers and mystics who revealed these things possessed knowledge and insight that we do not. Those who commune with the seers and mystics are the same angels who are watching us and guiding us, directing all human activity (Daniel 4:14). They know that we are headed towards an inevitable collision between our dimensional plane and theirs.

The point of time convergence, when the two universes collide, I believe, is that great and awful Day of the LORD spoken of throughout Scripture. This is the time of the coming of the Mashiah, and the beginning of fundamental changes in how our universe will operate, and how we will live in it. This collision of realities will so alter everything, that life as we know it will be radically different. This, however, is what comes after the End of Days, with the renewal of Heaven and Earth. It is not the topic of our present inquiry.

It is revelations of this kind that define the quantum nature of prophecy. Things are not as straightforward as they seem. When angels reveal to us future events, they are looking at those events from their own perspective, not ours. When angels see wars and battles they are not looking exclusively at the physical manifestation of these things as they transpire on Earth. Rather the angels observe, and thus reveal in prophecy, the actual spiritual nature of the battles going on.

Essentially these are battles, going on in Heaven, are the source of those that occur on Earth. Therefore, when Daniel records the great battle between the kings of the North and South, he is not referring to just the human counterparts of these kings, speaking about them within a singular historical context. Rather, Daniel is describing a psychic, spiritual reality that exists in simultaneous times, both in our past, and in our future.

The angelic princes fight their battle in Heaven and as they fight, their war materializes at different times, and in different places here on Earth. So, for us here what seems to be two separate wars, on two separate fronts, are actually one and the same. They are the same spirits fighting the same battle, yet their battle materializes on Earth in different times, and different places because the laws of the space time continuum that governs the angels is radically different from the continuum that governs us.

Therefore, Daniel 11 is speaking about a war in Heaven, and the revelation he receives speaks about how this war will materialize in both our pasts and future. With these insights we can now come to understand the final prophecies in the Book of Daniel, specifically in light of what we have already revealed in our previous lessons.

The War of the Kings of the North & the South

"And now, I shall tell you the truth. Behold three more kings will arise in Persia, and the fourth one will become wealthy with great wealth, and when he becomes strong with his wealth, he will arouse all against the kingdom of Greece. And a mighty king will arise and will rule a great dominion and do according to his will. And when he arises, his kingdom will be broken, and it will be divided to the four directions of the heavens, but not to his posterity, and not like the dominion that he ruled, for his kingdom will be uprooted and to others besides those. And when he arises, his kingdom will be broken, and it will be divided to the four directions of the heavens, but not to his posterity, and not like the dominion that he ruled, for his kingdom will be uprooted and to others besides those. And the king of the south will overwhelm [the king of the north] and his officers, and he will rule with great dominion over his ruling. And at the end of years they shall join themselves together; and the daughter of the king of the south shall come to the king of the north to make an agreement; but she shall not retain the strength of her arm; neither shall he stand, nor his arm; but she shall be given up, and they that brought her, and he that begot her, and he that obtained her in those times." Daniel 11:1-6

To begin an interpretation of these verses in light of the Grecian period would make proper sense. Yet, while we can do this, we also know that there is more to these words than a singular monolithic meaning. Now, here comes the hard part. Being that we need to understand this entire chapter also in the light of the End of Days, how do we go about doing this? In other words, what is Chapter 11 predicting for the End of Days, how do we decipher it, and learn from it?

A point well-made by classical Jewish commentators is that many of the prophecies are just not going to make sense until the time comes for their fulfillment. Only then, those with Pesher, (as described in an earlier essay), will have the keen insight and revelation to perceive that the then current events are the fulfillment of these words in their times.

Until then, all we can do is review what we have before us, and try to fit the pieces of prophecy together as we would a puzzle. Only one who has an image of what the whole is supposed to look like will understand where and how the pieces of the puzzle are meant to fit together. We have to look at almost the entire Chapter 11 in this light. We can speculate, and those who have Pesher insights can offer their revelations. However, we will all just have to wait and see how history is unveiled, and how it is that G-d decides to walk us through it.

Remember, as we learned above, all Earthly wars are expressions of angelic wars in Heaven. And angelic wars in Heaven do not unfold in accordance to the sequential passage of time here in our physical universe. Therefore, the battles spoken of in Daniel, from our point of view are on-going, even at this very moment. They manifest here on Earth in different ways, in different times, under the aliases of different players. Yet, regardless of whatever face is worn, underlying it is the power, force and motivation of the Watchers.

This is a crucial and vital point for us to remember, especially in light of modern politics, and current events. For the enemies we face today are the same old ones that we have always faced in the past. In Exodus (17:8), Israel faced their archenemy Amalek after they left Egypt. After an inconclusive battle, *"the LORD said Moses, Write this for a memorial in the book, and rehearse it in the ears of Joshua, for I will utterly blot out the remembrance of Amalek from under heaven... And he said, 'The hand [is] upon the throne of the LORD, the LORD will wage war with Amalek from generation to generation.'"* (Ex. 17:14, 16).

Amalek's angelic counterpart is with us in every generation. His name and face changes as the tides of political fortune ebb and flow. Nevertheless, as the verse says, the war will last from generation to generation, until in the End of Days, Amalek is finally defeated. Yet, just what is Amalek's final face has yet to be determined.

The Final Battles

It appears from these initial verses here in Daniel 11, that the Kings in question refer to the Kings of Persia and Greece. Yet, as we have already learned, and seen clearly in Daniel, Chapter 10, we are not necessarily speaking about human kings of flesh and blood. For if so, then we would indeed be severely limited to a precise and specific time period that could cover the lifespans of mortal human beings. But seeing how we flow through time from events in the near future to events in the far future, we can see that any references here cannot be to mere kings of flesh and blood, but rather to their angelic princes, spoken of in Daniel 10. It is they who wage war in Heaven and have done so since the days of Daniel, to our very own. Although modern government and religions change, the angelic princes that guide and control them do not change. Angelic wars are the topic here, and what we have is Daniel's revelations, always in symbolic metaphorical language, as to what is actually going on behind the scenes motivating human conflict here on Earth.

Persia is still Persia, and Greece represents all Europe, because Greece was absorbed into Rome, and Rome was, and still is all Europe. Persia today is the eastern domain of Islam. Greece today is the western domain of Christendom. It is these two major world powers represented here as the King of the North, and the King of the South.

It is these two Kings that were originally perceive in King Nebuchadnezzar's dream of the great stature whose feet were mixed of iron and clay. The iron and clay are these two kingdoms. It is here at the End of Days that they are destined to clash in a great battle of civilizations. The End Times scenarios are created by G-d specifically to rein in his wanton Watchers, and to elevate humanity and our world to their rightful places, robbed from us with the fall in Eden.

"And at the time of the end, the king of the south will clash with him, and the king of the north will storm over him with chariots, with horsemen, and with many ships, and he will come into the lands and inundate and pass."

Here we are now, *"at the time of the end."* The final words of this prophecy are definitively speaking about the End Times, so it is appropriate and possible for us to address them. Even some of the classical commentators recognize this, and continue to interpret this remaining portion of the Book of Daniel in this light, applying these revelations to those made by Ezekiel (38-39) about the great attack led by Gog and Magog.

Again, we see here the obvious use of prophetic metaphor. The King of the North attacks the King of the South with chariots and horsemen. While there are some modern armies that still maintain a cavalry, there are none to my knowledge that still fight with chariots. The Hebrew word used here for chariots is *Rekhev* and this is also the modern Hebrew word for automobile. Therefore, Daniel's words can be taken out of an ancient context, and understood in a modern context, one that Daniel himself might not have understood. Then the verse speaks of what we might refer to today as a naval armada. The King of the North attacks the King of the South by land and by sea, with a huge show of force.

"He shall enter also into the beautiful land, and many shall stumble; but these shall be delivered out of his hand, Edom, and Moab, and the chief of the children of Ammon."

It is clear that the *Eretz HaTzvi* "the beautiful land" is a reference to the Land of Israel. The King of the North is identified here in classical commentaries by the name given him in Ezekiel 38. He is Gog. In Ezekiel 39:2, G-d says to him, *"And I will turn you about and lead you on, and will cause you to come up from the uttermost parts of the north and I will bring you upon the mountains of Israel."* Gog comes to the Holy Land to conquer. His attack will be devastating, but he is not destined to conquer the Land, or to completely wipe out its Jewish population. As we learn from the Ezekiel prophecies, the armies of Gog are wiped out by a terrible earthquake that strikes them while in the Land of Israel.

What is interesting to note here is that Edom, Moab and part of Ammon escape Gog's onslaught. These names are not references to nations, but rather to the lands these nations once inhabited. These lands are present day southern Jordan, and northern Arabia.

Gog's armies come into the Land from the north, through modern day Lebanon and Syria, entering into Israel through the Galilee and Golan, destroying them totally, according to many later predictions. Gog is to march south towards the heartland before he is toppled by Divine retribution. Many in Israel, as prophesied elsewhere, will have to flee to the deserts in order to survive. These deserts are here identified. Fleeing Israelis will pour into Jordan and Arabia, and from there, fully armed militarily and spiritually with faith, will find haven from Gog's invading armies. Yet, the scenario does not end here.

"And he will stretch forth his hand upon lands, and the land of Egypt will not survive."

What Daniel reveals here about this final war is also reverberated in parallel prophecies found in Ezekiel, Isaiah, and even Zechariah. The complete destruction of Egypt is a prophetic theme repeated often in Scripture. The land of Egypt, and its populace, is foreseen not to survive.

"And he will rule over the treasures of the gold and silver and over all the precious things of Egypt, and the Libyans and the Cushites will be at his steps."

Again, the invading King takes possession of Egyptian wealth. Just what that might be is anyone's guess. The Libyans and Cushites (Ethiopians) will be in striking distance for attack. This is peculiar, for we see from Ezekiel's mention of Gog and Magog that Libya and Cush (Ethiopia) fight for Gog. If they fight for Gog, then whose lands are before them to attack? Maybe there will be elements in both places that will be divided, and those with Gog seek to "liberate" their homelands from those who, at that time, will possess them. This may be a subtle reference to the King of the South, properly identified as Al Mahdi, the Muslim messiah. The Kingdom of the South may very well be Islam's longed-for renewed Caliphate.

"And tidings will terrify him from the east and from the north, and he will go forth in great wrath to destroy and to exterminate many.

"And I will send a fire on Magog, and on them that dwell safely in the isles; and they shall know that I am the LORD" (Ezekiel 39:6). The armies of Gog may be entering Israel, not only to attack and destroy the Jewish nation, but also using the Holy Land as an avenue of attack to reach the King of the South. The Al Mahdi may be, at this time, ruling in Mecca, and the invading armies of Gog, King of the North, invade via Israel to attack him. But, as we see from both Daniel and Ezekiel, something happens to the nations of the North while their armies are here.

A terrible occurrence befalls their homelands, described as fire. This very well may be the same fire described by Joel (3:3), who spoke of *"blood, fire and pillars of smoke."* We have already identified these pillars of smoke as mushroom clouds, thus signifying a nuclear attack. It can thus be interpreted that Al Mahdi will launch a full scale nuclear attack against, what we today call, the western nations. This attack may be so devastating that it can off-set the balance of the entire planet.

The entire Earth could be disrupted, causing the great earthquake, spoken of in Ezekiel 38. As we see throughout Scripture, G-d often uses the natural forces at His disposal to execute judgment against the wicked. Gog's army is decimated but apparently he has enough remaining forces to "go forth with great wrath and destroy and exterminate many." Apparently, after the failure of this invasion plan, Gog will try another.

"And he will pitch his palatial tents between the seas and the beautiful holy mountain, and he will come to his end, and no one will help him."

Gog is destined to fall. This is the defeat of the Little Horn spoken of in Chapter 7. However, Chapter 7 is also very clear that after the fall of the Little Horn, the other kingdoms will remain for a "time and a season." The powers of the west are destined to come to an end. Yet, the King of the South, Al Mahdi still remains. What is implied here in Daniel is that in the great conflict to come between the Christian West and the Muslim East, it is the Islamic Caliphate that seems to win the war. This outcome however would seem to contradict the conclusions expressed in the Talmud (Yoma 10a), that it is the edict of G-d for Persia (Islam) to fall to Rome (Christian west).

However, the Talmud does indeed express opinions in both ways, although the argument for the victory of Persia is the more convincing. Still, maybe, the Talmud was following in the footsteps of the Sages prophetic ways and concealing matters about the future. For although the opinion expressed in the Talmud that Rome would defeat Persia and rule for 9 months is the final opinion expressed in the discussion, the Talmud does not overtly say, that this was to be accepted as the final word.

Indeed, Rav Ashi the compiler of the Talmud, was not one for declaring final words. As a master of the prophetic system and Pesher form of interpreting Torah, he knew very well to present matters as he did, in an open-ended form, which leaves us a lot of room to see multiple sides, not only of this issue, but in every other Talmudic issue as well.

What is interesting to note is that while Daniel's scenario here might be construed to conflict with the Talmudic version of the outcome, it coincides completely with what was written many years later in the Zohar. Zoharic tradition is almost unique in expressing that in the End of Days, it will be the King of Persia (Al Mahdi?) who will conquer most of Israel, only to fall at the gates of Jerusalem as described in Zechariah 14.

The End & The Transformations

12:1. "Now <u>at that time</u>, Michael, the great prince, who stands over the children of your people, will be silent, and <u>it will be a time of distress that never was since a nation existed until that time</u>, and at that time, your people will escape, everyone who is found inscribed in the book."

This is the time classically referred to as the *Hevlei Mashiah* (the birth-pangs of the Messiah). It is understood that this will be the aftermath of a world-wide nuclear war, with all its residual effects in the natural world. This will be a time of great testing for the righteous to see if they can withstand the onslaught of every natural problem that could possibly occur. Yet, all this happens for a reason, one so eloquently explained by Rabbi Avraham Azulai in his Hesed L'Avraham (Fifth Fountain, Eye of Judgment, River 36). He writes that these hard times to come are to test the righteous to cleanse their souls of any and all attractions for this physical world.

"From the level of Atzilut is the Torah elucidated through the emanated Sefirot. All subject matters of Torah are not according to how they appear, rather are to be interpreted according to the way of the Zohar, i.e. according to Sod (the secret meanings). When the end times come, when the klipot (the unclean shells) are to be nullified, Israel is to be sifted, like separating good food from garbage. Then all will be "good"; there will be no "bad" amongst them. Those who have adorned themselves with good deeds, who have performed their mitzvot and their prayers according to the Sod, in purity and cleanliness, will certainly sparkle in accordance to the secret of the Tree of Life, which is none other than the soul of the soul of Atzilut.

In the end times, these ones will not suffer from the travails, for the travails are exclusively for those of the Pshat (the simple meanings of Torah). They are of the Tree of Knowledge good and evil, their souls emanate from Beriah and Yetzirah and are thus surrounded by the wicked. These must be tested to see to which side they will adhere, whether good or bad. Of the ones who emanate from above, from the Tree of Life, the verse says "and they who are wise shall shine like the brightness (zohar) of the firmament" (Dan. 12:13) for they are of Atzilut. Thus the travails of the final days shall not befall them as it shall befall the transgressors.

G-d is going to remove from the righteous all impeding physical accouterments, and teach the righteous the age-old lesson found in the Torah that, *"He would make you know that man does not live by bread alone, but rather by, whatever comes forth from the mouth of the LORD does man live"* (Deut 8:3).

This will be a major transformational period for the righteous. They will not only be transformed psychologically and spiritually, this reawakening will also somehow "kick-start" a genetic change at the DNA level, and entire groups of righteous souls will start to evolve (guided by Heavenly design of course) into a newer and higher species of humanity. They will genetically be transformed from homo-sapient man to homo-superiors. The select of humanity will be forced to evolve, by Divine design, back to the original stature of Adamic man, before the fall in Eden. This will all come about as a result of the deprivations due to be experienced as a result of the terrible war to come and its aftermath. And still, there is yet no sign in Daniel of the coming of the Messiah!

"And many who sleep in the dust of the earth will awaken-these for eternal life, and those for disgrace, for eternal abhorrence."

Most interpret this to be a reference to the resurrection of the dead. Based on this verse, many accept a literal resurrection as a foundation of faith. How and when the resurrection is to take place will have to be addressed in another forum. It is not the topic of our present discussion. However, Rabbi Azulai, (Hesed L'Avraham, Third Fountain, Eye of the Land, River 22) passed down an interesting teaching on this subject, which may be applicable here. I first translated and published this in my book Yikra B'Shmi.

"Know that it is an accepted tradition in our hands that on the day that King Mashiah will come with the in-gathering of the exiles to the Land of Israel, there will be found in the Land only seven thousands of the children of Israel. On this same day, the dead of the Land of Israel shall be restored to life. On that same day also, the walls of Jerusalem shall be removed, and rebuilt from precious stones and pearls. Then, at the time, the dead of the Land of Israel shall be restored to life; they shall be new spiritual creations. Also, the seven thousand who shall be left alive at that time, they too shall be new creations, all of them with spiritual bodies, similar to the body of Adam prior to his sin, and the body of Enoch, Moshe our teacher and Eliyahu. They shall all float in the air, soaring like eagles. This shall be seen by all the people ingathered from the exile.

When these, their brothers, are made a new creation, soaring through the air, going to dwell in the (lower) Gan Eden to learn Torah from the Mouth of the Holy One, Blessed be He, then all together the children of the ingathered exiles, with worry in their hearts and anguish in their souls cry out to King Mashiah. They ask, we also are the nation of the Children of Israel, like them. Why have they merited to be spiritual beings in body and soul, and not us? Why are we less?

The Mashiah shall answer them saying, "The character of the Holy One, Blessed be He is already known and famous; He gives to each one 'measure for measure'. These also dwelled outside of the Land, and after great effort they succeeded to come to the Land of Israel, in order to merit a purified soul. They cared not for their physical or material well-being. They came by sea and by land, and were not dissuaded by the dangers of the sea or of being robbed along their journey. They suffered under cruel regimes, all for the sake of the essence of their spirit and soul. Therefore they have become complete spiritual beings, measure for measure.

However all of you, who had the ability to come to the Land of Israel, as they did, were discouraged over concern for your finances. You were worried about your physical safety and your money. These, you made to be the principle things in your lives, and not your spirit and soul. Therefore you have remained physical beings."

"And the wise will shine like the brightness of the sky, and those who bring the multitudes to righteousness like the stars forever and ever."

This is addressed in the quotation from the Hesed L'Avraham above. The righteous will be transformed into what Adamic man was supposed to originally be. Then all the righteous will be called by the term, "sons of man (Adam)." This is the context of the term when found in Ezekiel, and in later apocalyptic literature. It speaks about those select souls who are able to overcome the blemish instilled in all mankind through the eating of the forbidden fruit of the Tree of Knowledge, Good and Evil in Eden.

Those who partake of the fruit of the Tree of Life can then "live forever". However, in order to accomplish this, there will have to be fundamental changes in human genetics. These changes are potential in us even now. The prophetic meditative path is designed to help unleash them.

"And you, Daniel, close up the words and seal the book until the time of the end; many will run to and fro, and the knowledge will increase."

And here we have it, the command to make things confusing and concealed. Therefore, Daniel's entire book contains secrets that even to this day, we have not as yet discovered. Only those who walk the path towards the metaphorical Tree of Life, and develop a Pesher mentality towards Biblical studies will be able to receive revelation and insight into the concealed secrets as guided by the Higher Hand of Heaven.

"And I, Daniel, saw, and behold two others were standing, one on this side of the river bank, and one on that side of the riverbank. And he said to the man clad in linen, who was above the waters of the river, "How long will it be until the end of the wonders?" And I heard the man clad in linen, who was above the waters of the river, and he raised his right hand and his left hand to the heavens, and he swore by the Life of the world, that in a time, two times and a half, and when they have ended shattering the strength of the holy people, all these will end."

Here we go again with this, *Mo'ed Mo'adim VaHetzi* (time, double-time and a half). Does anyone have an accurate idea as to what this means? Absolutely every classical commentator who has tried to intellectually decipher this and the following verses to ascertain when the time of the "end of the wonders" is has failed miserably.

When it comes to identifying peoples, places and things, we have a good track record. However, when it comes to pinning down exact times, everyone has always been proven wrong. So, failing to be able to gaze into this text, and discover a secret hidden Pesher, I too must join along with all my colleagues of the past and confess I have no idea how to measure this time period to finally ascertain when it begins and when it ends.

All we know for sure, as seen clearly throughout Scripture and in this present work, is that G-d has His plan and Heaven has its schedule. We do not and cannot measure times for as we know, time is perceived quite differently in Heaven, as it is here on Earth.

The secret is that those who eat of the Tree of Life, rise above time and are thus able to see the End from on top, for it cannot be seen from down at the bottom. Contemplate my words, and learn wisdom.

"And I heard, but I did not understand, and I said, 'My lord, what is the end of these?' And he said, 'Go, Daniel, for the words are closed up and sealed until the time of the end. They will be clarified and whitened, and many will be purified, and the wicked will pervert [them], and all the wicked will not understand, but the wise will understand.'"

Knowledge and truth belong to the righteous. Pesher is the way the righteous come to learn and understand Scripture. Those who cannot walk in the proper paths of G-d will have to face their destinies during these times of trouble to come.

*"And from the time the daily sacrifice was removed and the silent abomination placed, is one thousand, two hundred, and ninety. Fortunate is he who waits and reaches days of one thousand, three hundred, and thirty-five. And you, go to the end, and you will rest and rise to your lot at the **end of the days**."*

From *"the time the daily sacrifice was removed and the silent abomination placed,"* when is this? Does this imply that a Third Temple is to be built in Jerusalem before the coming of the Messiah? Will this Temple be called a silent abomination in G-d's eyes? Certainly, without the Ark of the Covenant, it will have no connection to Heaven. And today, no one is in a state of ritual purity so as to build a Temple or to serve it in.

Yet, these point of Torah Law have never stopped determined people from acting as they will seem fit, even if it contradicts the very Will of G-d. Funny, how so many people go forward in their defiance and rebellion against G-d all the while thinking that it is G-d they are serving. Lies upon lies, truth twisted until it is no longer recognizable, all these are signs of the times, that indeed we are in the **End of Days**.

SECTION TWO

A GUIDE TO DREAM INTERPRETATIONS

Chapter 1

The Art of Dream Interpretation

"Both dreams and myths are important communications <u>from ourselves to ourselves</u>. If we do not understand the language in which they are written, we miss a great deal of what we know and tell ourselves in those hours when we are not busy manipulating the outside world."

Erich Fromm

In Torah Portion Miqetz, Yosef ascends to the leadership of the land of Egypt, second in command to Pharaoh. This remarkable elevation from slave to Prime Minister comes about due to Yosef's ability to interpret a dream. The parasha opens with Pharaoh's famous dreams of the sheaves of wheat and the cows. Yosef interprets these symbols as impending abundance and famine soon to come upon Egypt and the world. Impressed with his profound insight Pharaoh rewards Yosef.

We learn from this episode and others similar to it throughout the Bible that dreams have great significance. Rabbeynu Bahya writes in his Torah commentary to this section that dreams come from three different sources. Dreams can be caused by what we eat. Such dreams have no value or meaning. Dreams can be caused by our waking thoughts. Such dreams are exclusively psychological in nature. The third source of dreams is that they are messages. It is these dream messages that we will discuss now.

The Zohar (1:183b) states that "no occurrence materializes in the world that is not first revealed to one in a dream" and that "the edicts of the Heavenly Court are first shown to the children of man in dreams, then after a short time, the matter comes to pass." (Zoh.1: 251b).

As we can see, the subject of dreams touches the core of the human soul. Our Rabbis (Berakhot 57b) have said that dreams are a small portion of prophecy. It is through dreams that we humans communicate with all kinds of non-corporeal entities, be they disembodied spirits, demons, angels or even G-d Himself. A dream also is a communication between our conscious minds and our Neshama soul, which dwells in the unconscious.

A dream can reveal to us our innermost thoughts, our aspirations or our fears (ref. Berakhot 55b). A dream can bring us a message of future blessing or of impending doom. A dream can reveal, or explain, to us thoughts that have not yet congealed in consciousness. Many modern scientists have claimed that the idea for their latest scientific theories or even blueprints for inventions first came to them in a dream.

A dream is a tool of power. Therefore, a dream master, one who has the power to understand and interpret dreams, has the power to control the fate and destinies of others. A master of dreams can be compared to a seasoned warrior in combat who recognizes the subtle movements in a fighting opponent; thus knowing his next move before does the person himself.

As a warrior precipitates movement, so a dream master precipitates human thought, behavior and action, on an individual or collective level. This was the case of Yosef. Pharaoh recognized this power within him. This is why Pharaoh elevated him to such a high position. Having a man of such power as Yosef at his "right hand" assured Pharaoh of his own power.

Our Rabbis teach us that government leaders in general often receive messages from above that pertain to their countries. This was true of Pharaoh as recorded in Parashat Miqetz. Yet, whether it is a Pharaoh of old, or a President or a Prime Minister of today,

G-d (or His angel) communicates with them as they sleep to advise them of courses of actions.

It is public knowledge that the American President Ronald Reagan used the services of a professional astrologer to help plan his calendar. We do not know if he or any other world leader, past or present, uses a professional dream interpreter as Pharaoh used Yosef or as Nebuchadnezzar used Daniel. We see from the example of these two Biblical personages that for a world leader to have a professional dream interpreter could mean the difference between life and death for himself and for his nation.

We learn from the dreams of Pharaoh that messages are not always the most coherent or rational. Dream messages follow a language of their own. Their interpretation is paramount. Our Rabbis have said, "a dream uninterpreted is like an unread letter, it will be fulfilled even if one is not aware." (Zoh. 1:183b; 199b). In the case of a world leader, the letter is coming to him from G-d.

The language of dreams (and of visions) follows a language of pictures, rather than one of words. Picture language is the most primordial form of human communication. Infants, before ever learning to speak a word, have already learned a lot simply by watching the adults around them.

Communication of the eye precedes communication with the ear. In the spiritual plane, this same rule is followed; one is shown symbolic images and pictures that have primordial meanings. Due to our developed logical minds, the vast majority of people have lost the sensitivity and understanding of the primal pictorial forms that we understood so well as infants. Deep within our unconscious minds their meanings are still known, but these meanings seem to be stuck in the unconscious and have a hard time surfacing into consciousness.

When we remember a dream, we have a gnawing feeling that we know what it means, yet we fall short of grasping its meaning. It's like an inch you can't reach to scratch. A dream master helps to remind us what it is that we already know deep down within our minds. This was the case with both Yosef and Daniel. Both could, as if, read the minds of Pharaoh and Nebuchadnezzar respectively.

Yosef understood Pharaoh's mind and could tell him what his symbolic pictures were saying to him. Daniel did one step better and even told Nebuchadnezzar his dream and its interpretation. Upon hearing Daniel's words, Nebuchadnezzar immediately recognized them as true. Pharaoh too recognized Yosef's words as true, beyond anything anyone else was telling him. Pharaoh already knew the truth but it was "stuck" in his unconscious and thus could not bring it to the surface of his mind.

The dream message is unique in that its fulfillment can take on many different forms. Therefore, when Pharaoh heard Yosef's interpretation and that it meant vast wealth for Egypt, he was desirous for its fulfillment. Earlier the Torah relates the dreams of the cup bearer and the baker. Yosef interpreted one dream for good and the other for bad. Each dream was fulfilled in accordance to its interpretation.

Indeed the Talmud (Berakhot 55b) relates that in Second Temple times there were 24 professional dream interpreters in Jerusalem. Once Rabbi Bina'ah had a dream and he went to each interpreter for its meaning. Each of the 24 interpreted his dream differently. This might lead one to believe that dream interpretation is nothing other than subjective, however Rabbi Bina'ah relates that each of the 24 interpretations came true. The Gemara there states that dreams follow their interpretation.

The holy Zohar (Zoh.1:183a) adds that, "One should never tell his dream to anyone other than a close friend," for then one will be assured of a good interpretation and of a good outcome.

The Talmud Berakhot is replete with instructions for dream interpretation. Indeed in the 16th century, Rabbi Shlomo Almoli wrote his famous dream interpretation manual, Sefer Pitron Halamot (now available in English) which outlines a wealth of information. So valuable and respected is Rabbi Almoli's work that none other than Sigmund Freud makes mention of it in his work "The Interpretation of Dreams". Freud and especially Carl Jung recognized the symbolic nature of dream language and built their own systems based upon the principles that our holy Rabbis have used for centuries.

Dream interpretations are found in the Zohar as these examples show.

Seeing a camel (gamal) in a dream signifies that one has been sentenced to death but has been spared. (Zoh. 2:236a; 3:100b). The reasoning here is as follows: the word for camel (Gamal) sounds like the Hebrew word, "Gomel" which means to "compensate" or "bestow." A well-known phrase in the Amidah prayer (recited three times daily) refers to G-d as the "Gomel Hasidim Tovim" (one who bestows merciful good). Thus when G-d wishes to express the bestowal of His merciful good, He shows the dreamer the image of a Gamal, so that the dreamer would remember that G-d is the Gomel. The time when G-d bestows His merciful good upon a person is after a person is subject to punishment. G-d bestows His merciful good thus mitigating the forces of severity and judgment hanging over the person's head. Thus when a Gamal is seen, the implication is clear – the person was in trouble but is not any more. Upon awakening, such an individual has a lot for which to give thanks to G-d.

One who sees the letter Tet in a dream will see good. (Zoh. 2:230a). The reason for this is that the letter "Tet" is the first letter of the word "Tov" (good). Now, many other words also begin with Tet, yet Tov is the word most associated with the letter, therefore seeing the letter means "seeing" good.

One who sees wine in a dream, if he is a Rabbi, then it is good, if not then it means judgment (Zoh. 3:14b). Throughout the Bible, the study of Torah is compared to fine wine. Thus for a Rabbi, whose primary bond in life is with the Torah, to see a dream about wine is for him a symbol of Torah. This is not true of the layman whose does not have the same emotional and mental bond with Torah as does the Rabbi. The layman, therefore, must understand wine as it is interpreted elsewhere as a means to become intoxicated. As such, it is a sign of judgment for intoxication leads to improper behavior for which one is judged.

One might ask why the interpretation of a dream symbol changes from one type of person to another. Why does the symbol mean one thing to a Rabbi and a completely different, almost opposite meaning to someone who is not? The answer is that all dream symbols are highly individualized. As we are each different in our thinking, so are we each different in our unconscious minds. Nonetheless, there is a level of collective thinking where symbols mean the same things for a specific group.

In Jungian Psychology, he called these symbol groups "archetypes of the collective unconscious". Jung went further to state that every national or racial group has its own "racial sub-divisions within the collective unconscious" of all mankind. This sounds very similar to a mystical teaching that states originally all human souls were united as one within Adam. Because of the fall, the souls separated into "nations" with Israel being chosen by G-d to be His. Thus, each nation or race sees things collectively in a way unique unto itself.

Only an individual well trained and able to penetrate into humanity's collective unconscious will ever be able to tap into raw, unconscious, psychic content and be able to make sense out of the many confusing and contradictory symbols experienced therein.

Essentially, in order to be a tried and true "dream interpretation" master, one must be intimately connected to the Universal Mind underlying mankind, this being what we know as G-d. Racial subdivisions in the collective unconscious often prevent an individual of one culture to penetrate and understand the archetypal symbols of others from another culture. Overcoming racial subdivisions in the collective unconscious requires a deep, almost prophetic-like meditative bond with Elohim, G-d as revealed through nature. It is only this deep psychic, clairvoyant, telepathic ability that enables the one so trained to transcend the visions of symbols, to penetrate to their very essence.

This is why the dream interpreters for Pharaoh and later for Nebuchadnezzar could not delve into the depths of the minds of their respective kings. There must have been some racial differences between them, which prevented them from understanding. Yosef and Daniel, however, both having communion with Elohim/G-d, did not suffer from this difficulty.

Thus it is to this day with master dream interpreters. Only a one who is trained in these matters can understand dreams correctly.

One very important factor regarding dream interpretation is to know that not everything in a dream, even a message dream, is completely true. The Zohar (1:150b) states that "there are dreams which are true and dreams which are lies." More than this our Rabbis (Berakhot 55a) teach us that, "there is no dream that does not have some aspect of lies within it." When Yosef was young, he dreamed about the sun, moon and eleven stars bowing before him. This was interpreted by Ya'aqov his father as referring to himself, Yosef's mother and brothers bowing before him. Yet, herein lies the problem, Yosef's mother, Rachel, died when Yosef was still a child. His dream, therefore, contained an element of falsehood. (Reference Rashi on Ber. 37:10, Zohar 1:183a). Whenever a dream is interpreted, the interpreter must seek to weed out the peripheral information that is of no consequence to the dream.

A dream interpreter must also be aware that not all message dreams come from holy sources. Many dreams are related to sleeping souls from the forces of evil. Rabbi Yehudah Fatiyah in his Sefer Minhat Yehudah (Parashat Miqetz) explains in detail how to distinguish between dreams that come from angels and those which come from demons. He gives a warning that demons are not stupid and know very well how to seduce mankind as they sleep.

These unclean entities have learned the art of replication and can show an individual in their dreams false Heavenly and sublime spiritual symbols. The person will believe that he is receiving a holy Heavenly message, whereas in fact the soul is being deceived into becoming an agent of evil. Just as there are unscrupulous people in this world seeking to dupe and deceive others for their own personal gain, so are their spiritual beings that wish to do the same. The dream world is the realm of the unconscious; as such, it is the rightful domain of spirits both good and evil. Therefore, each of us when we dream must be very cautious. We must learn how to control our dreams.

"When a man's soul ascend above as he sleeps, if he is sinful then his soul is cast about from place to place by the forces of the powers

of evil, this is why one sees himself in a dream in another country or in another land." (Zoh. 3:222b).

Rabbi Fatiyah brings down examples how demons appear in dreams in the form of tzadikim or as "ascended masters." They can show dreamers images of the heavens, the holy throne, or even Kabbalistic symbolism. All this is their attempt to convince the dreamer to believe in that which they send to him. In this way, the forces of evil ensnare for themselves another soul. The demons always begin by showing one images of holiness to convince the person that what he is seeing in his dreams is kosher. Then after the soul is convinced and believes in what it is being shown, the demons then lead him step by step until eventually the person sinks into mental illness. In this state, the demons can control the person's mind and body.

The only way to avoid the onset of such a demonic attack is believed to be the recitation of the nighttime Shema Yisrael prayers, found in every Orthodox Jewish prayer book. The Sephardic Jewish prayer books, coming out of Israel, usually follow the Kabbalistic order of the Shema Yisrael nighttime prayers. This version is the best suited for spiritual protection at night.

Rabbi Fatiyah explains the difference between angelic dreams and demonic dreams as follows. An angelic dream is a message dream. Therefore, during the dream the dreamer will remain calm and reposed, almost unemotional, regardless of what is seen. The dreamer will watch the dream vision like watching a movie, while the image's inner meanings will somehow be imprinted in his mind.

Upon awakening, the dreamer is not frightened or alarmed. Although he is perplexed about what to do next, the next step always seems to become manifest. Such was the case with Pharaoh. After he awoke from his dream, he knew he needed it interpreted. Intuitively he felt inside himself that the interpretations his wise men were giving him were all wrong. He knew something was missing. Only then does his cup bearer speak to Pharaoh about Yosef. Pharaoh had never heard of Yosef to that day. Yet, that day forever changed the lives of both men, and both nations. G-d gave

Pharaoh his dreams. G-d inflicted Pharaoh's wise men with stupidity. G-d brought Yosef into Egypt, made him a dream master and brought him before Pharaoh, all in accordance to the Divine plan.

A demonic dream takes on a different form. During a demonic dream, one feels great agitation. One may feel a weight on one's chest as if someone is sitting on you. The dream images are confusing and blurry. No clear mental message is received. One awakens with feelings of anxiety and panic. One feels an inner conviction towards a certain course of action, yet no logical or permissible means avail themselves. The person then is led to believe that his family, friends or community is holding back from him some form of "unmanifest destiny." The forces of evil then return in dreams to confuse the person even further, making him suspicious of others around him. Eventually paranoia sets in and is soon followed by schizophrenia. All this occurred because the person opened himself to foreign outside influences without first being on a proper level of kedusha (holiness) to defend himself.

Many people see images in dreams that make them want to perform a ritual known as the dream fast, where one fasts the day of a bad dream to dispel some evil omen. The Zohar (3:105b) states, "not for naught are matters revealed in dreams, one is supposed to pray and ask for mercy." Rabbi Fatiyah writes that the demons are also aware of the specific dream symbols that when seen in a dream one is to fast. Since demonic activity is so prevalent today, Rabbi Fatiyah writes that rather than fast it is better that we pray, recite Tehilim (Psalms) and give tzedaka (charity). These spiritual acts increase one's kedusha (holiness) and are great mitzvot in and of themselves.

Another point about dreams that is important to remember is that the psychological element and the spiritual factor are often one and the same. Therefore, one should not quickly dismiss the psychological influence dreams can have on us or the control that we can have on our dreams. Dreams and hypnosis are closely related in that both can plant thoughts deep within our minds that only surface at a later time, but with all the intensity and conviction of absolute truth. Such people are, as if to say, possessed by their dreams, fantasies, or delusions. All these types of images overlap with the dream state.

The psychological state is so important that the Zohar (1:199b) states, "one needs to remember a good dream, and then it will be fulfilled; however, if the dream is forgotten in a man's heart, then it will also be forgotten above." This seems to signify that dreams and wish fulfillment have a lot to do with one another. In other words, if one can materialize a reality in one's dreams, then one has the ability to materialize that dream into reality.

This is exactly what happened with Yosef. After interpreting Pharaoh's dream, Yosef suggested to him what to do about the upcoming plenty and famine. It is truly amazing that Pharaoh would have ever listened to what in his eyes was a "heathen" Hebrew slave. Yet, Pharaoh heard the voice of G-d coming forth from Yosef's mouth. When Yosef proceeded to tell Pharaoh to appoint a Prime Minister over all of Egypt, he subtly intended that position for himself. Pharaoh was as if, under Yosef's spell. He could do nothing but to appoint Yosef to the position that he, Yosef himself, had created. For a moment, Pharaoh was shown a glimpse of the greater universe, one that was ruled by Yosef. He could do nothing but to overtly comply with Yosef's subtle power of voice. There are many secrets about the union of voice and speech, but this is not the place to discuss them.

When a person dreams a dream its reality predominates within the individuals mind and will change external reality to conform to the dream. This is seen clearly in the case of the dream of the Midianite guard whose conversation was overheard by Gideon (ref. Judges 7:13-14). When the guard interpreted the dream of his comrade to mean that the Children of Israel were coming, and that the Midianite army would soon be defeated, Gideon immediately knew to attack. Gideon realized that if the Midianite guards were already dreaming about defeat, then defeat was already in their hearts and minds. They could not win for deep down within them they had already lost their resolve.

"In a dream, in a vision of the night.... then He opens the ears of men...that He may turn man aside from his conduct" (Job 33:16,17).

Dreams are sent to us all in order to direct our behavior and help us return to G-d. Everyone dreams regardless of whether the dreams are remembered or not. While many dreams are caused by what we ate before we slept or by our waking thoughts, desires or fears, nonetheless the message dream is still a living and vibrant part of the psyches of most of us. Not having dreams is actually considered a sign that the soul does not ascend during sleep. The Zohar (3:105b) states, "one who does not have matters revealed to him in dreams is called evil." Dreams implant a message deep within our psyches. When we awaken we may not know it, but we have been "programmed." We have received a message and that inner knowledge will direct the thoughts in our minds, the feelings in our hearts and the course of the events in our lives.

There are many more details to the interpretation of dreams that cannot be discussed here. Cultivating awareness of the meaning of our dreams and their inherent power enables us to draw closer to our blessed Creator. What greater work than this is there?

Chapter 2

The Difference Between Dreams Originating from Angels & Demons

Translated from Sefer Minhat Yehuda (Parashat Miqetz 47) of Rabbi Yehuda Fatiyah

"And in the morning, his soul was agitated." (Ber.41:8) This infers that his soul was not agitated in his dream as he slept, but only in the morning when he awoke and contemplated the meaning of his dream. Then was he deeply troubled from within.

We find a similar case with regards to Nebuchadnezzar and his dream, where it says (Dan.2:1), "His soul was troubled and his sleep left him." For he was awakened from his sleep by his dream, and his soul was troubled within him. He could not return to sleep.

This then is the way of a true dream that comes through an angel. One's soul is not troubled while one sleeps when seeing the dream, only after one has awoken. The reason for this is that it is not G-d's desire to frighten a person or cause one trouble while that one sleeps. [A dream comes] specifically to make one aware of what [Heavenly] edicts have been made concerning oneself or others. This is so that one may make efforts to rectify their sins. If so, why then should one be bothered while one sleeps?

This is similar to the prophecy that Isaiah spoke to Hezekiah, King of Yehuda, that he would die, and not live (2 Kings 20:1). Our sages have said [regarding this episode] that [Hezekiah] would die in this world, and not live in the world to come. He asked [Isaiah] why. [Isaiah] answers it is because you did not marry and beget children. [Hezekiah] responds, if so, let me marry your daughter. Isaiah says that it is too late for that; the edict has already been issued. Hezekiah says "Isaiah, Son of Amotz, silence your prophecy and leave. For I have received from the House of my father's father [King David], that even if a sword is dangling over a man's throat, he should never stop awaiting [G-d's] mercy. For if the edict has already been issued, and there is no more hope, why then did G-d send you to me? You do have good news to tell me."

Thus, it is with a bad dream that is shown to a man through an angel. For were it not possible to nullify the edict by one's prayers, fasting, and charity, as well as one's repentance for what one has done, why then would the person be shown the dream at all? This is what our sages have taught [Ber. 55A] regarding the verse, "G-d has done this, so that you will be in awe of Him" [Koh. 3:14]. This refers to [showing one] a bad dream, so that one will be in awe of G-d. This being so, why should the dreamer be disturbed while he sleeps?

This then is the rule: The dream that comes through an angel will be neatly arranged. It will not be a mixture of conflicting matters. It also will not be fearful and terrorizing at the time of the dream. More than this [while within the dream] one will see oneself as if one were completely awake. If all these conditions have been met regarding a dream, know for sure that the dream is true, and that it has come from an angel, and that this is a 1/60 portion of prophecy [Ber. 57B.]

However, the dream that comes through a demon has another way to it. The demon stands next to the person while he sleeps a light sleep, and whispers in his ear frightening things, and fragments of things from various subjects. These things trouble the person's mind and make him afraid. His heart beats faster, and he awakens because of the heightened fear.

These demons remain standing there [at the person's side], and rejoice and laugh at him in that they were able to frighten him. When the person returns to sleep, they in turn bother [the person] all over again. They continually repeat this. No man will escape this until he repeats the bedtime Shema prayers.

There is also another way. When the person is awakened, he should say, "Tameh Tameh Barah Lakh M'kan" [unclean one, unclean one, be banished from here]. Say this three times. Then the demon will leave, and the person will rest securely. If one has an enemy then he should say, "Tameh Tameh Barah Lakh M'kan V'lekh Etzel Ploni Ben Ploni V'hav'hi'lehu" [unclean one, unclean one, be banished from here, and go to the home of so and so, and bother him]. The demon will then do whatever he is commanded.

If you wish to experiment with this, whisper in the ear of a young child while he is sleeping a light sleep, and say to him I have bought you all kinds of sweet candies, and I have placed them in this box nearby. When the child awakens from his sleep, he will ask about the candies, and where they are. This is what is written in Sefer Hasidim 135 and 441.

Therefore most dreams that are frightening and disturbing usually occur when a person is in a light state of sleep, such as at the beginning of one's sleep, or at its' end when one is about to awaken, for only then is the brain able to receive those [demonic] images, and not when the person is deep asleep.

Know, that even if one recites the bedtime Shema Israel prayers prior to sleep, if one is awakened from one's sleep by a crying baby, or for whatever reason and then returns to sleep, the demons can then have sway over him, to frighten and disturb his sleep with frightening images. One must recite again the Shema Yisrael prayer a second time. One must at least recite the first verse and Baruch Shem, as it is written in Sha'ar HaPesukim, Shir HaShirim on the verse, "I sleep" [SOS 5:2].

Also know, if a person has a demon bonded to them through sexual immorality, they [the demons] then have the power to breach the fence of the reading the Shema so as to fulfill their desires [through the person]. The regular reading of the bedtime Shema will therefore not be effective. One will have to read it with great devotion, word by word.

I will also reveal to you now new things. The demons have learned about the things that mankind cares about, and show them to people in their dreams. For example, one who sees [in a dream] that his tooth has fallen out, or that a cow is slaughtered before him, or that one is fasting, or wearing black garments, or going barefoot etc., a person [should no longer] be concerned about these [types] of dreams, with the exception if one is called up to the Torah by name. Even so, the one who is not concerned will receive a blessing.

Sometimes the demons show people bad things. If that person is a fool and believes these dreams, then the demons [themselves] bring the evil of the dream into physical reality, in order to fulfill the dream. [In this way the dreamer] learns to believe in his dreams. Sometimes when a Voice is heard proclaiming [a proclamation] in Heaven about some evil that is to come, [the demons] reveal this to a person in his dreams in order that the person will come to believe in his dreams.

Now this person needs to know that if he fasts over these dreams, or makes atonement or offers charity, and doesn't ask a Rabbi who knows how to differentiate between dreams that come through angels and those that come through demons, know for sure that this person will be destined to see horrible and evil dreams. For the demons rejoice that they did not work for naught over this person. These demons are called: "Shedim Nukhrain" (Gentile demons), who teach evil.

There are other demons called: "Shedim Yehudain" (Jewish demons) (Zohar, Bamidbar 253A). These have a different way about them. They make themselves appear as the ancient [Biblical] prophets, or as the Talmudic sages. There are those who make themselves appear as the judges of Israel and as great famous rabbis who have passed on to the other side. They all appear with great beards and crowns upon their heads, like the righteous and the pious. Sometimes they say that they are Abraham, Isaac, or Jacob, or Elijah the prophet or the like. One must be careful to ask them directly if they are the Biblical patriarchs [themselves] or if they just have the same names. Thus, you must also ask of Elijah. You must be very analytical regarding any answer [these demons] give you. For many a time they give an answer that is not exactly clear. If their answers are not clear, know that they are demons.

[These demons] can do even greater things than this. They can show to a person the image of the heavens, the image of the throne of glory, and the angels of heaven. [These demons] are careful not to frighten a person. On the contrary, they command the person to study Zohar and Psalms every single day. At night they arouse him to awaken to pray [the midnight service] Tikun Hatzot.

Sometimes they command the person to immerse a number of times in the mikvah each day, and to constantly change his clothes. [He is told] to abstain [from relations] with his wife. After all this [these demons] make the person accept upon himself all kinds of afflictions and fasts. If this person does all these things, [these demons] then strike him and command him never ever to reveal the vision of them or what they show him to anyone else (for fear that they will be exposed a demons).

In the end, the person's mind is completely caught up with [these demons], to the point that he goes insane. Eventually [these demons] cause the person to suffer seizures. May G-d protect us.

These demons come at the beginning of a dream. Afterwards they appear even while the person is awake. Sometimes they come just as a person is awakening. Many times people, men and women, have come to me, who have seen things while they are awake. I cannot get into all the details, but I will relate one story as an example.

In Tammuz 5671 (July, 1911), after the afternoon Shabat prayer, a young boy age 11 was brought before me. He said that he could speak with Elijah the prophet face to face, and not just in a vision or with puzzles. Any time that he would want [to speak with Elijah] all he had to do was call him, and he would immediately come. The only condition being that he [the boy] had to be alone, with no one else there [to see].

I said to him, enter this room, and ask him [Elijah] if he is truly Elijah the prophet. This the boy did. And he answered me; "I am truly Elijah, why does Yehuda doubt me?" (I am the Yehuda being spoken of). I said to the boy, this is none other than a Jewish demon whose name happens to be Elijah. This is not Elijah the prophet. You are being plagued by Jewish demons. Come and I will recite the prayer against demons over you, then will this Elijah flee from you. The child said to me, that this is certainly Elijah the prophet, and that you can do whatever you wish, and we will see who will be the victor.

After I prayed over the boy a number of times, he went into a private room to see whether Elijah would come. Elijah immediately came as he had done in the past. I was truly surprised by this. So, I took the child and went to see Rabbi Shimon Agasi zt"l, who was then alive, for him to examine the child. After he had examined him, [Rabbi Agasi] said that this was truly Elijah the prophet, and not a demon. I disagreed, and told him that it is a demon.

We both agreed that together we would all go after the Saturday evening prayers to see Rabbi Ya'aqob, the son of Rabbi Yosef Haim (the Ben Ish Hai) so that he may examine him. After he examined [the boy] in a number of ways, he too said that for certain this was Elijah the prophet of blessed memory. I disagreed with them both and nullified their proofs.

I requested of them to let me test [the boy] one more time. I said to the child that he should tell Elijah to translate to him the verse in Jeremiah, **"Ki'd'na Tem'run L'hom Ela'haya Di'Sh'maya V'ar'ka La Avadu Ye'vadu Me'ar'ah U'min T'hoht Sh'maya Eleh"** (Then shall you say to them, the gods that have not made the heavens and the earth, they shall perish from the earth, and from under these heavens. Jer. 10:11).

If [Elijah] translates this verse into Arabic (the spoken vernacular then), then it is possible to consider that maybe he is Elijah the prophet and not a demon. For the demons know the language of Aramaic (the language of this verse), for they [the demons] speak Aramaic and show evil dreams, and whisper into the ears of those who speak Aramaic. However, this verse speaks about their inevitable destruction. They do not wish to hear it, all the more so to translate it into any vernacular language.

Thus when the boy asked Elijah to translate the verse, Elijah said, that he had no time to waste there, for he had to leave [the boy] and *go write down the merits of the Jewish people [for the heavenly court]. Elijah said that he was in a rush. When the boy told me of this response, I said to him, go back and tell [Elijah] to translate the verse of which I ask, for it is very important [that he do so], so that we may know for sure that he truly is Elijah. Elijah again told the boy that he was in a rush. I said to the boy, say to Elijah, that he has been conversing with us for a good while [why all of a sudden is he in a rush?], when it should be easy for him to translate this verse, instead of wasting time trying to get out of doing it. Only in this way, by translating this verse, will the Sages be convinced.*

When the boy said these things to Elijah, he got angry and proclaimed "Hai HaShem" (As HaShem lives), I will never appear to you again for you do not believe that I am Elijah the prophet. Immediately [Elijah] disappeared and never reappeared to the boy.

After Elijah departed, Rabbi Agasi and Rabbi Ya'aqob said to me, that in their opinion, this was truly Elijah the prophet, for it is his way to swear by saying "Hai HaShem" (As HaShem lives). And our Sages have said (Meg. 3A) that even demons do not say the Name of G-d in vain.

I said to them that [this Elijah] was a demon, and that he did not say the Name [of G-d] in vain. Firstly, he fulfilled his word, he promised that he would leave and not return, and that is what he did, therefore, what he said was not in vain. And more than this, in essence [Elijah] never said the Name of G-d at all! He did not say Hai – Yod Key Vav Key [the true Name of G-d], nor did he use the Name Adonai. He said, Hai HaShem, using the word "HaShem" i.e., the letters Hey Shin Mem [this is a reference to the Name of G-d, and not the Name itself, at all]. This is nothing other than pure deception [on the part of this Elijah]. The Sages finally agreed that I was correct.

Now, to get back to our subject. Up until now, I have been explaining the difference between dreams that come through angels, and those that come through gentile or Jewish demons. Now, I will very briefly explain more about the essence of dreams and how they are to be interpreted.

One must know that all dreams come in very concealed images. This is for a number of reasons.

The first is that [the fulfillment] of the dream will not be for a number of years.

The second [reason] is [that the dream] comes to admonish a person for the sins that they have committed.

The third has to do with matters between a husband and wife. I will give you an example of all of these.

The first reason is a known thing, such as the dreams of Joseph who dreamed about his brothers, or the great image envisioned by Nebuchadnezzar, or the dreams of Daniel.

All of these came in the form of very concealed images because their fulfillment was still very far off.

In accordance to the level of the concealment within the dream vision, so is the distance [in time] of its fulfillment.

Chapter 3

Sh'aylat Halom, the Dream Question

Introduction

"Hear now my words, if there be a prophet among you, I HaShem make myself known to him in a vision, and speak to him in a dream."

Numbers 12:6

The Dream Question is a Kabbalistic tool, used for requesting guidance and information. It is addressed to the archangel Metatron, the Prince of the Presence, who as the Talmud teaches (San. 38), *"has the same name as his Master".* This is referring to G-d, who is called Shadai, the Almighty, the numerical value of Shadai and Metatron both being equal to 314. In matter of fact, the Holy Zohar teaches (Tik. Zoh., 14b) that Metatron is the garment in which the Divine Presence of G-d, the Shekhina, is cloaked. Metatron is also identified as the angel Raziel (Tik. Zoh. 127a), the revealer of the secrets of the Torah, which is why he is the chosen emissary for the dissemination of knowledge and wisdom.

It is for this reason that invoking the assistance of the great Metatron (Raziel) is considered an awesome task. Great preparations are to be performed in order to enable one to properly receive and channel his presence. The requirements of fasting and cleanliness are to be taken quite seriously; one must be sincere and not take these things lightly. The procedure, when followed according to directions claim to be tried and true, to reveal to the seeker that which is sought.

Sh'aylat Halom - Dream Question
From: The Book of the Angel Raziel

Fast for three days in purity, humility and awe. Dress in clean, white garments. Be clean of all impurity. Purify yourself for three days, these being Monday, Tuesday and Wednesday. Do not eat until Thursday. On Thursday night, light a candle in your home, lie upon the ground in the corner of your room, turn your face towards the light of the candle and recite your question or request. This is the formula:

"I adjure you by the Ineffable Name by He who sits upon the clouds of Heaven above, that you come to me this night with favor and a pure heart. Come to me only in love and speak to me the answer to my question, whatever it is that I request of you. Interpret for me my question, even as the angel Gavriel interpreted the dream of Pharoah for Yosef. His words were true, so may you come to me this night in truth. Solve for me my riddle, my request, by the power of your name, for your name is Prince Metatron. By the power of the Ineffable Name, He who sits upon the wheels of the chariot, by the power of He who lives forever, who sits upon Aravot, whose name is YAH. Rejoice before Him.

In the name of G-d who is Great, Powerful and Awesome, who is Beloved, Pleasant and Faithful. I adjure you, Prince Metatron by the name Ehyeh Asher Ehyeh who revealed himself to Moshe, the son of Amram, within the bush. "Blessed are you, Adonai who teaches me your edicts." (Tehilim 119:12). By the power of the Name that is interpreted in seventy languages, praised in seventy tongues and praised in seventy names. I adjure you in the name of He who rocks the world. The hosts of above and below tremble before His Name and from His wrath will the earth shake. No nation shall endure His fury. Blessed be the honor of Adonai from His place. Blessed be the Name of His glorious kingdom forever and ever.

I adjure you Prince Metatron in the name of the G-D of Israel, G-D of Avraham, Yitzhak and Ya'aqob and in the names of the eternal angels who stand before the great G-D. These are the seven angels: Mikhael, Gavriel, Rifael, Anael, Yitzuriel, Tariel, Aziel.

By Your Name and by Your truth, for Your Name is Merciful and Gracious. Blessed be the Name of His glorious kingdom forever and ever.

I adjure you, Prince Metatron in the names of the princes who govern the four seasons of the year. Those of the first season are Nuriel and Tzadkiel. Those of the second season are Aziel, Samakel, and Anael. Those of the third season are Zavadiel and Samaniel. Those of the fourth season are Gavriel, Rifael, Ashbirah, and Hasharon. Their dominion is over every season and every year.

I adjure you Prince Metatron by the blessed Name, by He whose Name is blessed, aloft, above all blessings and praise. For His Name is in yours and yours in Him. For before all is His Name correct, forever and ever will His name stand. Before His Name will the hosts of heaven and earth tremble.

Praised is Your name Adonai, all the supernal hosts, all praise Your Name. Your Name has not been foreseen; before Your Name shall all tremble. The sea shall fall back in awe of Your Name and its surf and waves shall give glory and praise to Your Name. The earth trembles before Your gaze at her, her pillars melt away and are in fear of Your Name.

Upon all is Your Name eternal. The dwellers of the universe fear and tremble in terror of Your Name. The dwellers of the depths and the netherworld, the wilderness and the great darkness are alarmed before Your Name. The Garden of Eden and all your righteous ones will sing to Your Name. All that has within it the breath of life, with the songs of their mouths, they shall give honor to Your Name.

And I, I am dust and ashes, worthless, of stricken heart and fallen spirit, a shadow that passes like a flower of the field. I come to lay before You my supplication, to request grace from before You and before the throne of Your glory. For You are near to all who call upon You, and present for those who seek You. Grant me, I pray my request with desire. Speedily bring me my answer in your grace. Do my will, for You are my Creator."

After all this recite your request with your face turned downwards, recite then these verses, all with pure intention and you shall see your desire.

"For He is full of compassion, forgiving iniquity and does not destroy, often He turns His anger, not stirring up all His wrath." (Tehilim 78:38)

"And Adonai came down in a cloud and spoke to him, and took of the spirit that was upon him and gave it to the seventy Elders, and it came to pass that when the spirit rested upon them that they prophesied." (Bamidbar 11:25)

"And Adonai descended in the cloud and stood with him there and proclaimed the Name of Adonai. And Adonai passed by before him and proclaimed Adonai, Adonai Merciful and Gracious, G-d, long-suffering, abundant in mercy and truth, keeping mercy to thousands, forgiving iniquity, transgression and sin." (Shemot 4:6-7)

"Adonai hear, Adonai forgive, Adonai hearken and act. Do not delay, for Your own sake, my G-d, for Your city and Your people are called by Your Name." (Dan.9:19)

"And Ya'aqob left Beersheva and went towards Haran. And he found a certain place, and rested there all night, for the sun had gone down. And he took of the stones of the place and put them under his head, and he lay down in that place. And he dreamed, and behold: a ladder set up upon the earth, with its top reaching into Heaven. And behold the angels of G-d went up and down on it. And behold, Adonai stood above him and said: I am Adonai G-d of Avraham your father and the G-d of Yitzhak. The land upon which you lie, to you will I give it and to your descendants... And behold, I am with you and will guard you in all the places that you will go." (Bereshit 28:10-13, 15)

SECTION THREE

JEWISH & KABBALISTIC MESSIANIC TEACHINGS

Chapter 1

Ezekiel 38 & 39
The Wars of Gog & Magog

The Book of Ezekiel, Chapters 38-39 contains the ominous prophecy of the war of Gog and Magog. This terrible war in the End of Days, is when a great army of many nations attacks the Land of Israel itself.

While the Book of Daniel only hints at such an attack, Ezekiel, an earlier contemporary of Daniel, also living in Babylon, was given a full-blown revelation, and prophecy about this terrible attack, and how G-d Himself is to intervene to pour out His Divine wrath upon the invading armies.

There are many misconceptions about the attack of Gog and Magog. These have arisen simply because most are not familiar with the original Biblical text and what is says, and more specifically, what it does not say.

Many interpret this battle to be the final war before the coming of the Mashiah, and expect the Mashiah to appear instantaneously after the war's Divine wrought conclusion. However, as we shall see, there is no scriptural evidence to substantiate this claim.

Indeed, many students of Biblical prophecy want to believe that the battle spoken of here in Ezekiel 38-39 is the same one prophesied later, recorded in Zechariah 14. However, as we shall see, even the classical commentators recognize that the battles mentioned in Ezekiel, and Zechariah are not one and the same.

Let us turn now to the text in Ezekiel, and learn it in context of the classical commentaries, and see what else we can discover.

Ezekiel 38

1. "Then the word of the L-rd came to me, saying: 2. "Son of man, set your face toward Gog, [toward] the land of Magog, the prince, the head of Meshech and Tubal, and prophesy concerning him. 3. And you shall say; So said the L-rd G-d: Behold, I am against you, Gog, the prince, the head of Meshech and Tubal."

Unlike the revelations in Daniel, here in Ezekiel we have full-fledged prophecy coming directing from G-d, and not through the intermediary angels.

Ezekiel is referred to here, and elsewhere, and "Ben Adam" (son of man). Although, in later literature, this title is aggrandized and given special messianic applications, here, in its original usage, Ben Adam simply means a human being, son of Adam, a mere mortal.

Indeed, in many of the Jewish translations of the Bible, this term Ben Adam is simply translated as Mortal, instead of the more literal son of man. The implication of the title suggests that G-d, who calls Ezekiel this, views him as what he is, a child and spiritual byproduct of His creation, the first man.

Adam was created by G-d, without sin or blemish, but not necessarily perfect. By calling Ezekiel this title, son of Adam, many interpret this to mean, that Ezekiel (and any other called this by G-d) may have reached a level of holiness akin to the first Adam before the fall. In merit of such an accomplishment in righteousness and holiness, G-d acknowledges the accomplishment by referring to the individual by a title that suggests the level of rectification achieved.

Now we must our attention to discussing the identity of Gog, Magog, Meshech and Tubal. While these names are not unknown in scripture, we must remember to apply here our rules of quantum prophecy. In other words, although these names can be traced with some historical accuracy, this does not by any means that such identifications are to be associated with their End Times applications.

Gog the individual, may very well be the angelic prince assigned over the nations under his control. Magog, Meshech and Tubal are apparently locations of his control. Yet, these domains may very well be spiritual and the references here archetypal and metaphorical. Therefore, to attempt to identity Gog with any type of historical accuracy appears to be irrelevant. This conclusion is not lost to the traditional commentators. The Malbim commentary comments as follows.

"Ezekiel prophesied that in the End of Days all the nations will wage war surrounding Jerusalem. The combatants on one side will be Egypt, Assyria and Elam, these are the Ishmaelites. The combatants on the other side will be Meshech, Tubal, the Princes of Edom and the Kings of the North. All of them will kill one another, and fall amongst the fallen."

"Our Sages received a tradition that Gog would come against Jerusalem three times. Here [in Ezekiel 38 & 39] are outlined the first two times. The third time is discussed in Zechariah 14."

"The identity of Gog, and the land of Magog, are unknown to us today. We only know what is written that Gog is the prince of Meshech and Tubal, these are [the names of] descendants of Yefet [son of Noah], and are not circumcised. They will be aroused in the End of Days after Israel has returned to the Land of Israel, and dwells there securely. They will then rise up against them because G-d will arouse them."

"The children of Edom destroyed the Second Temple, and Meshech and Tubal were with them. For the destroying Romans were at that time the head of the nations, and afterward all those nations were [generically] called Edom because of their [singular] religion...."

"In the End of Days G-d desires to gather these evil ones, and the children of Ishmael, together in one place, to the Valley of

Jehoshaphat, for Israel was exiled [into both of their lands] and there suffered horrible persecutions."

We see from the Malbim's commentary reflections of the great war of the Kings of the North and South, spoken of in Daniel 11. Again, Daniel and Ezekiel were relative contemporaries living in Babylon. Therefore, when it comes to Divine revelations about the End of Days, we should not be surprised to see that G-d reveals similar revelations to the two of them.

4. *"And I shall unbridle you, and I shall put hooks into your jaws and bring you forth and all your army, horses and riders, all of them clothed in finery, a great assembly, with encompassing shield and buckler, all of them grasping swords."*

As we learned previously in Daniel 4:14, G-d sends His angels, the Watchers, to manipulate the minds of men, to motivate them to take the actions that they do. This prophecy will undoubtedly be fulfilled.

What is ironic about it is that this prophecy has been around for close to 2500 years. Countless numbers know these words well and one would think that someone at some time might have wanted to take action to avoid its fulfillment. Yet, such endeavors have never arisen.

The underlying causes that are leading to this apocalyptic war remain unchecked. Humanity is heading straight into this war, with the words of this prophecy echoing in their ears, and still, no one seems to hear anything. This may very well be proof that certain aspects of human destiny are out of human control. Indeed, this is what Daniel 4:14 states outright, and what this verse clearly reinforces. Like a fish caught on a hook, these nations, and these armies, will be dragged into war, pulled by an unseen force, unable to escape its force and momentum.

5. *"Persia, Cush, and Put are with them; all of them with buckler and helmet."*

Persia is Iran, Cush is Africa, and Put is Libya. The implication is that these nations are joined together with Gog in common cause.

Yet, this is not what the verse actually says. The verse indicates their presence and their readiness for war, however, the term Itam (with them) does not have to imply "with them" meaning "on their side," but rather could just mean, "with them" there for battle.

One way or another, the armies described in Daniel as the King of the South are here present alongside the armies of the King of the North. While it may not be clear from here, it is clear from Daniel that these armies are not here alongside one another in brotherhood, and union. Rather they are together brought here by the Higher Hand to face one another in mortal combat. This will become apparently clear as the chapter proceeds. Therefore, the mention of these armies here should not be construed as a difficulty, because their presence does not refer to their allegiance, or their purpose.

6. *"Gomer and all its wings, the house of Togarmah, the utmost parts of the north and all its wings, many peoples with you."*

Again we have here identified peoples or nations not readily recognizable today. Different commentaries offer different identifications. Some agree, and many do not. Again, we must remember that although the names and faces of nations change, their angelic counterparts remain the same. And as we have learned earlier from Isaiah (24:19), "On that day, G-d will punish the hosts of Heaven in Heaven, and the kings of the Earth on the Earth."

7. *"Be prepared and make ready for yourself, you and all your assembly who are gathered about you, and you will be to them for a guardian. **8.** From many days you will be remembered; at the end of the years you will come to a land [whose inhabitants] returned from the sword, gathered from many peoples, upon the mountains of Israel, which had been continually laid waste, but it was liberated from the nations, and they all dwelt securely. **9.** And you will ascend; like mist you will come; like a cloud to cover the earth you will be; you and all your wings and many peoples with you."*

It is clear that this prophecy speaks about the "end of the years." This is a time, that verse 8 says the inhabitants of the land, meaning Israel will have returned from the lands of their exile, wherein which they suffered from the sword.

Modern day Israel is truly a conglomeration of Jews who have come to the Holy Land from many different points of origins. These many returnees rebuild the Holy Land and "made the desert bloom." The Holy Land it is said was liberated from the nations, an indication that the End Times state of Israel would be founded upon war, and not peace. Nevertheless, the newborn nation would dwell securely in their ancient homeland.

Then the enemy comes, like a mist, and a cloud that covers everything. The enemy is not a single nation but a combination of many, apparently all united under a single banner for a single cause.

The majority of commentators refer to this army as being the army of Islam, possibly under Al Mahdi, the Islamic messiah, under the banner of Islam, with the single cause of destroying the Jewish people in the Holy Land. One does not have to be prophetic to recognize that this scenario is very close to occurring in modern times when we look upon the current events in the Middle East.

The text is clear that there will be two armies descending upon Israel, one from the North, and one from the South. While tradition has always associated the personage of Gog as being the King of the North, as in Daniel 11, there are other opinions who suggest that maybe Gog is indeed the King of the South and that he should be identified as the Islamic messiah Al Mahdi.

10. *"So said the L-rd G-d: It will come to pass on that day that words will enter your heart and you will think a thought of evil."*

One can clearly see the fever pitch of the hatred of Jews and Israel today throughout the Muslim world. We see the nature of the depravity of Muslim terrorists in how they kill, and mutilate their Jewish victims. Even children and infants do not escape horrible torture and death. These facts are well documented, and is clear proof of the "thoughts of evil" made manifest in the deeds of this most bitter of enemies.

11. *"And you will say, "I shall ascend upon a land of open cities, I shall come upon the tranquil, who dwell securely; all of them living without a wall, and they have no bars or doors.* **12.** *To take spoil and to plunder loot, to return your hand upon the resettled ruins and to a people gathered from nations, acquiring livestock and possessions, dwelling on the navel of the earth.* **13.** *Sheba and Dedan and merchants of Tarshish and all its magnates will say to you, "Are you coming to take spoil? Have you assembled your assembly to plunder loot, to carry off silver and gold, to take livestock and possessions, to take much spoil?"*

The purpose of this attack is clear; the enemy seeks to despoil the land. When the intent of invasion is plunder, then needless to say, such acquisitions are acquired through violence, not only to combatants, but more specifically to civilians (those being plundered). The intent here is clearly seen that the attack is on innocent civilians, minding their own business, upon a land of open cities, without a wall or bars or doors.

Now, most modern individual homes do have doors, many even have barred windows. But the text is talking about the cities, not the individual homes therein. This prophecy is amazing in that it predicts a time when cities would be built without walls of protection. In Ezekiel's day, such a thought would be inconceivable. We see documented from scripture that the first endeavor performed by the returning refugees from Babylon to Jerusalem was the building its defensive wall.

The existence of a wall around a city was a vital matter in ancient times. This has been lost to us today in light of modern abilities to bombard from the air. Yet the value of a wall is still recognized.

The modern day State of Israel has constructed a large wall between its populated areas, and certain Arab areas, with the intent of keeping armed terrorists out. According to the Israeli government, the wall seems to be fulfilling its purpose. They claim the wall has been responsible for preventing many attacks.

Somehow, however, in light of modern weaponry, I do not think that the armies of Gog will be hindered by any Israeli wall.

Therefore, to conceive of walling modern cities for defense is antiquated. Therefore, no walls, and with no walls, there comes a sense of false security. While mankind does not notice their precarious and open position, Heaven does. The words of this prophecy are based upon this Heavenly insight.

Although the purpose of the great battle here is more so to kill the enemy, one must remember that this battle to come is very similar to battle like it fought long ago in the days of the Crusades. These were the first great wars between the Christians and the Muslims, with the battlefield and the prize, at first, as now in this prophecy being Jerusalem.

Needless to say, as it was in the Crusades so it is here to, that the Jewish population gets caught in the middle, becoming an object of slaughter for both sides. The ruthless bloodshed of Jews during the Crusades might rightly be called a holocaust. So too here the sides come for Jerusalem, and kill and plunder the Jews on their way to killing one another. As we see from these two chapters Gog, and his armies, are not destined to accomplish their goal at this time.

14. *"Therefore, prophesy, son of man, and say to Gog, So said the L-rd G-d, Surely on that day, when My people dwells securely, you will know.* **15.** *And you will come from your place, from the utmost north and many peoples with you, all of them riding horses; a great assembly and a mighty army.* **16.** *And you will ascend upon My people Israel like a cloud to cover the earth; at the End of Days it will be, and I shall bring you upon My land in order that the nations recognize Me when I am sanctified through you before their eyes, Gog."*

The verse says that when the nation of Israel shall dwell securely that the armies of Gog will surely know. This can only mean that the enemy has tested the defenses of the Holy land, and have found them strong. Therefore, after testing Israel to discover its weaknesses, Gog realizes that the only way he will be able to enter into Israel, to conquer it, will be through sheer, overwhelming power. Strategy will not be his plan; rather Gog will rely on an all-out, overwhelming hoard that will be able to simply swallow up any foe due to the mere size of its army.

The hoards are described here as riding on horses. So, unless we take a number of steps back away from our modern technologies, we will have to interpret these words as being metaphorical. Gog's army will move with all the swiftness a modern technological army can provide. The invading army will be enormous, yet it will not be hindered down because of its great size. It will move like a plague of locusts, overwhelming, speedy, unable to be slowed down, or stopped.

This efficiency, the dream of any modern army will be accomplished not due to the discipline of the army's officers, but rather because G-d is the one behind Gog's motivation. Gog will move forward with great zeal and focus, not knowing that it is G-d in Heaven who is guiding his every move. And while Gog is indeed being led by G-d, G-d is not leading Gog to victory, but rather to an ignominious defeat. Gog, the angelic Prince in Heaven will face His judgment as the nation under his charge suffers a terrible and debilitation defeat.

17. "So said the L-rd G-d, Are you he about whom I spoke in ancient days through My servants, the prophets of Israel who prophesied in those days many years ago, to bring you upon them."

The fall of Gog is here revealed to have been G-d's plan all along Even in ancient days, G-d had revealed through the prophets that the angelic prince of Gog would eventually face his destiny for his rebellion by coming down to Earth, and becoming entangled here against the Divine Will, and authority.

18. "And it will come to pass on that day, when Gog comes against the land of Israel, declares the L-rd G-d, that My blazing indignation will flame in My nostrils. 19. For in My jealousy and in the fire of My wrath I have spoken. Surely there shall be a great noise on that day in the land of Israel. 20. And at My presence, the fishes of the sea and the birds of the heaven and the beasts of the field and all the creeping things that creep upon the earth and all the men who are upon the surface of the earth shall quake, and all the mountains shall be thrown down, and the cliffs shall fall to the ground."

Like it was in the time of the Flood, or with the plagues in Egypt, G-d's chosen agent for punishing the wicked is the laws of nature that He Himself has created. As with these and numerous other examples throughout scripture, G-d is clearly proclaimed to not only be the Creator of the Heavens and the Earth, but also their Director. Not only does G-d send forth His Watchers to direct the minds of men, G-d also controls the very laws of nature. Although natural law is designed to take its course, G-d the Creator often intervenes, and acts as the Random Element, unleashing natural forces that just so happen to coincide with the Divine plan for judgment.

There are many secularists who, while not denying the Exodus from Egypt still wish to proclaim that all that transpired then, with regards to the plagues, were all due to natural causes, and not because of any Divine intervention. This attitude clearly expresses a lack of understanding of the movement of the Divine Hand.

Indeed, scripture is clear that the Parting of the Red Sea was brought about by a mighty wind blowing for hours against the waters causing them to part. This is the natural part. However, what a coincidence that the wind just so happened to have blown when it did, for how long it did, and how hard it did. This is the miracle, the timing! The act was indeed natural. The timing was indeed supernatural, or miraculous.

As it was with the Parting of the Red Sea so too will it be with the grandiose earthquake destined to shake the Holy Land however so conveniently when the nation of Israel is in dire need of Divine intervention to stop an unstoppable army.

This earthquake to come is not just another run of the mill earthquake the likes of which we have always seen. No, this earthquake is going to be at least a 10 point on the Richter scale event. In other words, this earthquake will do more than just devastate, this earthquake will topple mountains, and collapse cliffs. We cannot imagine just what an earthquake of this magnitude will be like. Yet, the scripture here is certain, it is G-d that is bringing forth this quake at this time so as to awaken all who witness it to the reality of the Higher Hand behind this, and all other natural phenomena.

21. *"And I will call the sword against him upon all My mountains, says the L-rd G-d, every man's sword shall be against his brother.* **22.** *And I will judge against him with pestilence and with blood, and rain bringing floods, and great hailstones, fire, and brimstone will I rain down upon him and upon his hordes and upon the many peoples that are with him.* **23.** *And I will reveal Myself in My greatness, and in My holiness, and will be recognized in the eyes of many nations, and they will know that I am the L-rd."*

The two armies will fall upon one another with reckless abandon. Gog and his forces are destined to be decimated. Yet, the battle with the enemy will be tremendous. Just where the armies of Israel will be at this time is never mentioned. The implication here is that they are not involved with the fighting.

This could be because the armies of Israel have already been defeated, and no longer exist, or because they will be ordered to stand down, and bow out of the fighting. One way or another, this great battle is not between Israel, and the armies invading the Holy Land. Rather, as Daniel 11 showed us, the battle will be between the Kings of the North and South.

Then, either because of the earthquake or in concert with it, all types of natural disasters break loose. Pestilence with blood, floods, hailstones, fire and brimstone. This does not look like a happy scenario to look forward to. Yet, as G-d is the L-rd of nature, we must ask, what type of natural occurrence could possibly occur that would result in this type of sudden natural upheaval. While we cannot possibly ascertain with certainty what will be, we can review some possibilities.

We are familiar with the words of the prophet Joel (3:3-4) who stated, *"And I will perform signs in the heavens and on the earth, Blood, fire, and pillars of smoke. The sun shall turn to darkness, and the moon to blood, prior to the coming of the great and awesome day of the L-rd."*

We have already discussed the "pillars of smoke," and their relationship to mushroom clouds, thus indicating a nuclear war. Yet, this nuclear war must be all-out and intensive if it is to blot out sunlight from the sky. Scientists have long taught that a full sale nuclear war would leave lead to such destruction that there would be a cloud over the entire earth for a good long period, blocking out all sunlight, leading to the death of almost all life on the planet. They call this a nuclear winter.

While I do not doubt the authenticity of this scenario, I do question if indeed this would be the Will of G-d. Although it may be the Divine edict to punish mankind, I do not believe it is the Divine edict to destroy the entire planet. Therefore, I seek to interpret both Ezekiel and Joel according to something a little bit less severe.

What else could be so devastating to cause an earthquake of unprecedented proportions, causing floods, hailstones and fire, not to mention, blotting out the sun's light for a portion of time? What could cause such overwhelming damage and still dissipate fast enough so that (we assume) shortly thereafter the messianic era could begin with a new dawn for mankind.

Being that using natural forces to create both natural and supernatural disasters, one might question whether or not the Earth is to be struck by either a passing comet or meteor. Such an event would clearly cause the catastrophic damage described above. I myself believe that the description of the damage and how it is caused certainly sounds like the Earth is to be struck with something big from out of the sky. Yet, if this is so, I wondered, why would there not be any mention of such a possibility in the majority of classical apocalyptic literature? It did not take me long to find some sources that do mention something.

Ezekiel 39

1. "And you, Son of man, prophesy about Gog, and say, So says the L-rd G-d, Lo! I am against you, Gog, prince and head of Meshech and Tubal. 2. And I will unbridle and entice you and lead you up from the utmost parts of the north and bring you upon the mountains of Israel."

This chapter is understood by the classical commentaries to be a completely separate attack on Israel, different from the first. It appears from the conclusion of this chapter 39 that this attack may very well be the same attack discussed in Zechariah 14, which we will review later at a later time.

Again, it is clear that G-d Himself is directing the course and events in human history. Gog, the man, who is identified by some as Armilus/the Anti-Christ, has no idea that it is G-d Himself who is directing his actions, for his own doom. Now, whoever Gog turns out to be in the near future, it can be considered a certainty that he will be familiar with these Biblical prophecies. Knowing their eventual outcome why would Gog be motivated to march forward just to face his own doom? The answer to this is that Gog will be so compelled that he will not be able to think straight. In his mind, he will believe that he is doing the Will of G-d to attack Israel, being assured of this, by these very scriptures we read here.

Yet, Gog will not be deterred by his prophesied destruction. That part of the prophecy, Gog will not accept. It so rather bizarre, how Gog and so many like him, turn to scripture to find justification for their actions, and yet at the same time ignore what scripture warns will be the consequences of those actions.

3. *"And I will smite the bow out of your left hand and make your arrows fall from your right hand."*

The mention here of bows and arrows we assume is classical prophetic metaphor. We do not expect the final battle to be fought with such antiquated weaponry. Yet, for the record, one should know, that a proficient bowman is as effective today in combat as was his ancient counterpart.

Most soldiers today do not go into combat fully covered with body armor and, therefore, are as susceptible to being shot with an arrow as they are with a bullet. Anyone knowing modern archery is familiar with today's compound bows and crossbows, all the more so hunter arrow heads. A good archer today can take out game at a good distance, and if under combat circumstances, he could just as easily take out human targets as well. While I do not anticipate modern or future warriors to be armed with compound bows or crossbows, nevertheless they are very lethal weapons. Learning their usage, in my opinion is highly recommended.

4. *"Upon the mountains of Israel shall you fall, you and all your hordes, and the people that are with you; to the birds of prey, to all the winged creatures and the beasts of the field have I given you to be devoured.* **5.** *Upon the open field shall you fall, for I have spoken, says the L-rd G-d."*

There is keenly no mention here that this army falls due to the natural plagues and disasters spoken of in the last chapter. Here it states that G-d will smite the bow from their hands, and make their arrows drop. How this is to be accomplished is not mentioned. If indeed this prophecy is a mirror prophecy of the one in Zechariah 14 (12-13), then we might expect the following to occur.

"And this shall be the plague wherewith the L-rd will smite all the nations who besieged Jerusalem; his flesh will waste away while he still stands on his feet; his eyes will waste away in their sockets, and his tongue shall waste away in his mouth. And it will come to pass on that day that there will be great consternation, sent by the L-rd upon them; each one shall seize the hand of the other, and his hand shall rise up against the hand of the other."

Apparently, the attacking soldiers are to be wiped out by some devastating weapon that wastes away their flesh. Literally, their organic structure simply disintegrates from over their bones. As the remainder of the prophecy here in Ezekiel 39 states, their remaining flesh will be eating by the beasts of the field, and nothing will remain other than their bones. These, as we shall see, are to be buried.

As to the nature of the weapon used against them, we can only guess. I would suggest that such a weapon is not now in human hands. While we humans can detonate an atomic bomb, I do not believe that the invading army is to be destroyed with such a destructive weapon. For this would wipe out everything, their flesh and their bones, leaving behind nothing other than ash. So, this cannot be.

Yet, some form of weapon will be used against them that will literally cause their organic structure to simply melt. Maybe this will be some kind of Chi or Orgone depletion weapon, one that literally sucks away the life force energy that holds all matter together, leaving behind just a melted empty shell. Only time will tell, exactly what it is the enemies of Israel, and G-d are destined to face.

Chapter 2

The Teachings About Mashiah Ben Yosef

Part 1

Jewish legends have for centuries discussed that prior to the coming of the Mashiah, the promised son of David who is to rebuild the Holy Temple in Jerusalem, gather in all the exiles of Israel, conquer all of Israel's enemies and to establish G-d's Kingdom on earth, another is to precede him to, as if begin his mission and to prepare his way. This other is also called a Mashiah, but of the tribe of Yosef, as opposed to the tribe of Yehuda. He is the Mashiah Ben Yosef.

The legends, predictions and/or stories about Mashiah Ben Yosef recorded in the Talmud and midrashim are rather consistent in that he is to appear some years before the final Mashiah, Ben David, and to fight the wars of G-d. However, unlike his Davidic counterpart, Mashiah Ben Yosef is predicted not to succeed in his endeavors. It is predicted that he is destined to fall in battle over Jerusalem, a victim of the evil emperor of the Edomic Empire, who in Jewish legend is called the Armilus.

The characterization and stories of Mashiah Ben Yosef have long been documented and are available in numerous translations. Yet, as with every legend that predicts an ominous future, its actual interpretations and applications become clouded over time, and thus grows the lack of ability to analyze the legend and to apply its essential teachings to current events and modern times. In light of this, a true understanding of the identity, role and career of Mashiah Ben Yosef might be totally missed unless one seeks to truly understand who he really is, what he really is practically and politically supposed to accomplish, and most importantly, when this is all to come about.

This series is dedicated to unraveling what has unfortunately become the mysterious identity of Mashiah ben Yosef and to enable us to recognize him and with G-d's help contribute to his ever so important task of preparing the world for the acceptance of the Kingdom of Heaven to be established with the advent of the true Mashiah ben David.

The original Talmudic/Gaonic era teachings about Mashiah Ben Yosef are relatively few and simple. They contain no involved theology or philosophy, just mere predictions of that which is yet to come. The legends/stories read similar to a Midrash, some more embellished than others, but together they all seem just to be telling a story instead of a involved abstract philosophical lesson.

This is important to keep in mind, for over the last five hundred years, since the advent of the Kabbalah of the Ari'zal, teachings about Mashiah Ben Yosef have proliferated and grown, expanded way out of the original socio-political proportion assigned to them by our Talmudic/Gaonic Sages. I must emphasize from the beginning that according to the original sources, Mashiah Ben Yosef is an actual historical individual who is to come and be active in the political and military realm. His mission and purpose is clear, and all the philosophical and theological embellishments added to his title, mission and purpose may or may not have any foundation in the unfolding political drama that will bring about his advent.

In other words, just because someone says something about the identity and/or purpose of Ben Yosef does not make that statement to be true. Of course, if a statement is made by a great Sage, many will desirously accept it as a Biblical truth. Nonetheless, with all due respect to our great Rabbis, not everything that they say is to be interpreted as either completely metaphorical or completely "al pi pshat" (straightforward). The words of our Sages have a way to them in that they have multiple layers of meanings. Nonetheless, regardless of all philosophical and spiritual interpretations of messianic teachings, one must above all remember that as RaMBaM has written the words of the Sages regarding messianic matters are merely opinions, and not absolute or obligatory opinions at that.

Discussions about messianic matters, be it Ben Yosef, or Ben David are not matters of Jewish Law (Halakha) and do not fall into the category of belief in the coming of Mashiah which is one of the Thirteen Principles of the Jewish Faith as outlined by RaMBaM (Maimonides). Messianic discussions are never really clearly set out and explained. There is much confusion about how messianic events will actually unfold in detail. The reason for this as outlined by our Sages should be obvious to all. When we are talking about the future we are talking about the unleashing of a chain of events, which is subject to monumental changes at every moment based upon the behavior of the individuals involved at any given moment.

Mankind, created in G-d's image, has the absolute gift of free will and choice. There is no pre-ordained destiny of doom and gloom to befall us. Although we have prophecy throughout the TaNaKh (Bible) and Talmud that will indeed come about in all their details, nonetheless, the ultimate fulfillment of prophecy is predicated upon the behavior of man.

Just like G-d sent Jonah to the city of Nineveh to proclaim its destruction if they did not repent, so is all other Biblical prophecy incumbent upon the condition of repentance on a national and global level. We have a choice, to accept upon ourselves the Yoke of the Kingdom of Heaven and thus to naturally evolve into a global higher spiritual state or to continue in our present course of action and face its inevitable consequences.

In actuality, this choice has already been made by us and for us. With regards to this, the scenario of messianic judgment already began over 50 years and we are today committed to the fulfillment of this course of action. This is a Heavenly edict and it will not and cannot be reversed or undone. Our collective human choice has already been made; the messianic scenario is already well under way.

Therefore, Mashiah Ben Yosef material must be understood in light of where we are at today, in light of current socio-political events as they are unfolding in our Holy Land Eretz Yisrael. The numerous philosophical conjectures of the past surrounding the character of Ben Yosef must not be viewed as an absolute mold of political reality into which we must fit our interpretation of current events. We must look first to see where we are at and then apply Ben Yosef teachings to this, only then will we be able to properly interpret the predictions of our holy Sages.

Fulfillment of prophecy is happening now in the way so ordained by Heaven. Mashiah Ben Yosef could have come in any number of forms or manners. Yet, he is here with us today, in his present form, based upon where we are today and how G-d in Heaven has ordained to respond to us and our choices.

In light of this introduction, let us proceed to outline in brief the original teachings about Mashiah Ben Yosef, define the common denominators and then look where we are at today and thus put all the pieces together to, pray G-d, get a glimpse of the fulfillment of prophecy happening around us.

In order to first explore the character of Mashiah Ben Yosef, we must first explore the nature of why he is said to be from the tribe of Yosef (specifically Ephraim). Why could he not be from any other tribe? Obviously by stating that this pre-Mashiah is of the tribe of Yosef, there is the implication of connection and identity with the tribe and its history.

Before we understand Yosef's Mashiah, we must first understand Yosef's tribe and the Kingdom that came forth under its tutelage.

Part 2

There are two very specific Biblical portrayals that properly define for us the character of the Tribe of Yosef and more so show us its relationship with the Tribe of Yehuda, from which comes forth Mashiah Ben David. From these two portrayals we will be able to draw a picture that will help us recognize the character of the "Benei Yosef" of today as well as clearly see the relationship of the two Mashiahs, Ben Yosef and Ben David.

The first Biblical episode of significance that outlines for us the relationship of Yosef and Yehuda also foreshadows the future inevitable meeting of their Mashiahs. In Genesis, Yosef and Yehuda meet for the first time as adults in Pharaoh's court. Yosef is unrecognizable to Yehuda having been raised an Egyptian for so many years. While Yehuda has maintained his cultural identity, Yosef looks ever so different. More than this, rather than following in the "family business," Yosef, is now a politician, a Prime Minister of Egypt, a man of the world, so very much unlike the House of Jacob, who are few, isolated and different. Yosef's name is Egyptian, as are his appearance, wife and children ever so opposite from his brothers. All in all, there is nothing left "Israelitish" of Yosef except one major defining factor. This is his heart.

In his heart, Yosef is still the son of Jacob and still a member of "the tribe." I use this term because although today we would call Yosef a "Jew" in good standing, he nevertheless never really was a "Jew" by the exact definition of the word. Yosef and his progeny are not "Jews" by the specific definition of the term, simply because the term "Jew" applies specifically to the descendants of Judah ("Jewdah").

In actuality, since the destruction of the Biblical Northern Kingdom of Israel, closely associated with the Tribe of Yosef, all Israelites have come to be termed "Jews" because of association to the Nation of Judah, which continued, was destroyed by Babylon, but yet rebuilt. The Northern Kingdom of Israel was never rebuilt. The exile under the Assyrians technically never came to an end. All recognizable survivors of the Northern Kingdom fled south into Judah.

Judah was later destroyed by Rome and it is Rome and the nations it has sired that continue to this day to look upon all descendants of the House of Israel as being members of the Nation of Judah, and thus Jews, regardless of their authentic tribal origins.

Back in Pharaoh's court, we see that G-d led Yosef down a very different path from the rest of his family which we should rightly call Israel, and later (in history) Yehuda. Yosef, while assimilated externally, remained faithful to Israel internally. Yet, it is Yosef's external and foreign posture/appearance that brings him into what our Sages taught was direct conflict with Yehuda. As is clear from the Genesis encounter, Yosef is testing his brothers to see if they are willing to stand together as brothers and defend Binyamin, whom he (Yosef) had set up and falsely accused of theft. Yehuda takes up the argument for Binyamin and his words are harsh and confrontational. Yosef recognizes the sincerity in Yehuda's words and shortly discards all pretenses and reunites with his brothers.

While this story is known to all, remember that the entire episode of the test and conflict stretched out over more than a year's time. On their first visit to Egypt, Shimon was taken prisoner. No one of his brothers came to his rescue or even spoke up for him. Shimon remained imprisoned for a year, and would have been there longer if the brothers did not need to return to Egypt for food.

Thus a year later needing to return, knowing full well the demand to bring Binyamin to Egypt, the brothers were at a crossroads. Should they not go to Egypt, they would have no grain, surely a recipe for suicide in a society dependent upon agriculture. Should they go, without Binyamin, who knows what the Prime Minister of Egypt would do to them? Yet, if they do go along with Binyamin, who knows what could happen to him?

Bearing for 20+ years the guilt and shame of how they treated their brother Yosef, they feared greatly what would happen to dear old Dad Israel, if they messed up again and harm came to Binyamin. Funny, how they shared no such remorse for Shimon. Yet, the brothers had learned their lesson. And Yehuda, son #4, takes charge; not by means of authority or Divine decree but rather because that was his personality. His personality made him rise up like a rocket and become a leader among his brothers. This is most unusual that the number four son should rise up and take a position of power and authority in the presence of his older brothers. Nonetheless, Reuven son number one, and Levi, son number three are not heard from. Apparently, they acquiesce to the leadership role of their younger brother Yehuda.

There is only one problem here; there already is a leader among the brothers, a mighty and powerful leader at that! This leader is Yosef! Although he is not a leader of his brothers by their choice, he is a leader by right and Divine design. Therefore we have two leaders, Yosef and Yehuda, one in the "family business" and one not.

What then is to happen when leaders clash? What happens in the "family business" now has to take into account the new leader, i.e., Yosef. Whether the Sons of Israel like it or not, their cast-away brother Yosef has risen to leadership in his own right and now that he is reunited with the family does not mean that his position and role of leadership is diminished. This is what psychologically underlies the conflict between Yosef and Yehuda as outlined in Genesis. The friction between their two personalities exists and existed even prior to Yosef's identity being revealed. As it was then, so it is today, as we shall soon see.

For our second Biblical portrayal, we must jump centuries into the future from the initial confrontation between Yosef and Yehuda and look towards the relationship of their descendants. As is known from later Biblical/Jewish history G-d chooses David from the House of Yehuda to be King over all Israel. This selection was not welcomed and accepted by all the tribes so quickly. Indeed, David reigned as King of Yehuda for seven years prior to being accepted as King over all the tribes. This is because throughout Jewish history to that time, it was Yosef who was naturally considered to be the leader of Israel.

Yosef became Jacob's first-born by his father's personal decree and received the appropriate double-portion of land inheritance in Eretz Yisrael. While Yehuda was certainly the singularly largest of the twelve tribes, the two Yosef tribes of Ephraim and Menashe were together bigger than he. Indeed, when Moshe Rabbeynu chose his own personal successor to lead the Jewish people, he did not choose his brother in-law Caleb from the tribe of Yehuda, husband of his sister Miriam and by all means a worthy individual who could by right lead Israel. Rather Moshe Rabbeynu chose his servant, his assistant Yehoshua, a man descended from Yosef. No one questioned this choice, not even Caleb.

Yehoshua was a man of Yosef and as such was fit and proper to rule. Throughout the days of the Judges, until the Kingdom of David, the Yosef tribes were always looked to for leadership in Israel. And when David's grandson took the throne and decreed edicts unacceptable to the people, what did the other tribes do? They rebelled and cast off Davidic (i.e. Yehuda) leadership and formed their own Kingdom under the leadership of no one other than a Ben Yosef!

Throughout the history of ancient Israel, there was always this conflict between Yosef and Yehuda, both the individuals and the tribes that they sired. The relationship between the Northern Kingdom of Israel and the Southern Kingdom of Yehuda was never really one of brothers. The relationship between the two kingdoms was tedious at best. Israel in the north claimed to stick to the psychology of the old ways, which of course never really happened. Yehuda on the other hand claimed to be true to G-d, and faithful to His chosen King and Temple, which in all due respect was not so true either. The Bible is replete with the conflicts and sour relationship between the Kingdom of Yehuda and the Kingdom of Israel, with titular leadership from Yosef.

Yosef, the individual, was a man of the world, an able leader of Egypt all the while faithful to the ideals of Israel, his father. His progeny carried on their father's traits of courage, outgoingness and fearlessness of interactions with other nations. The Yosef tribe excelled in their relationships with others. They were a very cosmopolitan group. However the influence from the idolatrous societies around the Northern Kingdom eventually proved too much even for the robust, proud and powerful Benei Yosef. In spite of all the prophetic warnings sent by G-d to them the Northern Kingdom, with tribe of Yosef at their spiritual head succumbed to the evil influences surrounding it and suffered Divine judgment because of its sins. Yehuda was not too far behind. Neither tribe, neither kingdom lived up to their Divine calling.

With the fall of both Kingdoms and centuries of assimilation the actual blood-lines of the tribes have become blurred and in many cases outright lost. To this day, although the blood-line identities of the members of the Yosef and Yehuda tribes have been for the most part blurred, the psychological conflict between them is still as strong and evident as ever. However being that we today have lost sight of the original historical conflict of the tribes we also do not know how to recognize its modern manifestation because we do not know how to recognize the modern day Benei Yehuda and Benei Yosef and identify them by their characters and behaviors as opposed to their names and blood-lines.

Yet, it is this identification that is paramount in importance. For how can we recognize a Mashiah Ben Yosef all the while that we so immaturely think that Ben Yosef can only mean of the blood line of Yosef? We must understand who Yosef is today, metaphorically and spiritually speaking. Only then will we be able to properly recognize and identify his messiah.

Let us then proceed to discuss more about the character of Yosef and the Benei Yosef and see from the description if anyone today can be associated with it.

Part 3

The character of the Benei Yosef, both past and present, can be summed up quite easily by reviewing what exactly the Bible has to say about the Northern Kingdom of Israel. Throughout prophecy the Northern Kingdom is always referred to as Yosef. Therefore whatever is said about the Biblical Northern Kingdom of Israel holds true for the Benei Yosef and helps us identify its characteristics.

By superimposing the Biblical descriptions onto modern personages and groups, we should be able to clearly identity those who embrace the "spirit" of Benei Yosef today. As mentioned previously being that for the most part specific physical blood-lines of the tribes of Yosef have been lost for centuries, the only way we can identify Yosef today is through their characteristics. Recognize the character and you recognize Yosef and can thus focus onto recognition of his Mashiah.

Biblical prophecies are certainly not very complementary towards Yosef. While his strength is praised he is on numerous occasion admonished, often rather harshly, because of wanton ways assimilating into the surrounding non-Jewish cultures and forgetting about his covenant with G-d and Torah. Yosef is often condemned in prophecy because he has fallen aside and follows his pleasures and lusts instead of staying moral and honest. From a summary of prophecy we can see that Yosef is not viewed well by Heaven. Nonetheless, Yosef's future is predicted to be bright because G-d is going to reunite him with Yehuda and make one nation out of the two of them.

Yosef as the representative for the Northern Kingdom is described as rebelling against G-d's chosen House of David monarchy and the Holy Temple, built by Solomon, son of David, but built for all Israel and not just for Yehuda. By rebelling against David, Jerusalem and the Temple, Yosef can best be described as rebelling against the very foundations of what today we define as the religion of Torah Judaism.

Indeed, allegiance to and faith in a Mashiah Ben David, the rebuilding of the Holy Temple in Jerusalem, the capital of a united Israel is the core of Judaism and the foundation of our daily prayers. By not accepting these Yosef has separated himself from the very essence of Judaism. Does any of this sound familiar or recognizable today? We will answer this question as we proceed. Yet, in order to properly lay the groundwork for this answer, let us look to the Prophets to assist us to further ascertain the identity of modern day Yosef.

According to one specific reference in the Prophets we are able to generally ascertain where the exiles of both Yosef and Yehuda went once they left the Holy Land so many centuries ago. The prophet Ovadiah (1:20) mentions that the exiled hosts of the Children of Israel went to dwell amongst the previously ejected Canaanites in a land called Tzarfat, which is the Hebrew name for modern day France. Interestingly, the same pasuk states that the exiles of Jerusalem, obviously the tribe of Yehuda who stayed faithful to the holy city were exiled to the land of Sifarad, which in Hebrew is modern day Spain.

Based upon this one pasuk many commentators have discerned that the Jewish inhabitants of France, Germany and Eastern Europe are descendants of Yosef, whereas those of Spanish origins are from Yehuda. In modern and direct terms, the blood-lines of Yosef are the original ancestors of the major portion of what we today call Ashkenazi Jewry, whereas the Yehuda blood-line is the source of the original Sephardic Jews from Spain.

There you have it, Biblical proof that Ashkenazim are from Yosef and Sephardim are from Yehuda. At least, this is how it was many centuries ago. Over many centuries, and especially in recent times, we see both personal and mass migrations, where individuals and whole communities moved from one country to the next. Today, the blood-lines of Ashkenazim and Sephardim, and who exactly is from a Yosef tribe or from Yehuda is very much intermingled. Personally, I view this as a blessing from G-d and a partial fulfillment of the prophecy to reunite the Houses of Yosef and Yehuda.

This being said, and the blood-lines being somewhat identified, let us now turn again to the characteristic traits of Yosef, their secularism, and rebellion against Jerusalem, the Davidic Kingdom and the Holy Temple and view this in light of the growth of radical secularism amongst European Ashkenazi Jews over the past two centuries and only then can we come into the modern realm and discuss secular Zionism. I believe the answer to the above question as to the modern identity of Yosef is becoming ever so much clearer.

Those who have ever studied the cultural, sociological and even psychological differences between Sephardim and Ashkenazim come to some rather striking conclusions. While there is of course much that is similar between the two peoples, there are specific traits in personality and world outlook that sharply divide the two types. Interestingly, but it should come as no surprise that the modern day differences between Sephardim and Ashkenazim ever so clearly parallel the differences between Biblical Yehuda and Yosef. Indeed, although the blood-lines are clouded, the identities of the souls still shine through bright and clear.

Yosef is portrayed in the Bible as cosmopolitan, world savvy, and what we would today call secular. It is then of no wonder that modern day Ashkenazim descendants of Yosef should follow in the footsteps of their ancestors. Yosef was clever, strong and ever so "bull-headed." Sound familiar? The difference between religious and secular Ashkenazim we will discuss later, but for right now let us focus on the secular and how these modern descendants of Yosef fit into the messianic scenario.

In order to discuss messianic matters, let us begin by delving into the centuries old prophecy, now fulfilled, that G-d would in the End of Days restore His people to our Holy Land. How was this to happen needs to be understood. For this let me share with you an ancient teaching from the writings of Rabbi Sa'adiah Gaon.

Over 1,000 years ago, Rabbi Sa'adiah Gaon wrote a most peculiar and most prophetic prediction about the return of the exiles to the Holy Land and the rebuilding of the Israelite nation. In his Emunot VeDeot (Article 8, Chapter 5) he writes:

"We already know that if our repentance is incomplete, we will remain [unredeemed] until the end comes. If it comes and we do not repent, salvation may come with us still sinners. With so much time having passed, G-d will return us to the Land without repentance. Only there is a prophetic tradition that we will be beset by troubles and distress through which we will choose to repent and will merit redemption. They also said that the catalyst for this will be a man from the seed of Yosef."

The beginning of redemption is clearly defined as the initial return of Jews to our Holy Land and our independence therein. This indeed has happened beginning in 1948, which itself is a year of prophetic significance. Over 100 years ago a Syrian Rabbi Yitzhak Alfiyya wrote in the name of Kabbalistic traditions that indeed the redemption would begin in the Hebrew year 5708, corresponding to 1948. The establishment of the State of Israel occurred right on time according to Rabbi Alfiyya and it was established exactly as Sa'adia Gaon said it would be, with us still sinners.

The secular State of Israel established by ardent secular Ashkenazi Jews from Europe, much to their own chagrin, fulfilled the Biblical, prophetic and Kabbalistic prophecies for the beginning of the redemption.

In light of all what we have covered, the Ashkenazi secular State of Israel must be viewed not as a re-establishment of Southern Kingdom of Yehuda, but rather as the re-establishment of the Northern Kingdom of Israel. Never in the history of Zionism was it ever conceived to re-establish the Biblical state of Yehuda. Never did the Zionists consider naming their new state Yehuda although the founders all considered themselves Jews.

Indeed, the founding Zionist fathers created for themselves a new name and a new identity. No longer were they to be called Jews. Now they are Israelis. This term has not been in use since the days of the fallen Northern Kingdom over 2500 years ago. The resurrection of the term Israeli to also include the members of the tribe of Yehuda (Yehudim-Jews) has not been heard since the days of King Solomon.

Like the Northern Kingdom, the present secular State of Israel rejects the authority of the House of David, enshrined as it is in the Orthodox religious leadership, they reject the concepts of both rebuilding the Temple and reconstituting the Sanhedrin. However, to their credit, they have accepted as fact that Jerusalem, capital of old Yehuda is now the one capital of all Israel.

The secular State of Israel today embraces the same rebellious spirit of the ancient Benei Yosef of the old Northern Kingdom of Israel. As such modern day Israel is the metaphorical Tribe of Yosef, if not the real tribe by rite of Ashkenazi blood-lines. We have now identified modern day Yosef. Now we must move along to investigate the identity of Mashiah Ben Yosef.

In order to do this, let us first remember that the term Mashiah, although it literally means "anointed one" actually means a redeemer and savior. Therefore Mashiah Ben Yosef is to be the savior of the modern day State of Israel. This therefore means that Mashiah Ben Yosef will somehow have to be an Israeli politician and some kind of religious leader.

Before we can investigate this further, we must learn more about what our Sages have taught about the nature, psyche and role of Mashiah Ben Yosef. Only then can we begin to identify him clearly and possibly point fingers at individuals who embrace these aspects of Mashiah Ben Yosef identity.

Part 4 - Conclusion

It never ceases to amaze me how the mind of man can run away into the most abstract imagination based upon the most simplest and practical of things. I consider this phenomenon of mind to be one of man's greatest assets whereas at the same time it is one of our greatest dangers. Spiritual existence is as real and tangible as physical existence. However, due to its "other-dimensional" status most just talk about or postulate about spiritual reality without having any personal experience whatsoever with its real details. This is where the imagination can become very dangerous indeed. These points must be kept in mind whenever there is discussion about the political reality versus the spiritual concepts of Mashiah Ben Yosef.

As can be seen throughout all literature on the subject, Mashiah Ben Yosef is to come as an actual political figure, a flesh and blood human being, who lives, fights and dies like any other normal human being. His role in history is to be political and sociological. He is supposed to be military warrior, a general, a man of violence and revenge. Nowhere in classical literature are any specific spiritual attributes ascribed to him. He is never described as an overwhelmingly holy man or righteous man. He is not described as an enlightened Sage or master of esoteric lore.

No, Mashiah Ben Yosef, has always been described in classical literature as just what he is supposed to be, a military general, and leader of latter day Israel whose role in history is to wage the wars of HaShem against the evil empire of Edom/Europe and to destroy their power and influence in the world. This is who Mashiah Ben Yosef will be, just as originally described, and all later embellishments to his career, soul, spiritual source and identity may or may not be true. Only time will tell with these. We will discuss more about the evil empire and its leader Armilus in the following lessons.

Throughout Ben Yosef literature it is repeatedly taught that he is supposed to die in battle with the enemies of Israel. General tradition teaches that he is to be killed by Armilus after waging a powerful battle that will destroy most of Europe and the civilization it has sired. The Zohar however teaches an alternative scenario. According to the Zohar, Mashiah Ben Yosef is to be killed by a King of Persia (Iran) who is to invade and conquer Israel.

Regardless of who it is that gets to kill Ben Yosef, apparently his fate to face death is agreed upon in all the sources. Although Kabbalists since the days of the Ari'zal have prayed that Mashiah Ben Yosef not have to die, such a change in fate would require drastic changes amongst the Jewish people, the likes of which have not yet happened. Therefore, in light of our current situation, we should however uncomfortably accept that Ben Yosef's destiny is right on target.

Ben Yosef is supposed to die in battle, yet the classic Midrashim relating the matter never actually reveal to us the reason why this has to be so. For the reason to this we must turn to the literature of the Kabbalists. Rather than proceed with an in-depth review of all the pertinent literature, let me summarize the major point.

Rabbi Hayim Vital, master Kabbalist and codifier of the Ari'zal system sums up Ben Yosef's fate by saying that his date with death is due to the fact that his soul emanates from the Tree of Knowledge, Good and Evil, instead of emanating from the Tree of Life. This metaphor is packed with meaning.

As we know in the Garden of Eden, there were the two trees; eating the fruits of one brought eternal life, eating the fruits of the other brought death. Adam as we know ate of the Tree of Knowledge, Good and Evil and thus brought death to the world. Mashiah Ben Yosef as the true "son of man" (Adam) follows in his footsteps and like every other human being since Eden is destined to "go the way of all the earth." Mashiah Ben David on the other hand is said to eat from the Tree of Life and as such will introduce to the world the radical removal of the concept of what we know as death. We will discuss Ben David in his place as we proceed.

Mashiah Ben Yosef is a man, born, and destined to die, like any other man. He is of the Tree of Knowledge and this seals his fate. Yet, the metaphor of the two Trees also goes beyond the mere applications to human versus spiritual life. The two Trees have come to represent the two ways of understanding the Torah, pshat and sod (Kabbalah).

Kabbalah (sod) has always been called the Tree of Life, whereas pshat (the study of non-mystical Torah) has always been called the Tree of Knowledge, Good and Evil. By saying that Ben Yosef emanates from the Tree of Knowledge, Rabbi Hayim is clearly insinuating something rather revelatory. Mashiah Ben Yosef is destined not to be a Kabbalist or student of the Kabbalah. As emanating from the Tree of Knowledge, Ben Yosef's outlook on life deals exclusively with life in this world, without too much concern for the life in the spiritual world.

Ben Yosef, might very well be a dreamer as was Father Yosef himself, but also like Father Yosef, Mashiah Ben Yosef will be a savvy, modern and to the eye very secular politician. In his heart and private practice he will be righteous, whether that righteousness as prescribed by Torah Law will be a known thing to the public remains to be seen. If Mashiah Ben Yosef is to be anything like Father Yosef, then indeed he will most likely follow in his footsteps and appear one way in public, and yet, be an entirely different person in private.

Another interesting point about Ben Yosef mentioned in classical sources is that similar to Father Yosef his brothers, specifically those led by Yehuda, are said not to recognize him. We know the significance this played in the Biblical story, but we really do have to consider the ramifications of what this would mean if modern day Jews do not recognize Mashiah Ben Yosef.

In light of the fact as we have discussed that Yehuda may be a metaphor for religious Jews and Yosef a metaphor for secular Jews, we can foresee Mashiah Ben Yosef being a Jewish leader who is not much recognized and accepted by the religious community at large.

As such Mashiah Ben Yosef would lead a secular Israel, similar as did any Biblical leader of Yosef rule over the ancient Northern Kingdom of Israel.

The wars of Mashiah ben Yosef are called the wars of HaShem. However, as with all wars of HaShem, this does not exactly mean that the wars are fought in the Name of HaShem. Remember Nebuchadnezzar who destroyed Jerusalem and exiled Yehuda acted as HaShem's agent. As the Divine agent he ruthlessly murdered tens of thousands of Jews, burned down the Holy Temple and perpetuated many other horrible crimes. Nonetheless, the scriptures are clear that he acted as the unwitting and unknowing agent of HaShem to punish Yehuda. Nebuchadnezzar acted for HaShem but not in the Name of HaShem. It is possible that Mashiah ben Yosef will be in a similar position.

Throughout scripture and classical Torah literature it is Yosef who is portrayed as the antagonist of Esau. Esau's descendants, Edom, have always been identified with the Romans, and the nations that succeeded them, modern day Europe, with the Church of Rome at their head. Thus the classical conflict of Mashiah Ben Yosef is said to be with Rome, which is Europe, quite possibly the modern day European Union. In light of recent European Union positions towards the sworn enemies of Jews worldwide and their constant anti-Israeli stand on a number of issues, political and otherwise, it is no wonder that a recent Israeli government report recently stated that there is a growing possibly of outright conflict and other hostilities foreseen over the coming decades between Israel and Europe.

World pressure against the existence of the State of Israel is growing. The United Nation has proven itself on countless occasions to not be a friend of the State of Israel. The European Union is fanning the flames of anti-Israeli positions worldwide.

The State of Israel is being pushed further and further into a political and military corner. The present political environment of pressure being put on Israel to leave itself vulnerable to its enemies leaves very little maneuvering room. One does not have to be a prophet to predict that eventually Israel will have to fight a great war just for the right to survive and exist. When the time comes to fight this war, Edom, with the European Union at its head is prophesied to spear-head the attack. Whether this will be directly with United Nations or European Union troops in a Bosnia type scenario or with political/economic sanctions and sabotage, time will tell.

Classical literature tells us that whatever the practical details of the scenario may be, the conflict between Mashiah Ben Yosef, a most likely secular Ashkenazi Jew, and the forces of Edom, who most likely are Europe and the United Nations is inevitable. Whether Mashiah Ben Yosef will die in this conflict as predicted is also subject to discussion, yet as with all details of this scenario, time will tell.

As pressure grows against the State of Israel and injustices against the State and her people continue, resentment grows amongst the populace. Somehow, at some time, something will happen in the body politic of the State of Israel that will cause an eruption of Jewish patriotism and lead to the rise of one who is destined to become Mashiah Ben Yosef, the savior of the modern State of Israel. He will lead Israel into bitter armed conflict against its enemies, who I remind you are not predicted to be led by Arabs. He is to be victorious, at least for a while, until Armilus comes.

The present world situation is ripe for the rise of Mashiah Ben Yosef. As we have described him, so shall he come. The religious will not welcome or accept him, whereas many of the secular will look to him as if he, Mashiah Ben Yosef, is in reality Mashiah Ben David. For this reason alone, he may be destined to die. Then again, like any other Jew, he may humble himself before his Creator in Heaven, embrace the Holy Torah and thus embrace the Tree of Life. In such a case, what will be is anyone's guess, and HaShem's Grace will decide the matter.

Much has been written regarding Mashiah Ben Yosef. There is an entire body of philosophy, speculations, calculations, and of course Kabbalah. Whether these add to our understanding of Mashiah Ben Yosef or merely cloud his identity time will tell once he comes. He has not yet come. We cannot point to anyone as yet being Mashiah Ben Yosef, although many have walked in his path. There are many who we can point to in Israel today who are likely candidates to become Mashiah Ben Yosef. Yet, as with all things, the final decision on what is to be is in the Hands of Almighty HaShem.

We have done now all that we need to in order to identify Mashiah Ben Yosef, the coming leader of the State of Israel who will defend our Holy Land from the encroachments of the nations of the world with Europe at their head. Europe, on the other hand will be led by a renewed Caesar, a new Alexander. In Jewish tradition this coming head of Edom/Europe will be called Armilus, based on the name Romulus, the legendary founder of Rome. In one Jewish source, Armilus is identified by his non-Jewish/Christian name. The Midrash Milkhamot HaMashiah calls Armilus, the "Anti-Christ." Being that this evil Mashiah of Edom is to play such a great role in the messianic scenario coming ever so quickly upon us, it is proper for us to continue our discussions and to focus on him.

Chapter 3

The State of Israel in Religion & Prophecy

Israel calls itself the Jewish State and opens its doors to Jews around the world to relocate there and to become citizens, if and when they have the need or the desire to do so. The purpose of the State, as it itself states, is to be a homeland for all Jews, to defend them in times of need, to fight with organized resistance in case another Holocaust is initiated against Jews anywhere. This is a laudable position and Israel has acted to save numerous Jewish lives over few decades of the State's existence.

Hatred of Jews, sometimes under the name of anti-Zionism, sometimes not, is a primary concern not only for the State of Israel, but for Jewish citizens of the many nations around the world. The existence of the State of Israel thus serves as a warning and guarantee that if and when hostilities against Jews breaks out anywhere in the world, the Jewish State claims the right to respond and to defend Jews, regardless of their nationality and location.

Israel makes great contributions to the world in many different fields of science. Regardless of these contributions, racism, prejudice and hatred of Jews still exists in many parts of the world.

Israel is a state for all its citizens, Jewish or otherwise. The State rightfully, following its own unique version of "separation of religion and state," is definably secular. The State does not claim to have any position of authority or significance within the religion of Judaism or in religious Torah Law.

There is an element within the religion of Judaism (and beyond) that views the present State of Israel in the light of Biblical and messianic prophecy. Those ascribing to these beliefs view the establishment and existence of the modern State of Israel to be a fulfillment of Biblical prophecy and a sign for the beginning of the End of Days.

Eschatology is the study of the End of Days, Based on Biblical sources, and later Rabbinic and Kabbalistic traditions and folklore, the period of the End of Days is supposed to be marked by a terrible world war between the Jewish people and its enemies. Those who see the modern State of Israel in prophetic light view it as fulfilling this role as the End Times "sons of light."

Needless to say, Israel rightfully does not see itself in this light, nor does it want to. The majority of citizens in the State do not desire and do not seek Armageddon and the Apocalypse.

End Times prophecies are numerous, confusing and often contradictory. The religion of Judaism does not enumerate a detailed, structured order of events that describe how the End of Days must unravel. Because of this ambiguity in the Jewish religion, the messianic element in modern Orthodox Judaism steps in and, like Jews in ancient times before them, seek to interpret every event in current events in light of the End of Days scenario and the fulfillment of messianic prophecies.

This desperate attempt to find meaning and relevance in daily affairs has led to an extremism of its own. They demand that the secular State of Israel follow a political agenda that embraces their messianic ideals. When the State does not act to live up to the ideals that they believe it should, members of this group often act on their own. Members of this group are known to have perpetuated acts of terrorism against Arabs and even against fellow Jews. Some even desire to act in ways to provoke a major World War. Those embracing the messianic ideals are more and more adopting a "cult-like" mentality that "you are either with us or against us." Needless to say, any such attitudes and the behaviors that they lead to are dangerous for the State of Israel and for Jews worldwide.

For the believers in religion, the End of Days will come, sometime. In the 1570's, the mystical Rabbi of Safed (in modern Israel) declared that then was the End of Days. Many others believe that the United States, founded in 1776 also was established to play a vital role in the End of Days. Therefore, in light of these views, the End of Days has been going on for a few hundred years and contains many different elements.

The End of Days did not start in 1948 with the establishment of the modern State of Israel. Therefore, from the religious, messianic and prophetic points of view, we must ask ourselves, are our days and more or less significant in the End of Days scenario that any other time before us? Must we face Armageddon and the Apocalypse? Is there no other human destiny? Must it be here and now?

For the messianic element within modern Orthodox Judaism (and elsewhere) the answer to these questions is a definitive, yes! They want to bring on the fight, for to them, G-d is on their side and desires them to act in this way. They are certain that in the end they will prevail and all their enemies will be killed, they will survive and live the embrace the dawn of the Messianic era. The Bible and later Rabbinic and Kabbalistic literature spells out this scenario and the eventual victory for Israel.

The messianic element, which considers now to be the time for the fulfillment of the prophecies want to do everything in their power to assist and bringing them to fruition. Therefore, many, as a first step will leave their homes in the various countires around the world, and move to Israel. They do not do this out of a sense of loyalty for the State of Israel, but instead so that they can "have a front seat to the fulfillment of prophecy and the coming of the Messiah."

While they aspirations may be laudable, rationally minded Eschatologists (experts in End Days studies) must ask, how do we know that now is the definitive time of the End of Days? Others in the past have also seen their current events in light of prophecy and led their lives accordingly. The Judean-Roman war which led to the destruction of the Second Temple in 68 c.e. was spurred on by the messianists in those days, who like their counterparts todays saw their time to be the fulfillment of Biblical prophecies. Their mistakes led to the destruction of Israel and the deaths of over one million Jews.

Modern Israel performs a laudable and important role in the realm of modern world Jewry. Nevertheless, the State was not designed and has no desire to embrace any type or form of messianic or prophetic role. The State is avidly and wisely secular and rightly so. For many of the religious this was totally acceptable and embraced. This was the status-quo for decades. Then the extremism began, the chauvinism started, and certain groups turned extreme, first in their philosophies and then in their actions. Secular Zionism was replaced with religious Zionism and religious Zionism became replaced with messianic/prophetic Zionism.

For those religious Jews around the world who seek to fulfill the Judaic dream of settling in the Holy Land, the doors are certainly open to them. For the first time since the days of the Second Temple, there is a dominant Jewish presence in the Holy Land. Jews are free to live in a country and an environment that for the most part reflects significant elements of the religious culture and identity. Yet, with all this being true, there is absolutely no evidence from either Biblical prophecy or later Rabbinic literature to verify that this is in any way a definitive sign that the advent of Mashiah is imminent.

The secular State of Israel and the End of Days prophecies do not have to be connected in any way. They may very well be connected, indeed! But, that is something that can only be known to G-d, and wished for by desperate individuals not willing for G-d's plan to manifest in accordance to the Divine Will.

Chapter 4

Two Messiahs for Two Trees

The Tree of Life brings life. This is no big surprise.

The Tree of Knowledge Good and Evil should rightly be called the Tree of Death. All those who eat of its fruit will die from its poison.

The Tree of Life, and the Tree of Knowledge are both symbols. They represent different stages and phases of human consciousness.

Therefore, one who thinks the way of the Tree of Life lives, and the one who thinks the way of the Tree of Knowledge dies.

There are two Messiahs to come to Israel; the Messiah son of David, and the Messiah son of Yosef.

Ben Yosef comes first, fights wars, and dies. Ben David comes after him, fights wars, and lives. Ben Yosef is destined to die. Ben David is destined to live. Why is this so?

Ben Yosef is said to eat of the fruit of the Tree of Knowledge; therefore, he is the Messiah of death. Ben David alone eats of the fruit of the Tree of Life and, therefore, he lives, and brings with him life for all.

Ben Yosef thinks according to the way of the Tree of Knowledge. It is his thinking that gets him killed. Ben David thinks according to the Tree of Life. It is his thinking that gives him life.

Thinking here is the key. We are talking about the mind. The mind is in the brain. The brain teaches us about these modes of thinking that we call life and death, the Tree of Life, and the Tree of Knowledge. In Kabbalah the brain is called Moah, and there are two Mohin, which are actually three.

We think in two general ways. The first way is the one most common to us today; this is thought as it is related to the external world. This is consciousness, the rational mind, directed by academic, intellectual reasoning.

The second way is most uncommon to us today; this is thought as it is related to the internal world. This is higher consciousness (which sometimes resides in the unconscious); this is the super-rational mind (although sometimes condemned as being irrational). This mode of thinking is materialized as intuition, the psychic and the domain of extra sensory perceptions, those beyond reasoning.

In Kabbalah, the first way is called the Moah (brain) of the Sefirah Binah; the second way is called the Moah (brain) of the Sefirah Hokhma.

Binah is the Tree of Knowledge, Good and Evil. Hokhma is the Tree of Life.

The rational mind directed by academic intellectual reasoning deals with external reality. This is the Tree of Knowledge, and it is the source of death. All those of the academic intellectual persuasion, by nature of their mental orientation imbibe death, breed death, and embrace death. Even their Messiah, Ben Yosef will, like them, die. For them, there is no other way. This is the price they pay for their lack of vision.

The psychic intuitive mind directed by internal awareness that comes from extra sensory sources looks at external reality through the vision of inner sight. As such, this enables the mind to see the world as it really is, instead of how it is thought to be, as seen in the eyes of those who cannot see within. This, and this alone, is the Tree of Life.

This alone is the Tree of Life for those who embrace it. It is psychic intuitive awareness that comes from a source beyond this physical world that brings with it light, enlightenment and life. Those who eat these fruits cultivate true life everlasting.

The Messiah of this Tree, Ben David, is one of life, and thus he never dies. Because he can see beyond the limitations of his physical eyes, he can teach others also how to see. He is rewarded for his grandeur of vision, and others who share his vision, will share both his grandeur, and his reward.

Ben Yosef, the Tree of Knowledge, academia and the intellect bring death. This is why Binah is said to be the source of all severity. Ben David, the Tree of Life, the psychic and intuitive brings life. This is why Hokhma is Atzilut, the domain of the Divine.

Torah teaches us to choose life. In order to choose the fruit of the Tree of Life, we must stop being so overly-rational, and divorced from natural intuitive psychic thinking. We must learn to unlearn. and then learn again anew.

The study of the Pshat (simple) of Torah is the Tree of Knowledge, Good and Evil. As such it teaches about the external world, the clean and unclean, life and death. All Torah study can be Pshat, including Kabbalah.

The study of the Sodot (secrets) of Torah is the Tree of Life. As such, to understand it requires an internal psychic intuitive awareness. Sod cannot be learned from a book; it is not a course of study. Sod is a way of study; it is the Way of Living Torah. All Torah study can be Sod, including Gemara.

Ben Yosef will be the Messiah of the Pshat world; therefore, when the Pshat world dies, he dies along with it. Ben David will be the Messiah of the Sod world; therefore, as Sod materializes, and manifests itself in the external world, it will transform it fundamentally from the ground-floor up. Everything will change; everything will come alive. It will be the time of resurrection and rebirth for those who can embrace its way of thinking.

The coming time cannot be avoided. What is meant to die will naturally die. Nothing will change this. Each of us has eaten the poisonous fruit of the Tree of Knowledge. Yet, we can still be healed.

First we must pass through the flaming sword that guards the path back to the Garden of Eden. After we have been burned down, we can then build up again, and arrive at the Tree of Life in the center of the Garden. We can then partake of its fruit alongside Messiah Ben David, and together with him, live forever in a rectified world of psychic intuitive awareness.

He will come from out of the Bird's Nest, from the midst of the living Garden that can be entered only through the bottom of the cave.

The path above requires the descent below.

Only upon reaching the inside will one be able to reach out and touch the sky.

Just beware the day when the sky touches back.

Chapter 5

The Fall & Rise
of the Primordial Kings of Edom:
Secrets of the United States & Europe

Part 1

If one wishes to understand the future then one must understand the past; for the future is just its reflection.

Before the coming of Mashiah, there must be what we call in Kabbalah, the Tikkun. While the word translates as rectification, almost no one, including the many academically trained so-called Kabbalists have any idea as to what this really means.

The Kabbalistic principles and teachings are outlined for us in many texts. If one has the proper insight one can clearly see that the currents and trends in the world body politic are following a specific predestined course.

This necessary course has been revealed by Heaven and has been known and passed down in Kabbalistic teachings for centuries. Yet, few know how to extract these teachings from the pages of books, and to apply them correctly to current events.

The great pre-Messianic Tikkun does not occur exclusively in the invisible spiritual dimensions. It has its parallel fulfillments here in our physical world.

Just as there must be great and significant changes in the invisible spiritual dimensions before Mashiah comes, so too will there be equally great and significant pre-Messianic changes here on Earth. Essentially almost everything that we have grown to be familiar with will be subject to radical and often violent change.

In order for me to discuss some details of this I must delve into some of the works of the Kabbalists and explain their meaning.

Let us begin our discussion with the teachings referred to as "the fall of the primordial Kings and their rectification." From this lesson, I pray, we will come to foresee that which must soon come upon us.

Prior to the establishment of the present order that we are familiar with, there existed a previous, more ancient order for the universe. This period was Kabbalistically referred to as the time when the "Kings of Edom" reigned.

When I use the term "prior" I am not necessarily speaking in an historical context of prehistoric times. Although this may be one application, the "prior" must be understood within a greater scope of psychic, spiritual or psychological reality. In other words, the Fallen Kings are as much a level of human consciousness and spiritual growth as they are a lesson about our prehistoric past. The lessons about these fallen Kings are based upon the Kabbalistic understandings of Genesis 36.

As recorded in Genesis 36, the number of the Kings mentioned is eight. Seven ruled and died. Only with regards to the eight and last King, Hadar is death not mentioned. He is also the only King whose wife's name is mentioned.

The Kabbalists understood great significance in these subtle and often overlooked details. The Kabbalistic identity of this eight King is not so relevant yet. What is more relevant is what caused these seven Kings to die, and what resurrects them from death.

The seven fallen Kings are said to be the source of evil in this world. They are seven in number and correspond to the seven lower sefirot. Another term used to describe the fallen Kings is the Shattering of the Vessels.

Essentially the teaching goes like this. Originally G-d when chose to shine His Divine Light into the primordial vessels of the sefirot; for reasons known and preordained, the vessels were not in proper alignment and thus not strong enough to receive the Divine Light. Thus when the Light shined into them, the vessels could not contain it and, like a light bulb receiving a charge too great for it to bare, broke and shattered.

This is all metaphorical language to describe how the previous epochs in time and certain present levels of human consciousness development both developed their parameters.

When too much Divine Light shined into them, it could not be comprehended and thus caused a shattering, which materialized as a twisting and perversion of the original Light. This then is the source of evil.

Good then comes into existence with the mission of taking that which is broken and repairing it. In this way, there is reward for proper performance and punishment for the lack of it. Ultimately, evil's destruction is its repair and rectification.

Although the Kabbalah places great detail in describing the fate of the seven lower sefirot that broke and shattered, there are less details that describe the original upper three sefirot that did not suffer such a fate.

The number of sefirot are always ten; not seven, nine or eleven. If seven fell and broke, what then was the fate of the upper three? The Kabbalists do explain that these upper three, were blemished, each one in varying degrees. Yet, still, they did not die. The original upper three sefirot, symbolically referred to as the head survived death.

The seven lower sefirot are said to emanate from the Realm of Mind (Beriah), also called the sefirat Binah. As such, Binah is called the Supernal Mother. For the Mind (Beriah) is considered the "mother of all feelings (Yetzirah) and actions (Asiyah).

Now that I have explained this material in the language of the Kabbalists, let me now explain what it means.

The fallen sefirot spoken of are metaphorically referred to as the "kings of Edom." They ruled in the "land of Edom" prior to their being a "King in Israel."

This lesson is about the present state of human spiritual/psychological development, in which we are not in proper alignment with Heaven to receive the primordial Light. As such our thoughts, emotions and actions are twisted and corrupted because we do not properly reflect the Heavenly model.

This present state of affairs is what we refer to as "the exile," one not only of Israel from the Holy Land, but also an exile of our conscious minds from our presently unconscious higher and truer selves.

Disconnected as we are from our own higher selves, we reflect the pattern of the seven lower sefirot, disconnected from the upper three. We are essentially spiritually and psychologically lost and bereft of direction.

Needless to say the necessary steps of realignment require the lower seven sefirot to first be reattached with the Supernal Mother, the sefirat Binah. While this does occur individually with each personal soul, Heaven also ordains that this happens over the course of human history.

As such, all human history is guided by Heaven for the sake of this great realignment. The more we embrace it with proper social and political change the greater we see the benefit for all humanity.

The specific details of how these lessons apply in our day and age and to the varying fluctuations of human consciousness are not important here. To digress to discuss them would distract us from our purpose here.

Still, how do we realign with the Supernal Mother? How has this manifested itself in human history? This mystery is answered by our Sages, although they used an entirely different set of metaphors to describe this wondrous truth.

Part 2

Our Sages relate a legend about the death of Esau, who is Edom. The legend states that when Jacob was taken to be buried in Makhpelah that Esau and his clan came to block his interment. This led to a war between the sons of Esau and the sons of Jacob.

In this war, Esau himself was killed and decapitated. Legend has it that as Jacob was buried, so too was Esau's decapitated head also placed in the family tomb, placed on the lap of his father Yitzhak. To this day if one were to visit the Cave of the Patriarchs in Hebron one would find the Caves of Avraham, Yitzhak and Yaakov (and their wives), and if one looked, one would also see a small little cave entitled, the head of Esau.

Whether or not this legend is accurate history or not is irrelevant to the point. What matters is the secret teaching as to what this legend means; for it is a reference to the "Mother of the fallen Kings."

The fallen kings of Edom who reigned prior to their being a King in Israel are a reference to the psychological/spiritual time that we are now living in. This is the time of exile, where the spiritual leader of the nations is Edom.

Edom is Esau, the twin brother of Jacob. Many times twins look alike. Many times, as similar as twins are on the outside, there are major differences to them on the inside. This is the case with Jacob and Esau.

Esau/Edom's descendants since Biblical times have been identified with Europe, specifically the empire of Rome. According to the Torah understanding, ancient Rome never actually fell, thus leaving the public scene. It was only replaced by the Church.

As we know the head of the Church always has been in the city of Rome. Therefore, Edom is Rome, Rome is Christianity, and thus Edom is all those domains to which the Christianity of Rome has spread. Thus we have identified the fallen Kings and see how they have indeed twisted and perverted the primordial Light of the original Torah.

In the end times, the great battle between Jacob and Esau is to come to its final fruition. Biblical prophecies speak of the resounding defeat of Edom and everything related to it. The seven Kings of Edom will fall and die. Yet, their death is described only within the greater process of their rectification. For in the end the fallen Kings are realigned with the Rectifier (Mashiah) who places their realigned forms into their proper places.

The seven Kings are thus no more. This does not mean that everyone literally dies, but rather, that everyone finally is able to see and receive the Light of Truth and thus a new dawn for humanity arises.

Yet, when discussing the fate of the seven Kings, all too few stop to ask about the fate of the Mother, the Sefirah Binah of the world of the Nikudim, who while blemished, still did not fall and die with the rest of Edom. Although the Mother receives her rectification along with the rest of "Edom;" still, where was "she" all along as this process proceeded?

The fate of Mother Binah is referred to in this ancient legend. She is the metaphorical head of Esau. That head, as we learned, is buried in Yitzhak's lap in Makhpelah.

Now, Makhpelah is the domain of holiness. It is the domain of Abraham, Yitzhak and Yaakov. It is certainly not the domain of Esau. What then is his head doing there?

The metaphorical head of Esau is a reference to the best of Edom, their head, so to speak. These had to be removed from the body in order for them to enter into the domain of Abraham, Yitzhak and Yaakov. Yitzhak is here also a metaphor to what we call the "left side" of holiness. This is a metaphor to describe the first stage or lower level of attachment to holiness. And Esau head rests in Yitzhak's lap.

The nations that comprise Edom have always been identified as Europe. The head of Edom must at one time been attached to its body and then somehow dismembered (metaphorically speaking).

The United States of America started out as a collection of European colonies that eventually fought for, and won its independence. This War of Independence might metaphorically be expressed as a severing.

We think of a decapitation as something that causes death, but remember in the world of symbolism and metaphors; analogies do not always have to be 100% accurate in detail.

Eventually the fledgling United States of America sought to remove as much European elements from its domain on this continent, thus forming the new nation.

The history of the United States is most peculiar. In one way the nation grew in typical Edomite fashion. It conquered and sought to destroy the indigenous peoples of this land and sought to make itself into a mighty power similar to Europe.

Yet, with all the Edomite influence of prejudice and evil against the Native and against the imported Africans, there was something about the United States of America that made it, in many ways, deeply different from its European counterparts.

In spite of all its fallings, there were still significant influences in the nation that did not tow the European line. There was significant support for African/American liberation, to such a point that it was one of the major causes of the first American Civil War.

America could not escape its Edomite origins, yet still, this representative of Edom was somehow peculiarly different from its European origins. America outshined the Europeans in the realms of morality and religion. America came to represent the best of what Europe had to offer. The creation of the United States of America was essentially Heaven's plan to emerge the "head of Edom."

The American culture has for decades been despised specifically by the Europeans. Although both cultures share a desire for secularism and both are rather opulent, still the American culture has for the longest time managed to hold on to its Protestant religious ethic and religiosity. To be blunt about it, America has always been more sincerely religious than the Europeans.

To this day, when traditional religion is definitely being targeted and rooted out of the public eye, still there remains throughout the United States millions of religious faithful from many different religious paths who all share the common values of traditional morals.

This American attitude is what makes America reviled in the eyes of many Europeans. And now that a younger generations of Americans are about to take over to lead the country; they plan to redirect the nation in their own course, a course set more in accordance to European standards than in common with traditional American standards.

The younger generation represents the seven fallen Kings of Edom, those who have rejected the realignment with the Supernal Mother.

The United States of America is thus taking a step backwards, away from its original purpose and destiny; a step that is taking it into the dominions of the New World Order, led by "Rome" and its chosen champion, Armilus, the legendary anti-Christ of Christianity.

Such a major shift and rift in society has already produced a cultural civil war. If such a cultural conflict can actually explode into a full scale military second civil war in the United States, time will tell; although, I must advise my reader that I am not the first to raise such an ominous fear.

From a Kabbalistic point of view, American as a religious culture separate from its European source indicates that the United States stands at the metaphorical head of European culture.

Maybe this metaphor also has other applications in that maybe we can indeed define the G-d fearing individuals of traditional morals and values as being the metaphorical "head of Esau." As such, their fate would be markedly different from that to be suffered by their other modern Edomite counterparts both in Europe and now also on American soil.

Part 3

Before Mashiah comes, the Kabbalists speak that the seven fallen Kings of Edom will die, and that this death is their rectification. Yet, this metaphorical death is described in Kabbalistic and earlier prophetic literature in rather frightening terms.

It is not enough that there is going to be social, political and economic upheaval; more than this the entire planet itself is destined to go through a transformational cleansing. Earthquakes, tidal waves, fundamental changes in weather, storms at magnitudes yet unseen and other natural events are prophesied to literally change the face of the Earth. By the time Mashiah comes, our present continental layout is prophesied to be radically altered.

Needless to say, the natural disasters will take even a greater toll on humanity than even the greatest of social or military disasters. Yet, all of this is necessary to realign our planet and those surviving on its surface to greet a brand-new epoch in the unfolding saga that is humanity's history and destiny.

The United States of America as I grew up in it is already no more. In its place has arisen a strange new Monster so dissimilar to the country I knew and loved.

Is it in human hands to fight this Monster? My concern is that maybe it is not the will of Heaven for the old America to be restored. The new America is growing now, being groomed in the image of its old and new masters from across the pond. Of the old America, as the song says, "G-d has shed His grace on thee." In the new America, any mention of G-d is quickly being removed from the public domain, just like it has been in Europe. Heaven watches this and is not pleased.

When the time comes for the great cleansing to occur, while it may begin with wars and terrorism, it will by no means end there. 9/11 was the first of many wake-up calls to the U.S. to turn back to Heaven or face the ultimate consequences of their choice not to be under Heaven's umbrella of protection.

One cannot continue to defy Heaven, violate Heaven's law and natural law and still expect to receive an abundance of blessings from Heaven. G-d is not some glorified superhuman being whose only wish is to smile, be happy and let everyone do what they wish. It is so sad that our understanding of spirituality is so mythological instead of being extraterrestrial, like it should be.

We are to be facing hard times for sure. Peoples of traditional religion especially will feel the pinch first. They are the head of Edom, although blemished, but still the living "mother" of the fallen kings. As our society turns a blind eye to Heavenly authority, so now those who were once held in the highest esteem for their religious convictions must now have armed guards at their churches, receive death threats, which have included mock attempts at biological terror attack (anthrax).

It is a funny thing about prophecy; one can rest assured that if part one of the prophecies is fulfilled then certainly part two is also sure to be fulfilled.

The G-dless corruption of modern civilization was long ago foreseen. Its ultimate implosion and destruction were also foreseen. Yet, what was also foreseen was that the righteous religious, Gentiles and Jews alike, would find safe haven in hiding when all these great natural and unnatural occurrences come to cleanse our planet.

This is the great secret, the righteous will be saved. Granted, they may not be able to save their homes and material wealth, but none of that is so important. Rather, they themselves will find a path etched out of the wilderness especially just for them.

As society turns more and more intolerant towards sincere and traditional Biblical sentiments, those who waver not in embracing them will become more and more ostracized, just as prophesied.

Then, they will see the proverbial handwriting on the wall and physically relocate into communities away from the coasts and away from the big cities. They will congregate into more remote areas where so many of their fellow co-religionists have lived for decades.

When this pattern begins, watch the big cities. For as the religious leave or as religion is continually pushed out of them, something else much more dreadful will come in to fill the gap. This is only natural, and when it occurs, the imbalance created will trigger the great cleansing. It is destiny; it cannot be and will not be avoided.

There is much confusion today in Jewish circles about Messianic prophecies. The vast majority of the religious and their Rabbis, with Kabbalists and Hasidic Rebbes amongst them have next to absolutely no clue as to what is coming down the pike and what to expect. The vast majority of these individuals have absolutely no meditative experience and therefore can have no Ruah HaKodesh (in spite of the protests of their devoted disciples).

This inability on their parts is unavoidable and regardless of whatever stories disciples wish to relate, most if they are honest, will acknowledge that stories and reality are very far from one another.

Too many have adopted a fantasy about what the coming of Mashiah will be. Essentially, they have adopted a false hope that I am afraid will end up getting many people into troubles and sufferings that they should have been able to avoid. All too many do not see the warning signs and are so out of touch with reality, both physical and spiritual, that they have no clue or insight as to what must happen before the intervention of the extraterrestrial Messianic armada.

Major changes are unavoidable. Prophecies will not go unfulfilled. Life as we know it will be drastically changed. It will be a process, but not one that will take more than a very short time. We should know this to be true and make the necessary preparations for its inevitability.

One should indeed prepare for hard times to come, building shelters, stockpiling weapons, and food. But in the end, not even these will save one. Rather, one should invest one's time and effort to explore the inner recesses of one's mind and cultivate the reality of living in G-d's presence. This is the realignment with the Supernal Mother, Binah. Only this is the rectification of the fallen

Kings. Those who embrace it will be embraced by Heaven. Those who reject Heaven will themselves be rejected by Heaven and left to face their destinies.

A true spiritual bond with G-d permeating one's mind and consciousness, this will serve as one's guide. One will know where to be, when to be there and how to get there all in the right way. With Heaven as one's guide, nothing can go wrong. We just might have to redefine our concepts of right and wrong and learn to see things as Heaven does.

When we live as the servants of Heaven and allow G-d's Hand to move through us; we become the vehicles of Divine movement here on Earth. Such a vehicle in Hebrew is called a Merkava, such surrender is called in Hebrew the Ma'aseh Merkava, it is the deepest and greatest of Kabbalistic teachings. Heaven desires this of us, more than anything else.

The great realignment is inevitable and unavoidable. Everything the great world powers are presently planning is all part of Heaven's greater plan. We are not destined to change or interfere with the plan. Our job is to go along with it and do our share when the time comes.

Edom has no idea who it is that is giving them their marching orders, but in the end the Eight King will reign, along with his wife, and they shall not die forever. For the Eight King of Edom, number Eight; let us just say that "she" is the eight sefirat Binah, the Supernal Mother. She will be properly repaired and her children restored, all by the Hand of the Rectifier, King Mashiah.

Have I left you with many questions? I am sure that I have. Now it is your turn to do the studying to seek out that which you need to know. Don't worry; Heaven will guide your path.

Chapter 6

Esau & His Messianic Restoration

Family affairs can sure be complicated and the complications of youth can last a lifetime. Sometimes they even last a whole lot longer than that.

Gen. 25:23 relates a strange prophecy about the birth of two brothers, later to be named Esau and Jacob. "Two nations are in your womb, and two kingdoms will separate from your innards, and one kingdom will become mightier than the other kingdom, and the elder will serve the younger." From the out-set conflict was inevitable. Just like long ago G-d revealed to Avram that his children would be foreigners in a land not their own, so now too, destinies are foretold, even before birth.

We should ask some questions here. We accept that right from birth the two brothers Esau and Jacob are markedly different, and that conflict between the two of them would last a lifetime (and beyond). Knowing all and seeing all, why then did G-d ordain that these two apparently divergent and radically different souls come to Earth sharing a womb and a family? In other words, these two were twins in name only, why have their souls come to Earth born as physical twins, when spiritually there is absolutely nothing twin about them?

Now, no one can perceive the secrets of G-d or fathom Divine reasoning, but we can look at the facts and discover some amazing principles. First and foremost, Esau and Jacob are brothers. This cannot be denied. Esau by birthright is as much a grandson of Abraham as is Jacob. This right of birth grants him great privilege. Yet, as it becomes apparently clear over the continuing chapters in Genesis, although Esau is the first-born son of the chosen Isaac, he takes after his Mommy's side of the family more than his Dad's. This is where all Esau's problems arose from.

Although Esau was the first born son of the promised son, a position that should have entitled him significant blessing and status, by the nature of his actions, his own personal choices, he made decisions that led to him losing almost everything that he could have had. This goes to show us that even one born "with a silver spoon in the mouth" does not necessarily get to eat with that silver spoon all one's life, unless one lives up to it, and works hard to maintain it.

As we know Esau lost his birthright and later was duped out of his paternal blessing. But should we look at him with pity, thinking him a poor dolt, intellectually incapable of standing up to the wiles of his younger brother? Was Esau really the victim here, or was there something in his personality, inherent within him from birth that led him, or maybe even compelling him to make the poor choices that he did and to reap the consequences of such behaviors?

Nowhere in G-d's prophecy to Rivka, Esau and Jacob's mother was there any reference to either of her future sons becoming wicked, evil men, or for that matter one being smarter or dumber than the other. The prophecy simply stated one would be greater and the other lesser. With the birth of twin sons, and the pecking order strictly embraced in those days, it was only natural and expected that the two brothers would have developed a relationship of one being dominant and the other subservient.

The surprising thing about the prophecy was that the younger brother was to take dominance over the older brother. This was most unusual, but not unheard of, especially in the House of Avraham. After, all did not Isaac the younger brother receive all the blessings and household authority over his older brother Ishmael? One may argue that younger Isaac and older Ishmael had different mothers and that sealed their fates. Yet, in ancient times, such a concern was no concern at all.

Isaac's dominance over Ishmael was most unusual, so unusual in fact that it had to be Divinely ordained in order for it to be established. As it was with Isaac and Ishmael, so too was it here with Jacob and Esau. It was by Divine design that the normally subservient younger would rise up and dominate the naturally dominant older brother. G-d sure has His ways to make day-to-day family life interesting! Yet, as Isaiah (55:8-9) so eloquently spoke G-d's Word centuries after these things saying, ""For My thoughts are not your thoughts, neither are your ways My ways," says the L-rd. As the Heavens are higher than the Earth, so are My ways higher than your ways and My thoughts [higher] than your thoughts."

What can anyone say about this? How can anyone respond? What is there to say? The answer is, nothing! We are dumbfounded into silence before the Wisdom of G-d and all we can do is to go along with the Divine plan to discover what it really is and then to go along it.

Between Esau and Jacob, the revelation of the Divine plan was not long in unfolding. The first episode recorded of Esau's foolish choice was his selling of his birthright to his brother. We are all familiar with the Biblical story. Esau is out hunting; Jacob is at home cooking. Esau comes home famished and extremely hungry and asks his brother for some of what he is cooking. Jacob says he will give to Esau what he desires if only Esau would first sell Jacob his birthright. Esau agrees and sells his birthright for a bowl of soup. Unfortunately for us, we no longer understand the meaning of a birthright, nor do we understand its financial and spiritual value. We also seem to overlook the dynamics of brothers.

Esau was famished but he was not at death's door. He would not have died had he not eaten of his brother's food. I am surprised that after hearing Jacob's request that Esau did not overpower his weaker brother, punch him in the nose and take whatever soup he desired. If he was to be scolded by either his Mom or Dad, he could have easily told them what Jacob had demanded and it would have been Jacob who would have gotten in trouble for asking such a price, not Esau for denying it to him. But, as we know, this is not the way it happened.

A birthright by modern standards can be compared to being named as primary inheritor in a will as well as its executor. Esau was supposed to inherit the House of Isaac, just as Isaac inherited the House of Abraham. Judging from scripture, the financial value here must have been considerable.

Imagine this, you are named the inheritor of a large estate worth tens of millions of dollars. One day, a family member takes advantage of you in a moment of weakness and asks that you sign over your rights for a minor, paltry sum. How out of your mind will you have to be to agree to such an agreement? Yet, for whatever strange reason Esau thought so little of the future, of his family status, and of his own honor that he agreed to give away an inheritance of millions for next to nothing.

Scripture describes that Esau did not even put up a fight, he did not even object to the terms. This is a clear sign of a significant problem. A hungry strong young man could have easily punched his brother in the nose for making such a request and then taken whatever he wanted. Knowing the animosity between these two, would we really be surprised if the two did come to blows earlier in their childhood in episodes not recorded by scripture? Why then should this be any different. But apparently Esau was not thinking "big time" and he made a legally binding contract giving away an inheritance of millions for next to nothing.

Although later scripture records that Esau blames his brother for deceiving him into this, the original narrative shows no such deception. The incident is clearly black and white. Esau knew what he was doing and did it consciously and willfully. Thus, scripture says that he despised his birthright, and indeed he did. One must wonder what his Mom and Dad thought when either he or Jacob told them of the transfer. Scripture does not record it, but we can guess that father Isaac must not have been too happy with either of his sons, not the crafty one and not the dumb one.

The issue of the paternal blessing however is another story. For when it was time to receive the family blessing, notwithstanding the issue of the sale of the birthright, Father Isaac is about to bless his favorite son Esau. Scripture is clear that Jacob did not intervene to do anything about this. Rather it was Mother Rivka who concocted the plan for Jacob to wear his brother's clothes and to masquerade as him. As we know, Jacob receives his brother's blessing, angering Esau to the point of wanting to kill him. Yet, how is it that the sale of the birthright was apparently overlooked by the family? Could not the reception of the family blessing equally be overlooked? Apparently not. The patriarchal blessing seemed to be irrevocable as was Esau's anger for losing it.

Another example of Esau's bad character is seen in his choice of wives. Unlike father Isaac and later brother Jacob, Esau saw no need to marry in the family, as was so important to grandfather Avraham. Esau chose local wives and scripture is clear that his mother Rivka most certainly did not like the women Esau chose. Now, in the days when matchmaking was the rule, how was it that Esau went and took for himself not one wife, but two, apparently without the approval of his parents?

Although Isaac's objections are not recorded, one would suspect that he would have agreed with his wife rather than with his son over the choices. Yet, scripture records only Rivka's objections, not Isaac's. Later, it is recorded that Esau tried to rectify the situation by taking for himself a third wife, this time, from within the extended family. He married a daughter of his uncle Ishmael. Yet, scripture is clear, he did not divorce the other two! Now Esau had three wives, and the impact of wife number three on the foreign ways of wives numbers one and two is not recorded in scripture. So, Esau despised his birthright, desired to kill his brother and took wives who did not follow in the family religion, thus making sure that neither would his sons.

Isaac however still loved his son Esau. There is never any mention of his ever-having rejected Esau or banishing him for his bad ways as Abraham had parted from Lot. The next we hear about Esau is when after so many years and siring his own family Jacob is returning home from the House of Laban. Scripture records that

Esau is living in the land of Seir, apparently not with his father Isaac anymore. There is no scriptural record to indicate that Isaac cast him out. Therefore, we must assume that as with the taking of his wives, Esau acted on his own accord. It must have become apparent to Isaac long before this that Esau because of his poor choices was not fit and thus could be destined to carry on the family mission received by father Abraham at the Covenant Between The Pieces. While scripture makes this glaringly clear, still nowhere are these words or sentiments actually put into the mouth of Father Isaac.

Isaac's relationship to Esau must have been strained by the events that occurred with Jacob. Still scripture never portrays Isaac as having rejected his son. Later, when Esau and Jacob reunite after years of separation, on the surface everything seems to be all forgiven. Yet, although scripture may give this appearance, later Biblical record and numerous later Torah legends contradict this entirely. What most have never considered is that when Jacob returns from the House of Laban now with his own family and wealth, Father Isaac was still alive. One can simply calculate this from the Biblical narrative to verify it. Esau would have never harmed his brother while his father was alive. Maybe this is why Jacob made sure to put good distance between himself and Esau, fearing the day of their father's death.

Esau's descendants are then said to have established kings and kingdoms prior to there being a King in Israel. The end of Genesis 36 enumerates their names. Yet, according to the secret traditions of the Torah, these scriptural verses contain a code that conceal within it spiritual wisdom about the origins and nature of evil itself. The study of the "fallen kings of Edom" is one of the deepest subjects of the philosophical Kabbalah. Not for naught has Esau come to represent the forces of evil in this world.

Esau has become the image of the "devil incarnate," the eternal enemy of Jacob and his descendants the Jewish people. This image is reinforced by almost every later Biblical mention of Esau found in the later books of the Bible (the Neviim, Prophets). Esau is prophesied to face eternal destruction and devastation for the way he treated his brother Jacob. These prophecies of course speak about the descendants of Esau. Their fate is sealed.

Yet, one of the profound lessons taught about the "fallen kings of Edom" in the code underlying Genesis 36, is that even to Esau there is still some good left in him. The good in Esau is symbolized as his head. Torah legends relate that when Jacob died and was carried to Makhpelah Cave to be buried, a war broke out between the sons of Jacob and Esau and his sons. Esau refused to allow Jacob's burial in the family plot. In the conflict, Esau himself was said to be killed and as a compromise, his severed head was buried in the lap of his father Isaac as Jacob was buried alongside. To this day if one is to visit the Tomb of the Patriarchs in Hebron, Israel, one will find rooms in the location named for each of the Patriarchs (and Matriarchs) as well as a small side location called the Cave of the Head of Esau. Whether or not Esau's head is actually buried there, no one can verify. But it does go to show how old this legend is.

The meaning of this legend is what is important here. For although scripture portrays Esau as the arch-enemy of his brother Jacob, nevertheless, there is still good in Esau, his symbolic head, those souls who still cling to holiness through their father Isaac and therefore have merited a place in the Tomb of the Patriarchs alongside them. Although the historical man Esau made poor choices that caused him to become the epitome of evil, still he must have sired descendants who over the centuries clung to their brother Jacob and refused to follow in the way of the majority of the body of Esau.

Esau has come to represent the "world of the shattered vessels," "the fallen kings" and misalignment of Divine Lights. Yet, his metaphorical head is still considered complete. Its rectification is said to be that it becomes bonded to the head of Israel, and the two heads merge together to serve as one, in almost an active/passive relationship. To the Kabbalists this is known as the Yihud of MAH and BEN, mystical terms used to describe the union between the rectified and the rectifier.

Scripture is clear. Malachi 1:2-3 sums it up when G-d Himself says, "I love Jacob and I hate Esau. Esau is prophesied to be destroyed, "his mountains desolate and his heritage into [a habitat for] the jackals of the desert." Yet, the head of Esau is buried in the lap of Isaac. In the end there will be a grand sifting of Esau. For just as Jacob is made up of many souls, so too is Esau. Not all souls of Esau are born into Esau, some are actually born into Jacob (Israel) and the opposite is also true. Some souls from Jacob are born into the bodies of the descendants of Esau.

G-d judges the souls of men. How they are born is of minor consequence. Esau was born into the most noble of families but chose to abandon his nobility to become something else much less. Yet, from his descendants, many of Esau's seed choose to reconnect to their noble heritage in Isaac and brotherhood with Jacob. These souls are our true brothers and everyone in Jacob should welcome them to our side.

There is however one last bit of "dirty laundry" to be dealt with. There are souls from Esau born into Jacob who, like Esau, choose to deny their nobility and to act with the denial and rejection of Torah that has come to be identified with Esau. They are symbolically referred to as "the souls of Amalek" and "the mixed multitude." These wolves in sheep's clothing, these Esau souls in Jacob are exposed by how they live.

They are the some of the worst secular, religion mocking Jews who are a disgrace and embarrassment to not only the Jewish religion, but to the Jewish people as a whole. They are the ones who by their deplorable behavior are responsible for giving all Jews a bad name. These hypocritical Jews stoke the fires of antisemitism and are rightly called "Amalek," the eternal enemy of G-d.

In the end, Jews who are Jews in name only will return to their rightful place, in Esau. They will finally be cast out of Jacob (Israel) so that the People of Promise can be complete. In G-d's eyes, Faithful Israel is defined as the community of like-minded souls, not limited to the "accidents" of birth.

This realignment of righteous souls is what the Kabbalists call the Tikun, the unification of MAH and BEN, the restoration of the Fallen Kings, when BEN will be restored and again become SAG, fulfilling the prophecy recorded in Zechariah 14:9. Although this mystical language will be unfathomable to most readers unfamiliar with the deep Kabbalistic metaphors, those familiar should be made aware of the great shifts coming and the realignment of loyalties that is necessary for the coming of Mashiah.

Twin souls are funny things. G-d knew in the beginning that many Esau souls would be attracted to Jacob and that many Jacob souls would become attracted to Esau. Thus, they were born here on Earth as twins because they were originally twin souls in Heaven.

Earth was created to be the place where rectification of divisions can be accomplished. In Heaven, the twin souls were two halves of the same whole. Here on Earth a process of sifting and repair transpire over the entire history of the human race. Now, towards the end, the repair is almost complete. The souls above are uniting as are their bodies here below on Earth. The righteous are finally realizing that unity in spirit is a bond greater than that of body, flesh or blood. The purpose of Heaven is almost compete.

May G-d bless us that all righteous souls return to their homes and that the chaff finally be burned away and their ashes scattered into the wind. Long live the righteous. May Esau's head (BEN) rest in peace alongside his brother Jacob (MAH) in the lap of Father Isaac. "On that day shall the L-rd be one, and His name one" (Zechariah 14:9).

Chapter 7

Countdown to Mashiah:
Kabbalistic Prophecies Outlining
a Timeline to the Messianic Scenario

Note: This essay was written in 1999, when Messianic expectation was heavy due to the circumstances of the day. This essay reflects the concerns of those times. While many points in it might seem obsolete, they are in fact archetypal, and transcend the limits of any single time period. For this reason, this essay has been included here in this book.

"The length of the days of this world shall be 5,760 years."

Midrash Talpiyot, letter Gimel, Sec. Geulah (the redemption)

*"The blood that was shed in the land
will be atoned only by the blood of those who shed it,
and the atonement must come:
total dismantling of all foundations of contemporary civilization,
with all their falsity and deception, with all their poison and venom.*

*The present civilization will disappear with all its foundations - literature and theatre, and so forth;
all the laws founded on inanity and iniquity,
all evil etiquette will pass away.*

*Therefore, the entire contemporary civilization is doomed
and in its ruins will be established a world order
of truth and G-d consciousness."*

Rabbi Avraham Yitzhak Kook, Orot M'Ofel, 8

What do the years 1840, 1948 and 1999 have in common? They are all years of prophecy! They are the years that were spoken of in ages gone by.

The holy Zohar is full of messianic prophecies. Rather than speak about them nebulously, in general, as does the Talmud, tractate Sanhendrin, the Zohar in numerous places speaks quite specifically about what will happen and when.

Before we view modern day events, let us review a Zoharic prophecy that announces the beginning of the redemption. The first step in the redemption cycle is to be the opening of the "gates of wisdom" from above and the "sources of wisdom" below. This is to begin the process of the rectification of the world, preparing it to enter the 7th millennia. (We are presently in the 759th year of the 6th millennia, i.e., the year 5759).

"In the year 600 of the sixth millennia (i.e. the Hebrew year 5,600) will be opened the gates of wisdom from above and the sources of wisdom below in order to rectify the world to prepare it to enter into the 7th millennia (i.e., the year 6,000)."
Zohar 1, 117A

Here the precise year 5,600 is given. This corresponds to the secular year 1840. So, what event can we describe as the opening of the gates of wisdom? I am sorry to tell you but no one real event sticks out being such a monumental "opening" of the heavenly gates.

While no specific event stands out, there was yet revolution occurring in world society. In 1840, the Industrial Revolution was well under way. Technology is indeed a wisdom that comes from Heaven. Technology has changed our world. However, does it prepare us for the year 7,000, when according to Kabbalistic tradition, the messianic age of peace will have dawned?

According to the Gra, the famous Rabbi Eliyahu, the Gaon of Vilna, the development of modern industrialization and technology enabled the human mind to become free of our superstitious and mythological views of nature. Indeed, the work, "Kol HaTor," the author, who was a top student of the Gra, outlines his philosophy that technology is the opening of the gates of wisdom from above and below spoken of in the holy Zohar. Freedom of the human mind is the best preparation for the messianic era to come. Indeed modern technology enables us to see the inherent Divine force within creation.

Yet, the advent of modern technology only ushers in the ketz hayamim (end times). These in and of themselves can last until the Hebrew year 6,000, which will only come in the secular year 2240. If Mashiah is to come only then, then we have a long wait ahead of us.

The Zohar Hadash (Bereshit 21B), however mentions that while the Mashiah is to come in the sixth millennia, his coming will not be at the very end, but rather sometime before it. Again, the Zohar (1, 170A) warns us that the redemption is not to happen all at once, but rather a little at a time.

Therefore, apparently, we will not have the wait for the secular year 2240. The next obvious questions then are what is next to occur, what will trigger it and when will it happen?

One of the most obvious messianic prophecies needing to be fulfilled is the ingathering of the Jewish exiles from around the world back to the Holy Land of Israel. This began back in the 1940's with the establishment of the new State of Israel in 1948. Is this year 1948 a year of destiny? According to the Kabbalistic scenario, indeed it is.

At the turn of the 20th century, a Syrian Rabbi Yitzhak Alfiyyah wrote an interesting text entitled, "Kuntress HaYekhieli." In it he wrote a section entitled, "remez hageulah" (a hint about the redemption), wherein which he details the Kabbalistic significance of the secular year 1948.

Basing himself on the Torah of the Ari'zal, Rabbi Alfiyyah endeavors to portray for us the bigger picture. He wants us to understand the time of redemption in relationship to time in general. I will in brief sum up his teachings here.

In brief, according to the Ari'zal, when Adam sinned in the Garden of Eden, he not only blemished himself, but he also blemished the six days of creation that preceded him. As he was responsible for their blemish so must he be responsible for their rectification.

The now six blemished days would be rectified in six thousand human years. One day being a thousand years, as the verse in Psalm 90 suggests.

At the end of six thousand years the blemish would be rectified, and mankind (Adam's offspring) would be restored to the Garden of Eden. This then is the proverbial coming of Mashiah. Thus the significance of the Hebrew year 6,000. Mind you the Hebrew calendar starts with creation.

According to the correlation of each day being a thousand years, then 5,000 years would equal five days in the cosmic cycle. ½ day or twelve "cosmic hours" would be equal to 500 years. So in the cosmic scheme of things the "cosmic" Friday morning began 259 years ago in the secular year 1740, a full 100 years before the "opening of the Heavenly gates" referred to above.

According to this correlation, if 500 human years are 12 "cosmic hours," then each and every "cosmic hour" would be the equivalent to 40 human years and 8 human months. This becomes of significance when we recognize what is to come after the six thousand years. What comes is the cosmic Shabat, the holy time of rest. Yet, as the weekly Shabat fits into the human cycle, so can its lessons be applied to the cosmic cycle.

The radiance of holiness of the weekly Shabat can begin to be felt from the fifth hour on Friday. At this time, the radiance of Shabat begins to descend upon us from Heaven. At this hour, the pious begin their Shabat preparation.

In the cosmic scheme of things, the "cosmic Friday morning" began in the year 5,500 (1740). At the rate of 40 human years and 8 human months corresponding to a "cosmic hour," then the "cosmic fifth hour of cosmic Friday" would have occurred in the Hebrew year 5,708. You guessed it, this corresponds to 1948.

Therefore, according to the greater Kabbalistic cosmic cycle the year of the founding of the modern State of Israel corresponds to the beginning of the cosmic Shabat. Thus, the birth of the State of Israel is indeed the birth of the cosmic Shabat, the messianic era.

Everything appears to be happening right on schedule. Yet, what is to come next? For the answer to this, we must turn to a text much older than the Kuntress HaYekhieli.

In the mid 1600's Rabbi Avraham Azulai, a master Kabbalist of both the Ari'zal and Prophetic schools wrote an extraordinary book entitled "Hesed L'Avraham." While most of his teachings are Zoharic and Cordoveran in nature, nonetheless, he is one of the few Kabbalists that have put into writing many teachings that were only passed down orally.

One of these oral teachings that originated in Hesed L'Avraham deals with the lengths of the days of our world and when the redemption is to occur. Since its original publication, this Kabbalistic oral tradition was only rarely repeated. It was, however, included in a mini-encyclopedia published in Izmir, Turkey entitled, "Midrash Talpiyot." The following is the full version of the Midrash Talpiyot version of the original Hesed L'Avraham text.

"The measure of the days of the world is the same as the measure of (the waters of) the mikvah. A mikvah holds 40 seah (of water); each seah is 144 eggs. 40 x 144 equals 5,760. Thus, the length of days of this world shall be 5,760 years. Then shall the world be renewed. For as the mikvah purifies the unclean, at this time the Holy One, Blessed be He will remove the unclean spirit from the world, there will not be left any remnant or trace. But this is only the beginning of the redemption."

Midrash Talpiyot, letter Gimel, Sec. Geulah (the redemption) Pg. 114A

According to this obscure Kabbalistic teaching, the world is only to last for 5,760 years. This is just short of 6,000 years and would seem to coincide with the Zoharic teaching recorded earlier (Zohar Hadash, Bereshit 21B).

We, however, might consider this problematic, being that the Hebrew year 5,760 begins on Shabat, September 11th 1999. "At this time the Holy One, Blessed be He will remove the unclean spirit from the world." In addition, I am sure that the unclean spirit will not be removed without difficulty. Apparently then, the year 5,760, the secular year 2,000 is going to be a time of great turmoil.

In tractate Yoma 10B, there is recorded an interesting discussion about a war that is to take place in the future between the forces that built the Second Temple and the forces that destroyed it. The Second Temple was built by permission of Darius, King of ancient Persia and thus its building is attributed to him. As is well known, the Romans destroyed the Second Temple.

Now, neither the ancient Romans, nor the ancient Persians are around anymore to fight it out in any type of war. However, their descendants still survive and today these descendants are extremely hostile towards one another. The descendants of the ancient Persians are the modern day Iranians, the Moslem fundamentalists. The descendants of ancient Rome are the western powers, with their head being the United States (symbolized by the eagle, as was ancient Rome).

Does anyone foresee the possibility of hostilities ever breaking out between an axis of Moslem fundamentalist states and western allied forces under the leadership of the United States? No knowledgeable person in the political or military arenas would ever dismiss this scenario. In fact, most people in the military, political and intelligence communities are working overtime specifically to prevent such an event from happening. Yet, even they admit, it is only a matter of time before something "big" happens.

Recently, in the July 23, 1999 edition on the Jewish Press, a story was reported that Iran is now ready to test intercontinental ballistic missiles, which will have the capacity to deliver nuclear, biological or chemical warheads onto American soil. Will they have the same discretion, as did the Russians before them not to initiate WWIII? Alternatively, will the zeal for a world Islamic empire make them put their faith in Allah and reign down death upon America, their "great Satan"?

The question is will time run out in the year 5,760? And if so, what will happen? Will a new war begin with Iran, or in another part of the Middle East? Maybe it will start in the Balkans or in

Kashmir? Will non-conventional weapons be used? Will nuclear weapons be introduced? Will the whole world become involved and the resulting conflict lead to apocalypse?

So many questions, not so many answers. Nevertheless, time will tell. In addition, if the 5,760 scenario is to be played out, then time is at a premium.

The Zoharic messianic tradition goes even further into details about what has been discussed above. The specific hour of the "coming" of Mashiah does not appear to be known to anyone, even the Mashiah himself (Zohar 2, 9A). Nonetheless, the time of his arrival, in this the last quarter of the sixth millennia seems to have to do with a secret meaning associated with the Hebrew letter, Vav (Zohar 1, 119A).

In this section (1, 119A), the Zohar, in its typical obtuse style speaks about specific sets of years revolving around the secret of the (sixth letter of the Hebrew alef bet) Vav, which is said to correspond to the sixth millennia (from the Hebrew year 5,000) onward.

"In the year 66, King Mashiah will be revealed in the Galilee... And all the nations shall gather against the daughter of Jacob to push her out of the world."

Zohar, 1, 119A

Many things are said to happen at this time, in the year "66." I suggest that you read this section of the Zohar for all the details. (It is fully translated into English in the Soncino edition of the Zohar (vol. 1, pages 369-371). Referencing all the details here is outside the scope of our present discussion. Yet, we must ask, when is this ominous year "66"? As is typical of the Zohar, no specifics are given.

However, I might be so bold as to suggest that maybe the "66" is to come after the year 5,700 as we have learned above. That would make the year of the messianic revelation to be 5766 or the secular year 2006. Of course, such an interpretation of the Zohar is my own. However, I chose it in light of something that I have read elsewhere.

Recently, a new style of Torah research hit the public like a storm. I am referring to the "Bible codes." It has been discovered that concealed within the Torah text there exist words and phrases that only become visible when viewed by equal distance letter skipping. For example, if one were to count every 1,234th letter for a sequence of ten times it would be found that the ten letters just so happen to spell out a word.

In his New York Times best-seller book entitled, "The Bible Codes", author Michael Drosnin claims to have discovered a code that refers to events that are to occur in the year 2006.

In chapter six of his book entitled, "Armageddon", Drosnin reveals a code that he says spells out disaster. According to this code, Jerusalem, like Hiroshima before it, is to become a victim of a nuclear attack. And when is this ominous destruction to occur? According to Drosnin, the code can be pointing to the year 2006. However, the code can just as easily be read as referring to the year 2000. It all depends if one adds or subtracts the next letter in the sequence, which just so happens to be a Vav.

On page 125 on the text, Drosnin clearly shows a code that reads (in English translation) "atomic holocaust in 5760" (or 5766, if you add the next sequential letter, Vav, 6). Close by is the name Jerusalem and Ariel (a Biblical poetical name for the city). Continuing in this chapter one finds names such as "Assad" (President of Syria), "China", "Armageddon", "Gog", "Magog", and "a mighty army."

While the authenticity of this code is subject to controversy, its warning is, nonetheless, clear, ominous, and right on schedule alongside the Kabbalistic time table.

From all these sources, it does appear that something is predicted to happen in the year 5760 (2000). The Zohar does go into details about the messianic scenario and these details read more like a modern day newspaper than an ancient mystical text. Let us review some more of these Zoharic messianic prophecies.

In the Zohar (1, 119A, 2, 32A) an interesting prophecy is stated that in the days prior to Mashiah the children of Ishmael (the

Arabs) would gather the nations of the world togther to wage war against Jerusalem.

Now, the text is quite precise. It does not say that war would be waged against Jews or Israel in general, but rather against Jerusalem in particular.

In light of:

1. The world not recognizing Jerusalem as the eternal and undivided capital of Israel, and

2. In light of Palestinian demands to make Jerusalem the capital of their State, and

3. In light of the United Nations call for the internationalization of Jerusalem under the directorship of the Vatican, one can clearly see that the issue of the city of Jerusalem is a hotbed of political trouble.

This however, is prophesied in the Bible. G-d speaks to the prophet Zechariah (14:3) saying, "It shall be on that day that I will make Jerusalem for all the peoples a burdensome stone, all who will lift it will be severely injured, and all the nations will gather against it."

It appears from this Biblical prophecy that no matter what political deal regarding Jerusalem's future is worked out between Israel, the Palestinians, the Americans and /or the Vatican, it is destined to somehow fail due to the Divine Will to subvert its success. If G-d has His agenda, what plans of man can stand against it.

The Zohar, also, sheds light onto this Biblical prophecy. According to the Zohar, it is the Arabs (Ishmaelites) who are to bring this about.

And when is this to come about? In light of the imminent establishment of a Palestinian State and the ongoing pressure against Israel to relinquish control over the city, my guess would be that the armies might march against Jerusalem somewhat sooner than later. Very possibly, we could see these events occur somewhere between the years 2000 or 2006.

The Zohar (2, 32A) continues and says that the Arabs will only be removed from the Holy Land after Mashiah has come. The implication is that they will not be removed beforehand. Therefore, any mere mortal political attempts to do so appear to be doomed to failure.

The Zohar also relates a scenario regarding the pre-Mashiah. This is the Mashiah ben Yosef. This individual is spoken about often throughout all Rabbinic literature, kabbalistic and otherwise. He is destined to come prior to Mashiah, initiate the messianic wars and to die fighting in them.

Probably the best collection of messianic midrashim is a recently published Hebrew work entitled, "Otzrot Aharit HaYamim" by Rabbi Yehudah Chayoun (Benei Brak, 1993). This text brings together well known messianic material alongside much that is not so well known. This text has even been condensed and translated into English under the title' "When Mashiah Comes" published by Targum Press (NY, 1994).

Traditionally, midrashic literature (found in Rabbi Chayoun's work) relates that Mashiah ben Yosef is to arise only after all the nations of the world have been defeated in a horrible world war by Edom-Rome (i.e., the Western powers, possibly with the U.S. at their head).

The new leader of the "New World order" is said to be "Armilus" who in one midrash (Milkhamot Melekh HaMashiah), is actually referred to by the Christian term, "anti-Christ." After subduing the world, Armilus will turn his attentions towards Israel. He is to approach Mashiah ben Yosef and demand of him that all Jews convert and accept him (Armilus) as our long expected Mashiah. Mashiah ben Yosef of course will refuse. A great war is to break out, where Mashiah Ben Yosef is to be killed by Armilus, the children of Israel are to be persecuted and cast out of all civilized areas of the world.

Only after a period of hardships is the true Mashiah (ben David) to appear out of the clouds with an army of angels. He will destroy Armilus and usher in the messianic era. This is in brief the traditional messianic scenario.

There is, however, one slight problem.

The Zohar has a different reading of events than the traditional midrashic story.

According to the Zohar (3, 166A), indeed there will be a great war between Persia (Iran) and the West. According to the "Matok M'Devash" commentary to this section of Zohar, the Western powers are supposed to fall, not to Persia, but to Mashiah ben Yosef.

Only after the defeat of West by Mashiah ben Yosef does Persia then attack Yisrael. The "King of Persia" is then said to kill Mashiah ben Yosef and to proceed to rule over Eretz Yisrael for a full year, killing countless numbers of Jews at this time.

Only after a full year is Mashiah (ben David) to be revealed with an army of angels. He will come and kill the King of Persia and then establish the messianic kingdom.

Being that today's Iran (Persia) is at the forefront of fundamentalist Islam, which is the Ishmaelite religion, the Zoharic scenario is internally consistent. If the Arabs are to remain in Eretz Yisrael until the coming of Mashiah ben David, this would only be helped if Yisrael were indeed conquered by Arab-Moslem armies led by Iran.

Is this what is destined to happen? Could such a scenario be triggered by a nuclear terrorist attack against Jerusalem this next year? These are all legitimate and sound questions. But no one but HaShem has the answers. Indeed the course of human history may not have been decided yet. Maybe, similar to the days of both the first and second Temples, HaShem is being patient and providing the Jewish people with time for collective national repentance. Again, who knows?

Returning to the prophecies, we are left with two different scenarios with drastically different details. Either Persia (Iran) is to win WWIII and thus persecute the Jews or the West is to win and then they will persecute us. No matter which scenario plays out, it doesn't look to good for the Jewish people.

Whether either of the scenarios will occur or if indeed, there will be a WWIII, we will all find out in time.

Chapter 8

The Reality of Mashiah

Still waiting for Mashiah? Yeah? Well, so is G-d! Still waiting for some kind of a magical, Heavenly intervention to save us all from all our self-made human problems? If you are, then you had better be careful what you wish for, and what you pray for!

Let's ask this! What if, yes, what if, all of a sudden, out of the sky, there would appear, as if out of a wormhole, or something equally bizarre or supernatural, a large space/inter-dimensional armada, claiming to be the army of Mashiah. Would such a sight be welcomed by all as the promised messianic salvation, or would everyone run in terror, and cry "invasion," as if reality was imitating our best science fiction thrillers?

How would anyone know the difference between an alien invasion, the coming of Mashiah, a demonic deception, or a false-flag government conspiracy? The answer is that no one would be able to tell anything about anything! While everyone would draw his own conclusion, and act based upon what he believed, there would be no proof that what the one believed was true, and what the other believed was false.

If something or someone were to come, appearing with extraordinary "out-of-this-world" power, and claiming to be the long awaited Mashiah, who would have the courage to stand up to face him, and, if necessary confront him? Who would have the

236

courage to approach this "mashiah," and ask him for his credentials of authenticity? The answer is no one!

While many people might suspect many things, who will have the courage of conviction to stand up, and thus, stand out, and do something significant? Ultimately, most people are simply cowards, who freeze in the face of fear, and shun all kinds of confrontation that may be too uncomfortable. Most people do not stand up for themselves under normal circumstances, why would anyone expect for there to be a birth of courage and resolve under such extraordinary circumstances?

The average, assimilated, western Jews, of all kinds, are a clear example of this. With the exception of small groups of Israelis, most Jews fear violence and run from it in terror. Most would do anything rather than have to stand up, and get literally bloodied in a fight.

Most Jews refuse, with passion, to own a firearm. Most Jews refuse with passion to train themselves, either physically or psychologically, to deal with threats to either themselves, or their communities at large. It is this type of cowardliness, shielded under tons of justifications and rationalizations, which make Jews such a welcome target for crime, racism, racial violence, and bloodshed. Almost everyone knows that most Jews never fight back. Because of this adverse reaction to violence, these Jews invite the violence that they seek to avoid. Maybe the coming "mashiah" won't be theirs?

So, what do you think the Messianic army is going to look like? Maybe it will look like something out of a movie, or from a comic strip? Maybe the Messianic army will be a bunch of peace loving, happy, singing, blood hair, blue eyed female angels whose only desire is for everyone to kiss and make up. Of course those who believe this kind of delusion would be best served under the care of a mental health professional. While we wait for Mashiah to come, most never give any real thought to exactly what it is that they are waiting for, and how they would recognize it, from a forgery, if indeed, it were to come!

So many today are convinced that we are living in pre-messianic times, the legendary "End of Days." This predilection is nothing new, it has been around for a very long time. In the late 1500's the famous Kabbalists, Isaac Luria and Hayim Vital proclaimed that they too were living in the "End of Days." These "End of Days" must go on for a long time, if they have been going on now for close to 500 years. At this rate, who knows when the "End of Days" will finally come to an end.

An interesting thing about apocalyptic beliefs, and "End of Days" Biblical prophecies is that everyone who reads them tends to interpret them literally, whereas the professional, classical Torah commentators often do no such thing. With regards to the actual meanings of prophetic texts, the Sages all agree that how the Biblical scenario will actually materialize remains a mystery, and a minor mystery, at that. How the Mashiah is to come, and how the End of Days are to unfold, are not considered to be essential matters of the Torah faith.

One thing is certain, when Mashiah does come, if there is anything extraordinary in his appearance, as Zechariah 14:5 suggests, how this experience will be understood by a world watching the events unfold on television, and the internet, will be something other than religious.

So when the Mashiah does show up, how will he be recognized? How will he be welcomed, not only by the world, but by his own nation Israel, and not just the secular who may not care for him, or his message, but what about the religious who are supposed to be anticipating and expecting his arrival every day? How will the religious respond, once the prayers they have been praying daily for thousands of years are finally answered?

If indeed humanity, as a whole, were to become subject to an invasion force from outside of anything within our presently known parameters of reality, we can rest assured that the global reaction would be one of panic and collective shock. If Mashiah comes, as described literally in the Bible, with overwhelming Heavenly force, we can rest assured that such an advent will be messy at least.

It is easy to give people what they want. It would be easy to fool the world into believing that a "mashiah" has come, when indeed one has not. In our modern age of global media and entertainment, one can project any news story, and make it believable.

So, when the time comes for the real Mashiah to come, it may be that he will have to make a real mess, in order to get noticed, in the way that he might seek. Personally, this is one mess that I do not seek to see, to create, and certainly not to clean up.

So, while I wait for Mashiah daily, as is our Torah way, I am also very well aware of what it is that I am waiting for. And, unlike many of my peers, I am not afraid to ask the uncomfortable questions, or to raise what I consider to be necessary controversy.

We want Mashiah now, really? We had better get a grip on what it is that we are asking for, and what the ramifications of such prayer and request will be!

Chapter 9

When is Mashiah Coming

Before we ask when is Mashiah coming, we must first ask, what does it mean for him to come?

Does Mashiah come as a master magician, to magically make all our problems disappear? No! There is no legitimate prophecy or prediction that makes any such claim.

Mashiah comes and his role is one of hard work. There will be no magic, but instead, there will be tremendous efforts, struggles and wars. Mashiah will dominate and be victorious, but not because of any magical interventions, but rather because he will do what needs to be done, in the right way, in the right time and in the right place.

When will this happen? This has already been answered over the many centuries by our people in the wise. Long ago, the Talmud recorded a legend, a story about one of the great Sages who met the Mashiah sitting at the gates of Rome. He asked Mashiah when he was planning to come and redeem both Israel and the world. He answered the great Sage and said to him, "today."

Bewildered the Sage turned later to the immortal prophet Elijah and asked him what the Mashiah meant by such a strange and seemingly untrue response. Elijah answered him in the words of scripture, "today, but only if you hear His Voice."

Mashiah gave the condition for his coming, we must learn first how to hear the Voice of G-d as it speaks telepathically within our minds. This is what the Bible calls G-d writing His Word upon our hearts, and what the Sages later called, Ruah HaKodesh, Divine inspiration. When this occurs Mashiah will come.

Many years later another Sage stated it ever so eloquently. He said that each of us has a spark of Mashiah within us, and that it is up to each of us individually, to bring the Mashiah first, into our own selves, our minds, our psyches, and our lives. When we can first embrace Mashiah internally and personally, only then can we expect Mashiah to come into the world.

We have always been taught, to first bring Mashiah to the individual from within, and then the unified and transformed people will bring Mashiah out, from within themselves, to the outside world.

We are a long way off from this. There is no wonder then why Mashiah has not yet come, and may not come for a very long time. War may come and destruction may follow, but there is no promise now or in the past that Mashiah will come to save us from such a destruction or to rebuild us if and when such a destruction occurs.

G-d has placed our fates in our own hands. What we chose to do with it is up to us and the Watcher Angels, along with their ward, Mashiah son of David is watching and waiting. Truly they must be very patient, for we have kept them waiting for a very long time.

We can change matters, if we please, it all starts with one person, YOU! You influence collective humanity. Your individual influence will influence one more, who in turn will influence another, who in turn will influence yet another. One after another, after another. This is how we build, and this is how we restore the fallen tabernacle of David, one stone, one soul at a time. Today, if only we hear His Voice.

Chapter 10

Can a Torah Faithful, Orthodox Jew Believe that Jesus Was (or Will Be) the Messiah of Israel

Note: This essay expresses my thoughts and ideas about how to build bridges between divergent religious communities, for the sake of honoring the name of G-d, and creating peace on Earth. I have expressed these thoughts to try to help enable people understand one another. Work with me (not against me) in this sacred endeavor.

To my Christian readers, what unites us is far greater than that which separates us. In order to properly proclaim the glory of G-d and to speak His Divine truths, it is incumbent upon us to build bridges over the chasms that presently divide us.

Let me begin by first addressing and putting aside two issues. Number One, Torah law prohibits Jews from accepting that Yeshu (or any other human being) is G-d or a G-d, and as such worshiped, or prayed to. The concept of "the word of G-d becoming flesh and dwelling amongst us" (CB John 1:14) is, (in alternate terminology), actually well-known and embraced in Judaism. However, this concept as originally spoken of, and understood in Judaism, is not what is embraced by Christianity today. Further discussion of this issue is outside the scope of our present discussion.

Number Two, Torah law prohibits Jews from abandoning the ritual observance of the Divinely ordained commandments by which Jews live by. Surprisingly, Yeshu taught exactly this, but his original intent has, over many centuries, gotten lost under mountains of Christian theology. These two issues are what divide Christianity from Judaism, not the issue of whether Yeshu was (is, or will be) the Messiah.

Remember this, the concept of a Messiah, as being one who saves one's soul from sin and eternal damnation, is not at all a Jewish concept, and never was. This is an exclusively Christian concept. The Messiah according to Torah, the prophets and Judaism, is a savior in this world, who restorers the lost Kingdom of Israel, physically, in this world. The Torah/prophets/Jewish Mashiah has nothing to do with the spiritual world. The Jewish Mashiah is a political title, not a spiritual one.

With this being said, can a Torah faithful, Orthodox Jew believe that Jesus was (or will be) the Messiah of Israel? Well, it might come as a surprise to both Jew and Christian, but the answer to this question is actually a conditional yes! It all depends upon how what such belief is, and what it means. Let's explain.

First and foremost, I say with assurance that among the many Jewish law codes that outline Torah law, practices and beliefs, none of them include a statement that in any way states that it is out rightly forbidden to believe that the historical Jesus (best to be referred to by his actual historical name Yeshu) was, or will be the Messiah of Israel.

There is no law in Judaism that forbids one to believe that anyone could be the Messiah. The identity of the Messiah is not known, and therefore, the Messiah could end up being anyone who fulfills the messianic prophecies, and has the verified, proper Davidic lineage. The Messiah could thus be you, me, or Yeshu if any of us met the proper Biblical requirements.

Now, with regards to Yeshu, we have a problem. We Jews, unlike our Christian neighbors, believe that Yeshu is long dead, dead and buried. And, with the exception of the Lubavitcher Hasidim, Judaism does not believe that the Messiah can come from the dead. But, let's examine this belief and see, how, from a Jewish point of the view, it could become true.

If the Lubavitcher Rebbe, who is dead, is himself to become the Messiah, then he must be resurrected from the dead. This, in and of itself, would be a miraculous feat, but it still would not substantiate him as being the Messiah. Resurrected or not, he would still have to fulfill the Biblical requirements of being verified from the proper Davidic bloodline, and only then, fulfill all the other Biblical prophecies of rebuilding the physical Temple in Jerusalem, make world peace, and the like. If a resurrected Rebbe can do all this, great, all the more power to him.

Yet, as of today, the Rebbe lies in his grave, and we have no signs of his imminent resurrection. So, how else could he or anyone else dead then come to be the Messiah? Without resurrection, there is still one other way, reincarnation.

Now Orthodox Jews believe in reincarnation (except for a fringe extremist element), and Christians used to believe in reincarnation, but do not any more. So, if the dead were reincarnated, then the soul of someone from the past can indeed, be born again as someone new in the future (or present).

But, here we have a minor glitch. You see, the newborn will now have a new identity, and thus technically is no longer the previous person. We can say that such a one is the reincarnation (gilgul) of the past person, but we cannot say that the newborn is actually that same person. This would be true about Yeshu, the Lubavitcher Rebbe, or anyone else.

Now, Christians circumvent the reincarnation issue, and go directly to the resurrection argument. They claim that Yeshu has already been resurrected, and that right now he is in Heaven, alongside G-d and the angels, which must include the angels Metatron and Sandalphon. Yet, one thing I find interesting, and disturbing, about the Christian record (recorded in the Christian Bible), with regards to Yeshu's ascent into Heaven is that it is strikingly different from other recorded ascents into Heaven. There are definitely certain things missing from the Yeshu account that cast very serious doubt upon its historicity.

In Judaism, we have accounts of two who have ascended to Heaven previous to Yeshu. I speak of Enoch and Elijah. The Bible records Elijah's ascent, whereas Hekhalot (Enochian) literature (prominent in Temple times, and popular in Yeshu's days) records the account of Enoch's ascent. In both of these cases, both men were taken up to Heaven in chariots of fire, and then transformed genetically into creatures very alien to this Earth. Enoch became Metatron, and Elijah became Sandalphon, both creatures of fire, with many wings, and eyes. Essentially, both became angels in Heaven, and therefore, fundamentally, are no longer human.

For Elijah to return to Earth, he must again take on human form, and when he does, he does so only temporarily, and then divests it, to again return to his now permanent form as the angel Sandalphon. Elijah does not reincarnate. He is never born again.

Now, what about Yeshu, how did he ascend into Heaven, and how has he been living there ever since? Did he become an angel too? Some associate Yeshu with Metatron, but this is problematic. For we say that Metatron was Enoch, how then could he be Yeshu?

Granted, Enoch ascended into Heaven, but to suggest then that Enoch/Metatron was later born as Yeshu suggests that a soul once born on Earth, has now been born anew, a second time. One cannot get around it, this would be reincarnation. Is Yeshu the reincarnation of Enoch? If we were to associate him with Metatron, we would have to think so, and this poses a deep theological problem for Christianity that rejects reincarnation!

Also, an angel is no longer human, and thus cannot fulfill the role of being a blood line descendant of House David, such a being is therefore ineligible for the Messianic title.

Can an angelic being be born as a human being? We believe that it can be. However, if Enoch/Metatron was indeed Yeshu, and then he was to be physically born again in modern times, we would again have reincarnation. And, if we were to accept the possibility of this concept, how many charlatans and cult leaders would arise claiming to be the incarnation of Enoch, Metatron or Yeshu? It has happened in the past, why would we think ourselves immune to such deception today?

For a resurrected being to fulfill the role of the Messiah, he would have to remain in the grave, (and thus on Earth), and not have ascended to Heaven. This might work for the Lubavitcher Rebbe. It might also work for Yeshu if, like Jews believe, he is dead and buried. But this cannot work for Christians who believe that Yeshu is in Heaven, and thus cannot possibly be considered human anymore.

When we deal with Biblical prophecies, we have to accept them as they are. The prophecies are clear that the Messiah must be a verified descendant of House David, and if Yeshu was of House David, and if Yeshu did ascend into Heaven resurrected, then he has given up his human identity, and thus cannot legitimately claim it anew.

Then again, there have always been other issues with Yeshu's earthly identity, and claim to the Davidic throne. For Christianity has always proclaimed that Yeshu has no earthly father, be he Jewish, Davidic or otherwise. Anyone familiar with Torah law recognizes that this here creates a serious problem. For G-d's Law so ordains that a son inherits his father. If Yeshu had no earthly father, then he is not in line to inherit anything here on Earth. He is thus not eligible to claim House David lineage.

Granted, if Joseph, the husband of Yeshu's mother, wished to grant him a financial inheritance, he could do that. But, as not personally being a direct blood line of House David from his father, (who is not Joseph, according to Christianity), Yeshu would, therefore, not be qualified for the Messianic title.

And even if we were to overturn all of Christianity's beliefs about the so-called virgin birth, we are still left in a conundrum, in that there are two genealogies recorded for Yeshu, neither of which can be validated, and both of which seem to include information, that if verified, would disqualify him for the Messianic title.

Unfortunately, the Gospel record does not help, or encourage, an authentic Jewish, Messianic claim for Yeshu. But, be this as it may, Jews do not accept the Christian accounts as "gospel truth," so

Jews are not bound by them. Nevertheless, the questions of legitimacy remain.

In his historical lifetime, it is possible, if the genealogy issues were not a question, for Yeshu's followers to have believed that he would, in the future, become the Messiah. Like we said above, there is no Torah law to prohibit one from believing that anyone could be the Messiah. Yet, once Yeshu was dead, the concept of a Messiah from the dead would not have occurred to those in his day. So, for Yeshu's followers to have believed that Yeshu could have been the Messiah, or would have been the Messiah, if he had lived, is not in violation of any Jewish law. But this was then. What about now?

Can a Torah faithful Jew believe today that Yeshu was the Messiah? The answer is no! Once Yeshu died, and did not fulfill all the Biblical prophecies, he can no longer be believed to be the Messiah. If one wants to believe that the Messiah, who is yet to be born, will be the reincarnation of Yeshu, this is a possible belief. But of course, who can prove or disprove any claims about reincarnation?

Yeshu cannot be the Messiah now, because we have no Messiah now, at least not a Messiah in accordance to Torah and Biblical prophecy and law. Therefore, to believe that Yeshu is now the Messiah is unsubstantiated. So, while Yeshu might have had the opportunity to be the Messiah in his day, that opportunity passed with his passing. So, any present consideration about Yeshu is equally disqualified.

All a believer in Yeshu can hope for is the future. Theoretically, it is possible for the Messiah to be a reincarnation of Yeshu, but we have already reviewed the problems with this. And indeed, if Yeshu is dead and buried, like Jews believed, then maybe, like the Lubavitcher Rebbe, he could be resurrected and thus eligible for the Messianic title, if and when we can overcome the huge obstacle of the confusing birthright issue, and conflicting genealogies.

So, there we have it. Technically speaking it is not forbidden to believe that Yeshu will come again someday, and be the Messiah. Yet, as we have learned this can only occur within certain parameters. And under such circumstances the Messiah would technically not be Yeshu, but rather his reincarnation.

As one can see, this issue can get rather confusing. Therefore, it has never been a Jewish concern to try to identify the Messiah prior to his fulfilling all the Biblical prophecies spoken with regards to him. It is really hard to see how Yeshu could ever become the Messiah, and it is definitely impossible to say that he actually was the Messiah in his own lifetime.

The historical Yeshu never accomplished anything that the Mashiah of Torah/prophets/Judaism has to accomplish. The concept of Yeshu having a "second coming" is considered a comfortable theological justification to attempt to justify the lack of Yeshu's fulfillment of Biblical prophecies.

Christianity has developed its theology and stand firmly on it, in faith. So be it! Christian faith and beliefs are not a challenge to Judaism. On the contrary, as long as Christianity continues to embrace Jewish teachings, and the Jewish code of morals, indeed Jews applaud this warm embrace.

And what Jewish teachings do Christians embrace? Almost everything that is recorded in the Gospels, spoken by Yeshu, can be seen in the writings of the Rabbis of the period. It is a true shame that most Christians are not familiar with the Jewish origins of much of what Yeshu taught. If they were so educated, Christians would develop a great appreciation and love for Judaism, a love that I say, is long overdue.

If one wishes to believe that the historical Yeshu was a wise, good and kind Rabbi, one is not prohibited from such a belief, even though such a portrayal goes against every recorded Jewish/Torah tradition. Many missionary groups claim a Jewish affiliation with either Yeshu directly, or some pseudo "First Century" pre-Christian Christianity. Yet, while doing all this, they still maintain allegiance and loyalty to traditional Christian doctrine, theology and beliefs, which in and of themselves are later creations, and not the original teachings of Yeshu, and his Jerusalem followers.

In conclusion, I say that one may, and indeed should, believe as one wishes. One does not need proofs for one's religious beliefs. This is why such beliefs are called "faith."

We can continue a two thousand year argument, or we can move forward, and give glory to G-d, by emphasizing that which unites us, instead of that which divides us. Instead of fighting to the bitter end, let us instead agree to disagree with regards to unprovable theology, and move forward with our common agenda of morality and righteousness.

One day the true Messiah will indeed come. He will fulfill the prophecy in the Book of Zechariah that states on that day, his feet will stand on the Mount of Olives. When that day does finally arrive, I pray that both righteous Jew and righteous Christian will jointly welcome the long awaited Messiah.

On that day, I pray that the first words out of our mouths will not be, "solve our argument, and tell us your name." Rather, I pray that together we will say, Barukh HaBa B'Shem Adonai, Blessed is he whom comes in the Name of the L-rd.

Chapter 11

What to Expect When Mashiah Comes

The nature of Mashiah is often misunderstood. Granted, Mashiah is supposed to come as a savior, to step into the middle of a very nasty war between Israel and its enemies and to destroy those enemies with an overwhelming show of force. Then once Israel is safe and its enemies no more, we are all supposed to live happily ever after. Everyone is supposed to love one another; we expect all to live carefree lives, and life will be blissful and utopian. This is what the majority expect the Mashiah is to accomplish. There is however one simple problem with all this; this utopian fantasy is not what the Biblical prophets prophesied.

The same prophets of the Bible who informed us that there would be a future intervention of superior force to overwhelm and destroy the enemies of Israel also tells us that what follows is no "kumbaya" love fest, similar to a gathering of 60's-style hippies. On the contrary, Mashiah is expected to overwhelm and destroy a lot more than the military enemies of Israel; he is prophesied to also destroy entire segments of human civilization that have not lived up to certain expectations.

Mashiah comes to rule as a king and dictator. Nowhere in any Biblical or later Torah literature does it state, suggest or even insinuate that Mashiah will rule by force of love. The hippies aren't going to make it; neither will the "kumbaya" crowd. Mashiah is not going to be very open to variables or questions to his rule, authority and power. The future King will rule with a rod of iron, not one of rosebuds. Symbolically our Sages referred to this when they said that in present times Torah Law follows the lenient views of House Hillel and when Mashiah comes Torah Law will follow the strict views of House Shamai. Of course this is a metaphor, not to be understood literally, nonetheless, the intent is clear. When Mashiah comes, there will be "no more Mr. Nice Guy."

King Mashiah will not be known for his sweetness, but rather for his swift and quick judgment, which the prophecy states, he will execute by literally smelling the litigants. No trials, no testimony, no deliberations. One sniff and he'll know whether you're guilty or innocent. Mashiah will know all hidden truths and judge telepathically. Some today might not consider this to be the proper liberal way. Then again, where throughout all of Biblical literature is Mashiah ever referred to as a liberal?

Biblical prophecy and later Torah literature all describe the coming of Mashiah as an event of global if not galactic proportion. The consequences of his intervention in human history will certainly not be limited to the nation of Israel. It is prophesied that Mashiah comes with an army of angels from out of the sky. In other words, they literally come from out of this world. And this signifies that not only will Mashiah's invention be global but its influence and affect will reach far beyond the reaches of our planet, and possibly beyond the confines of our presently known universe. After all, where did this "angelic" army really come from? The term Heaven is mythical. It obviously refers to some real place; yet where this place is, in our universe or in another is not clearly understood.

The prophet Zechariah clearly states that Mashiah marches on Earth backed by an army of angels. It amazes me how so many are oblivious as to what this prophecy seems to suggest especially in light of modern technological knowledge. Angels are clearly described in the Bible, some are humanoid entities that seem to glow with some kind of energy; others are clearly described as having multiple faces, animal-like features and other traits that we can only describe as un-earthly. So, when Mashiah appears in the skies over Jerusalem with an army of these entities, I do not believe that such an advent will be recognized in the religious context. I do not believe that those witnessing this event either live or on world-wide television, will be saying, "Look, up in the sky, Mashiah has come!" I think they will use words very different from "angel" or "angelic" to describe the invading Messianic army.

Rather than call out "Hooray! Here comes Mashiah," I believe those witnessing this event will rather call out "Aaahh! Invasion from Outer Space!" Yes, you guessed it, the world will call the coming of Mashiah as an invasion from outer space. In light of today's loss of Biblical religiosity and the embrace of secular science as the new world religion, the world will interpret the fulfillment of Biblical prophecy in light of modern myths. Therefore, Mashiah's coming will indeed be interpreted as an invasion from outer space. And who amongst us can say what is science and what is spirituality, and what exactly is the difference between the two?

Judging from how prophecy describes the way Mashiah and his army is supposed to act, extraterrestrial invasion might be the proper way to understand the coming event. After all, Mashiah's army will display superiority over all the world's technology and weapons. With the greatest of ease, the Messianic army will completely demolish the forces opposing it, just like what we would expect from an invasion from outer space.

Just like in our worst-case scenario science fiction movies, where the evil aliens come, smash the Earth and take over, so in reality, according to Biblical prophecy, Mashiah comes, wipes out a massive army of resistance and then takes over the world. Once he does this, he is not transformed into a loving sweet grandfatherly-type of guy. Nowhere is Mashiah prophesied to go around singing, dancing and hugging everyone in the streets.

Mashiah is not going to be personally accessible to the general public any more than any other present political leader today. No one is going to be able to travel to his seat of government, walk in on him and just say hello. If today one were to attempt to approach a President, Prime Minister or King without permission and clearance such an endeavor would be prevented by a wall of security. Why on Earth would anyone expect access to King Mashiah to be any more lenient? Such a wish or hope is beyond wishful thinking, it is delusional and unrealistic in the highest sense. Even G-d is unapproachable to the angels, so much more so Mashiah will be to the everyday common person.

The prophecies clearly state that during Messianic times much will be expected of the nations of the world and any failure (or rebellion) on their part will be met with terrible consequences. True, all Messianic prophecies speak of a world finally in an utopian state, but arriving at this state and maintaining it is never described as being a simple, free and easy process.

While enlightenment is supposed to be enjoyed by a good portion of the world population, not everyone is to be so blessed. True, they will reap the benefits of the Messianic utopian state but they will still have the ability if not the will to rebel. Mashiah will thus maintain order for a very long time with stern vigor. True, they will beat their swords into plow shears and their spears into pruning hooks and nations will no longer wage war, but where does it say that these events are going to transpire willingly? Just because prophecy states that they are destined to happen, nowhere does prophecy state that they will be desired to happen.

One thing is clear about the Messianic age, religion will become a thing of the past. The entire world's religions, and these include Judaism, will cease to exist in their present forms. The entire human race will be exposed to a grander reality about the universe, our own human past and our collective human future in the greater universe. We will finally have the real answers from those who were there as to what really happened on Sinai, who really were Moshe, Yeshu and Mohammad and all similar questions arising out of religions and spiritual traditions world-wide.

Kabbalistic Messianic prophecies state that during messianic times the human race will advance to such a point that the very wall that divides the physical/spiritual divide will finally be broken down. We will be able to interact with what today we call the spiritual on a regular basis in a very regular way. Spirits will be recognized as another form of real actual life, living in a parallel dimension of sorts. No longer will spirituality be a subject of religion, but rather of science, and not science fiction, but actual science fact. This reality alone is what will shatter everything that is old and usher in upon us all a truly new age for all humanity. But don't think for a minute its revelations will be warmly welcomed and easily embraced.

Even the coming Third Temple is not going to be the religious edifice and return to the past that many today think it will be. The oldest tradition in Torah, recorded in the Talmud itself speaks of the Third Temple descending down from Heaven fully built and that it will "land" of the top of an earthquake adjusted now very high peak that was once Moriah, the Temple Mount. When this grandiose edifice is witnessed descending from Heaven; what will the witnesses call it, a building, or something else? Possibly in the UFO/invasion mindset that will be so prevalent at the moment, many will interpret such an event as the landing of the "mother-ship," something akin to recent Hollywood films.

I pray that I have shown here that the long awaited coming of Mashiah is not going to be what the vast majority in religious circles think it will be. The dawn of the Messianic era will bring with it tremendous iconoclastic upheavals. Almost everything that we all know and believe will be altered, changed or gone. It will indeed be a whole new world and a fresh page in a new chapter for the continuing saga of humanity.

Personally, in spite of all the good that we have today, I am willing to trade it all in for the better world promised to come to us on that day. The great Messianic intervention is a natural process in the continuing evolution of humanity and our world. There is a definite schedule for it, one not of our making, or subject to our influence.

All the Biblical prophecies will definitely come to pass and they will definitely happen in the frightening and other-worldly way which is described. All recent attempts to water-down prophecy and to make it more palatable to modern-day desires will soon be shown up to be the bankrupt deceptions that they truly are. As for me, I say so let it be! I can't wait. Because regardless of where or how I will then be, in this life form or in a parallel one, I'll be there on that day and I'll be darn happy for that!

Long live the King!

Courses Offered Through the KosherTorah School

Available through our website www.koshertorah.com

The following is a selection of courses available at the present time from the KosherTorah School. All course lessons are in audio MP3 for easy downloading and access. Fees and instructions for acquiring the courses are included herein. Please go to our website: www.koshertorah.com for a much larger selection of courses, and classes on many topics in the Bible, Judaism, Kabbalah, Meditation.

1. The Hebrew book of Enoch
Sefer Hanokh also known as, The Ascent of R. Ishmael

A Seventeen (17) Lesson Audio Course Taught by Ariel B. Tzadok

Course Outline

Lesson 1, Chapter 1. **An overall introduction into the experience of *Merkava* ascent.** Ascent is a psychological, astral phenomena. This is why the ascent is properly called a "descent," meaning a descent into the deepest levels of the unconscious, and from there, astrally traveling outside. **This series is geared towards explaining the practical realities of such travels**, with pointers from my personal experiences. The meaning of the Gates and the Guardians, and how their appearances change in accordance to the eye of the beholder (*especluria sh'ayna me'ira/kilpah*). This is not a class just about academic or philosophical ideas and concepts. The connection between the spiritual, psychological and extraterrestrial is fully explained. For those seeking actual spiritual experience and guidance, this is the class for you.

Lesson 2, Chapters 2 – 4. **Secret of the Metatron Race.** Identifying the different races of extraterrestrials that we call angels. How these entities view the human race with disdain. Why Enoch is called Metatron and "Youth". The 70 names of Metatron (and God), how each is understood and perceived differently by all the nations of the world. The race of the Metatrons, preexisting the universe, and where they are now, and what they are doing. How Enoch joined the already existing race of Metatrons, and who they really are. Secrets of the pre-Adamic dragon race, the *Teli*. Secrets of Atlantis, and the fall in Eden, secret of the *Nahash*/Serpent. The objection to Enoch's ascent, and how this led to a rebellion in *Rakia*.

This lesson is the source material of many later *midrashic* teachings. It discusses the great Heavenly plan, and emphasizes why astral ascents of this nature are so vital to one's personal spiritual growth and for the betterment of the entire race.

Lesson 3, Chapters 5 – 7. **The Fallen Angels & the Origins of Idolatry.** Secrets of the tangible life-force energy field called the *Shekhina* / Chi / Orgone / Vril / *Nefesh*. It was an actual energy source that connected ancient Earth to its source world *Aravot Rakia*. After the expulsion of the Adamic race from Eden, human beings searched for a different source of energy and technology in order to run the planet. They tapped into other natural forces. They were taught how to do these things (technologies) by angelic entities who disagreed with God's plan and direction for experiment Earth. Rather than surrendering to the Divine plan, humanity decided instead to forge their own plan, and entities from above assisted them in this effort (both in the past, and in the present). This then is the true form of idolatry. Enoch was taken up to Heaven to serve as witness and proof that project humanity could be successful and that Adamic souls can be successfully integrated into homo sapien bodies. Just how Enoch was genetically transformed for life off Earth will be the topic of the next lesson.

Lesson 4, Chapters 8 – 11. **Genetic Transformations & the Secret of the YHWH Princes.** Enoch was prepared to be altered from a homo sapien human being into whatever form he became. Enoch was placed at the gates of *Aravot*, the place of connection between what the later Kabbalah would call the *Beriatic* and *Yetziratic* universes. In other words, Enoch sat in the 7th Heaven at the veil that conceals the higher 8 – 10 levels of Heaven. Many terms and numbers are referred to which clearly are some kind of code, which to this day, seems unbreakable. Enoch/Metatron serves YHWH as His Divine representative in the lower worlds. *Mashiah* Ben Aharon & the heavenly High Priest. Michael/Metatron. Enoch/Metatron serves as the *Zeir Anpin* (using the later term). There are however Higher Princes, angels who also share the Name YHWH with their Creator. This class discusses the secret relationship of YHWH, Adam and Torah, and concludes with a brief discussion as to what really is the Torah, and what exactly are its secrets.

Lesson 5, Chapters 12 – 14. **Enoch/Metatron, the Little YHWH, Who is Not God!** Enoch becomes Metatron, and Metatron is called the Little YHWH, but this does not make him to be YHWH Himself. Metatron can bear God's authority, but not God's essence. God's name is IN Metatron (as in the angel of the Lord, in Exodus), but he is not God. This relationship between Enoch/Metatron and the

Son of Man discussed in Daniel, and First Enoch, became the foundation of the Christian belief that Yeshu was somehow God incarnate. This class explains the history of this concept, how it began, and how it became what it is today. Enoch/Metatron's authority is over all the Heavens and Earth, that which the later Kabbalah calls the realms of *Asiyah* and *Yetzirah*. All in these domains are under Metatronic authority, and this includes Samael, and all the powers charged by God to test humanity. This class continues to reveal more about the Metatronian race, and humanity's relationship to it, at present, and in the future.

Lesson 6, Chapters 15 – 16. **Metatron, Moshe and Elisha Aher.** We begin with the nature of Enoch's transformation into another life-form capable of permanent existence in his new realm. We also reference Elijah and how his ascent was different. Enoch is Metatron, Elijah is Sandalphon, Metatron in *Yetzirah*, Sandalphon is *Asiyah*, and what this all practically means. Moshe ascended above in astral form. Upon appearing "above," he too is confronted as was Enoch before him. Metatron is dispatched to defend Moshe, but this is not their first meeting. They met earlier at the burning bush, when Metatron served as "the angel of the Lord". Later, Aher ascends. Seeing Metatron, he proclaims that there are two "gods". What he meant was that there appeared to be two different sets of rules as to how the universe operates, the rules of Heaven (under the name YHWH), and the rules of Earth (under the name *Elohim*). Aher is corrected, but makes a terrible choice, requiring the Sages to disavow him because of this choice. More about Aher is discussed in our Legends of the Talmud series, in the class about the Four who ascend Above (from Tractate *Hagigah*). We conclude with practical and relevant lessons about religious extremism.

Lesson 7, **The Seven Heavens & their Angels.** How Rabbinic Judaism is as much a descendant of the Essene school, as it is the Pharisee school. References from the books, *Shoreshei Shemot* and *Malakhei Elyon*, on the names of angels, and how our list in Hebrew Enoch is unique, and not found in later literature. How it is strange that the angels and heavens, as discussed in the Zohar, do not always coincide with the Enoch sources. This class emphasizes the fundamental differences between systems based on personal experience, and those based upon philosophical speculations. Examples are made from the Talmud *Hagigah*, and an episode from Rabbi Yaakov of Merush, who would communicate with angels, and ask them what Heaven says about Jewish ritual law practices. References are also made to Josephus, Qumran, the laws of teaching *Ma'aseh Merkava*, and the difference between the original *Sitrei Torah* (secrets of the

Torah), and the later Kabbalah (Jewish mysticism). Introduction into the 72 Angelic Princes over the nations, and their relationship to the planets.

Lesson 8, **The Angelic Hierarchy, Introduction into the Galactic Government.** First, we discuss the age-old controversy, are angels all incorporeal, or are there those that are physical. We see from the text that their physicality is definitely implied. These entities travel by some means of transportation device, herein called, "horses". Angelic authorities form a strict hierarchy, each with their individual realm of authority and responsibility. Many angel names given herein are not found anywhere else, and may be words in a language that we humans cannot identify. Many angels names are codes, and others are titles, describing the entities field of responsibility. Then come the YHWH angels. These are above *Aravot*, and using the language of the later Kabbalah, reside in *Olam HaBeriah*. Above these stand the one angel, who is two. One over life, and the other over death. We conclude this lesson with deep secrets about the relationship between Metatron and Samael, bringing us an understanding about the Devil and evil as it is revealed through the *Hekhalot* and the Torah.

This class also includes the most direct, and practical full instructions on how *merkava* ascent and astral travel is to be performed.

Lesson 9, Chapters 19-21, **Angel Tech of the *Merkava* Chariot.** Rekhaviel, Hayaliel and the *Hayot*. This lesson indicates that the *Merkava*/chariot (as recorded in Ezekiel) is something more than just a mere form of transportation device. Individual "angelic" entities are responsible for specific parts of its operations, and these entities are endowed with tremendous power and authority. **This class discusses the actual nature of what is the *merkava*/chariot, and what insights we can glean from our text to reveal what its actual function and workings might be.** *The merkava is a life-force, life-giving "machine". It is inter-dimensional, whose function is the sustenance and maintenance of life in existence.* The entity "angels" associated with it at the different levels therein are both individual beings and machines both at the same time. While we read their names in Hebrew, these names are only titles for our present understanding. This class explains more about the visualization/meditative exercises used to glimpse a view of the psychic *merkava*, and how this can be accessed within human consciousness. We also discussed the Golden Spiral, the Fibonacci sequence, and how this fits into, and possibly helps explain, the actual function of the *merkava* living machine.

Lesson 10, Chapter 22, **Secrets of Keruviel YHWH, and the *Cherubim*.** Mission of the *Cherubim*, Crossing the Bridges of Fire. We open with a review of the difference between theoretical religious knowledge and direct spiritual experience. Hebrew Enoch is a book written in code that describes actual, direct experiences with higher realities. We discuss the differences between astral projection (*haluka d'rabbanan*), and seeing higher worlds in expanded consciousness. *Cherubim* are not little babies, but something entirely foreign, and frightening. They serve as part of the *Merkava* machine. We discuss Keruviel YHWH as a *Beriatic* being, and then proceed to describe and identify *Cherubim* from the *Merkava* vision of Ezekiel, chapters 1 and 10. Also mentioned is Ezekiel 9, and the "X" mark placed on the righteous, in the past (and the future). Keruviel YHWH as a *Beriatic* being is a *Neshama*, not a *Malakh*. As such he is one of "Israel" above. What "Israel" above is discussed and how it differs from Israel below. *Cosmic Torah are the laws of nature. Torah on Earth (halakha/the commandments) are how human souls align themselves with the cosmic polarities.*

The *Cherubim* are the entities which, as part of the *Merkava*, serve as the conduit transferring Divine energy and directives from above to below. This is why their form is on the Ark of the Covenant, and why it is specifically a *Cherub*, with a sword of fire, that guards the way to the Garden of Eden. We briefly discuss the Inner Earth Temple, and how the Ark is there being serviced by modern-day Zadokite priests.

We conclude with a discussion of the bridges of fire, and how they are the pathways of psychic/astral ascent, and how each of us, individually, is destined and required to walk this path, no matter how long it takes for us to do so.

Lesson 11, Chapter 26, **The Original Purpose of Apocalypse.** Seraphiel, the *Seraphim* and the Satan. We open with an understanding of the poetic nature of angelic descriptions, and how the original Hebrew texts are used as chants to attempt a personal visual experience of the realities of the individual entities described. How experiential literature (prophetic/*merkava*), starting with Ezekiel and Daniel in the Bible, continued throughout the Temple period and into the Talmudic period, and where this genre of literature is today. The relationship of *Beriatic* angels to souls, souls to the Name YHWH, and how these both relate to *Yetziratic* entities. How there are human souls and "Israel" in every world, on every planet, regardless of dimension or galaxy. The *Seraphim* are the higher *Teli*, the *Beriatic* entities of fire. Their function is to burn the tablets of the Satan, written by Samael and Dubiel that recounts the sins of

Israel. It is clear that Satan is not Samael. These three, Seraphiel, Samael and Dubiel correspond above the triad below of Rome, Israel and Persia. These powers exist on our planet as part of the great Divine plan for the evolution of our world. This is discussed in some detail. *Readings from the book Malakhei Elyon by Rabbi Reuben Margolis showing a relationship between Seraphiel and Adam. Readings from the book Shoreshei Shemot by Rabbi Moshe Zacuto showing a magical formula using the angel Seraphiel.*

Lesson 12, Chapters 28-31. **The Watchers & the Heavenly Court, the Princes of YHWH.** We begin with a discussion about understanding natural law and how everything in the universe requires natural balance. We then review how existence operates under specific parameters and how conscious, sentient entities are part of the fabric of everything to ensure that the Supernal Mind is manifest properly in all its multiple parts. There are a chain of Watchers, from the highest in *Aravot* to the *Teli* here on Earth. We briefly discuss the history of the ancient, holy dragons, and the ones who broke from them in the fall. We discuss how all the individual nations of the world each have equal access to, and relationship with Heaven, each in their own way. How judgment of a soul actually occurs and why. Judgment, including mercy is part of natural law, and part of the operations of the great "machine" of creation. The Princes of YHWH are the members of the Heavenly Supreme Court, who are each called by the name of YHWH. They are part of the collective. We explain what a Throne is, what judgment is, and how it is a natural, ongoing process of alignment of all integral parts into the greater whole which is YHWH. Perspectives of the *sefirot*, internal or external, and why this is important.

Lesson 13. Chapters 43-44. **Journeys Around the Afterlife with Metatron & R. Yishmael.** This class begins with an introduction about the true nature of souls, and the realities they experience outside of human bodies. How the afterlife is perceived as a projections of one's thoughts during life. The *Gan Eden* of Earth and *Gehinom* are considered to be physical locations in Inner Earth, where souls reside all the while that they no longer inhabit human bodies. The nature of souls trapped here on Earth, and what is needed for them to be freed. Righteousness and sin are both calibrations of life force energy, pro and con respectively. Those who calibrate towards righteousness align with life, and ascend, and vice versa for the opposite souls. The reality of the Throne of Glory and the *Beriatic* realm. Newborn souls (*beriatic*) that will only be born once *Mashiah* comes. The nature of disincarnate intermediate souls and how they are rectified. A brief discussion about possessions and exorcisms. The nature of

Divine Justice and the foundation of existence, prayers for mercy and redemption, what delays redemption, and what we must practically do to assist in the great scheme of things to help bring redemption closer. Mention of a meditative exercise to assist one in discovering one's true inner identity.

Lesson 14, Chapters 45 – 46. **The Generations of Man & the Souls of the Stars.** Secret relationship of space/time and consciousness. The invisible universe above ours, the invisible mind (unconscious) within us, and the invisible order and structure that guides them all. The Higher Torah, the natural, universal way, how it existed before Sinai, and how, even now, this Torah exists everywhere. Every nation has this Torah and every nation has its prophets. All is structured and ordained in accordance to quantum probabilities, and in accordance to reverse time, where the future marches backwards into the past. The vortex of meeting when the future past meets the past future is the time when *Mashiah* dawns in our world. The source of astrology, the souls of the stars. Readings from RaMBaM (Maimonides). Stars are alive, living, sentient, self-aware beings. Our future relationship with stars. The natural, way according to Higher Torah, how to understand Jewish Law, through Gemara study.

Lesson 15, Chapters 47 – 48a. **Souls of the Angels, God's Right Hand & the Coming of *Mashiah*.** Angels do have souls. These souls descend into forms for the sake of being conduits of life-force energy. Yet, sometimes these forms are improper, and the "song" they "sing" is wrong. Their forms (bodies) are then deconstructed in the *Nehar Dinur* (River of Fire) that separates the higher and lower dimensional planes. God's Right Hand, a metaphor for the *sefirotic Partzuf Zeir Anpin* (ZA), who is in a state of *dormita* (concealment) during the time of exile. This is symbolically called God's right Hand being tied up behind his back. The redemption begins in this state. Human righteousness contributes. Righteous human consciousness projects into the collective mind seeds of influence to "speed" things up if possible. Yet, the redemption comes "in its time". When redemption comes there will be a comprehensive transformation of human consciousness and the dimensional planes in which it exists. Reference is made to many messianic prophecies. Secret of Inner Earth, the *Kan Tzippur* (Bird's Nest), the age and birth date of *Mashiah* ben David, and the secret identity of the army that supports *Mashiah* in his establishment of the Kingdom of Heaven upon the Earth. Reference is also made to many current events, including the purpose of the existence of the present State of Israel

Lesson 16, Chapter 48b. **Enoch's Ascent & Metatron's Authority.** A review of the entire Enoch legend. How and why a human being was chosen from Earth to ascend to realms beyond, to serve in a position of authority over already existing higher races of beings. The necessity of understanding science and natural truth, and how these themselves are Torah. Therefore, whatever be truth, and wherever it is found, this is Torah. There is thus no separation whatsoever between science and real religion. The scientific understanding of life transforming from one form into another, or how exactly could Enoch be translated from a human being into a being of either pure energy, or into another form that we cannot imagine, and most likely could not even recognize as a life-form.

The race of Metatrons, and where Enoch the former human fit into them, and into God's greater plan for humanity and our planet. Metatron as general over his army of lesser ranked messengers (angels). Metatron in charge of the Watchers (Daniel), and how the Watcher interact with him, and how they can (and do) equally fight with one another. Metatron's relationship with human souls, and the true nature of repentance, how Hebrew *Teshuva*, and eastern Karma differentiate. The fate of the souls of human children who die before having fulfilled their Earth missions.

Lesson 17, **The Seventy Names and Identities of Metatron.** In this final lesson of the series, I summarize and reveal all the secrets of how Metatron is known to all the different nations of the world, (and to citizens of other planets), each by a name and context unique to their individual cultures and religions. We discuss specific names Yahuel, Eved, Ruah Piskonit, the little YHWH, Na'ar, Taftafyah, and clear up the garbled forms of the angel Zagnugael, who appeared to Moshe in the burning bush.

We discuss Moshe' ascent into heaven in his astral body, and how in that body consciousness shifts into astral consciousness, maybe this being what we today call theta and delta brain waves. When he descends back into his body, he forgets the Torah because in the flesh he is back in his alpha-beta mind. Moshe was thus altered to be able to use all four together in perfect harmony. This gave him the ability to read God's Mind, and thus making Moshe, chief of all prophets. Quantum Torah was given on Sinai, the entire Torah is its primordial, non-physical state. This is the universal Torah, the Torah of *Mashiah*, the true secrets of the Torah. All have access to this Torah, whereas Israel alone embraces the Torah of Moshe.

The importance of *Halakha*, the living flow of the living Torah. Who alone has the right to be called a *Rav*, a teacher of Torah. The argument in Heaven between Metatron who taught Moshe the Torah and the angels who were angry at him for doing so. **The healing tradition of Torah, and how it is similar today to that found in certain aspects of traditional Chinese medicine (TCM). The Jewish connection between Native American beliefs and peoples, and Chinese beliefs.** The secret order of using the seventy names from the book *Sefer Heshek*, by R. Eliezer of Worms. This is the order found on my Metatron *Shiviti*.

Course Details
The cost of the course is $340.00.

To purchase this course: Log on to our KosherTorah School website. Click on any one of the links that say "support" or "donate". This will bring to you to our generic payment page. Make payment in the proper amount.
Upon checkout make sure that you note in the "comments box" which course you are purchasing. Write: **"for the _____ Course".** Once your payment has been received you will receive in turn via email a PDF document that includes the class outlines, as well as the links to the online classes.

2. The Kabbalah of Spiritual Contact
The Cultivation of Expanded Consciousness and Extra Sensory Perceptions in the Torah Tradition

Based on the Kabbalistic classic, The Gates of Holiness (Sha'arei Kedusha), Section Three by Hayim Vital. A seventeen (17) lesson audio course taught by Ariel B. Tzadok

Course Outline

Lesson 1 – Chapter 1A. **An overall review of the worlds we call YHWH**
We begin with readings from *Sefer Ba'al Shem Tov* (*V'et'hanan* 71, 69, 66) to establish that our discussion about the supernal worlds is indeed a discussion about the psychological worlds inside us.
All references to worlds, *sefirot*, emanations and the like must be understood metaphorically, and symbolically. We do not associate to them any literalness at all.

There is the Supernal Emanator and then there is the Emanated. The Emanated is YHWH, which is the pattern of all the worlds in existence.

There is a difference between emanation and creation. Discussion explains the relationship of God manifest (YHWH) and the Unmanifest (*Eyn Sof*).

This class outlines the existence of the four/five worlds and their relationship to the ten *sefirot*, which again, are understood a levels of consciousness within the human psyche.

This first class lays the foundations for everything that we will build in the following classes of this course.

Lesson 2 – Chapter 1B. **The Seven Heavens & Extraterrestrial Life**

An overall review of the Seven Heavens understood to be varying degrees of physicality in the universe.

An extended discussion of extraterrestrial life, and the forms that it may take. Relationship of these forms to traditional religious understandings, with reference examples to modern science fiction.

All life follows the general pattern of the worlds, and *sefirot*, therefore, all forms of life to be found on other worlds while physically different, will share similar qualities of consciousness.

Speculations with regards to the subdivisions of *sefirot* levels within *Asiyah/Malkhut* and their relationship to modern discoveries of Dark Matter, and Dark Energy. Comments on the mistake of Geocentrism, and why according to Torah such a belief, while at one time acceptable, (and the norm), is no longer acceptable, or even tolerable. The levels of soul, and how even Maimonides understood that planets and stars were actually sentient life forms, with self-awareness, and cosmic consciousness.

Lesson 3 – Chapter 2A. **The Purpose of Humanity in the Universe, and on Earth**

Why was humanity created in the form of body and soul? Why do we have inclinations towards the highest good, and at the same time, the lowest evil? What is our relationship to other sentient species, those who we call angels? These are the questions R. Vital raises as we begin this chapter.

We review the order of the worlds, emphasizing their psychological nature, and not their metaphysical reality. We speculate about the nature of higher domains in relationship to matter and the speed of light. Levels of consciousness are what define our humanity, and these levels, psychological as they are, also reside in their own domains, which very well may be higher dimensional planes, each being its own independent universe.

We introduce the concept of YHWH of 45 (*MAH*), as it is a reference to "Man" above, and to the many "images" of "Man" below.

We outline the "image of Man," as it refers to the domain of the *sefirot*/*Atzilut*/Creator, and the lower worlds together called creation/the Tree of Knowledge. We elaborate many details regarding this biblical metaphor.

Lesson 4 – Chapter 2B – **The Kabbalah of Human Essence**

The inner domains of the human being, with startling revelations of how the individual and collective unconscious is influenced by specific other-worldly intelligence who definitely do not share human moral values. This is the secret of the "dark light" that masks the angelic races who direct the forces underlying the physical universe. Reference to Daniel's Watchers, the *Teli* dragons, and those of their number who came to Earth with powers and abilities far beyond those of mortal men, and who yet do not at all share human moral values. The forces of life and consciousness that R. Vital takes from traditional Greek philosophical teachings.

Lesson 5 – Chapter 2C – **Human Potential, and the Fifth Element**

All life-forms are conscious sentient beings. Yet, some levels of life have higher levels of consciousness than others. This class reviews the five level, with emphasis on humanity, and the minority within humanity that forms a fifth element, not based on ethnicity or religion, but rather on consciousness, crossing all cultural divides.

The nature of human enlightenment, and its relationship to prophecy and the messianic age.

Lesson 6 – Chapter 2D – **Souls, Angels, Humans**

This lesson describes the relationship between our true Adamic reality as parts of a greater collective which transcends individuality, and every finite physical form. Adamic entities can exist in any form in any dimension, including other physical worlds, and still contain "the soul of man".

What exactly is "the soul of Man (Adam)".

The intermediary function of entities whose role it is to serve as conduits from the collective source of things down to the individual forms in the finite plane. How these intermediary forms are clearly superior to that which is beneath them, but inferior to that which is above them. How and why these intermediary forms exist.

Further discussions explaining levels of consciousness and how these apply to different levels of soul.

Lesson 7 – Chapter 2E – **The Purpose of Good and Evil**

The relationship of the *Neshama* higher Self to the *Nefesh* lower self is explained in detail with the psychological application to the relationship between the conscious mind, and the personal unconscious.

The two inclinations, the *Yetzer HaTov*, and the *Yetzer HaRa* are explained to be emotional factors used to properly calibrate and correlate the *Nefesh* to the *Neshama*.

Good and evil exist within the subjective context of application. The concepts of good and evil are then extended to collective proportions is relationship to the requirements directing human social behavior, and the need for commandments.

This class addresses many relevant, modern issues about religion, tolerance, extremism, and explains many deep theological concepts in a easy to grasp way.

Lesson 8 – Chapter 2F – **The Purpose of Human Incarnation on Earth.**

This lesson is a comprehensive review of everything that Torah, Kabbalah, prophecy, and our KosherTorah School teaches about the truth of human existence, potential, and future.

A comprehensive realistic, and psychological understanding of the "five worlds," what they really mean, and how they are experienced in normal life.

The purpose and practice of meditation and spirituality. The expansion of human consciousness includes intellectual revelation, emotional balance, and all its relevant physical applications, including technological development.

The actual meaning of the messianic era, and the role of future technologies.

Lesson 9 – Chapter 3, **The Hindrances that Block Prophecy.**

Prophecy is the expansion of human consciousness that brings a widening imaginative faculty into strong alignment with the rational mind. When the two are in complete harmony, and communication, consciousness can expand to perceive greater, deeper levels of reality. Such awareness always is attached to some form, object, or things. These become symbolic messengers from one's higher self. These then are one's personal angel, spiritual guide, and guardian angel.

The hindrances are anything from whatever cause, intellectual, emotional, or physiological, that causes confusion in the mind and heart, and/or congestion in the physical anatomy.

Religion is meant to serve as an archetypal expression that gives form to inner, deeper psychological truths, which are the foundation of our humanity.

Religious sin is understood in its proper context as psychological imbalances. This class addresses relevant social, and political issues in light of their affect upon the collective unconscious.

Lesson 10 – Chapter 5, **The Levels of Consciousness, 1**
All souls form a singularity. The path of meditation is to expand individual awareness into higher realms of thought, and perception. The path is for one to discover one's unique individual place. This path is the way of discovery to reveal "the spark of *Mashiah*" within the soul of each of us.

Lesson 11 – Chapter 5, **The Levels of Consciousness, 2**
The differences between dreams, meditation, and astral travel.
When does the soul leave the body to travel into other realms? When does the mind/soul stay put, and instead of ascending into Heaven, bring Heaven down to Earth?
The active and passive nature of developing psychic abilities of the mind.
The power of the imaginative faculty, the point of union between rationalist philosophy, and prophetic Kabbalah meditation.
Practical examples of meditative experiences, with references to Eastern meditative practices, to emphasize the psychological nature of this topic, and thus its global appeal.

Lesson 12 – Chapter 5, **The Levels of Consciousness, 3**
Prophecy and Clairvoyance. The practical development of psychic abilities according to the Torah/Kabbalah and Psychology.
R. Hayim Vital, like Abulafia and Maimonides before him, accepts the belief (originating from the Greek philosophers) that psychic development (in Judaism called prophecy) is a natural development of the refined individual. Psychic powers are not a gift, but can be acquired by anyone who cultivates them. Discussion of using mental constructs to provide forms for higher realities to manifest within the conscious mind. Example of tarot cards and how they are properly read.
The ascent up the *Sefirotic* Tree of Life, and how this image forms the general pattern that enables us to seek internal emotional balance.
The importance of passion (*yesod*) in accomplishing psychic development. Practical examples about sexual attraction, and marital relationships.

Lesson 13 – Chapter 7 – **Prophetic Consciousness in Modern Times**
Understanding the psychological nature of spiritual practices.

Orthodox Judaism is a path for Orthodox Jews, but it is not (and has never been) a path for everyone. The Torah path is a subjective path, it is one of many that leads to the development of the mind, and through this to the development of psychic abilities, which in earlier days were called Prophecy and *Ruah HaKodesh* (Divine inspiration). Reference the teaching of the *Tana D'vei Eliyahu*.

This lesson is geared towards dispelling the myth of the importance of external paths, as opposed to internal paths.

Lesson 14 – Chapter 7 – **Psychic Phenomena in the Kabbalistic Tradition**
There are all kinds of Kabbalistic methods for making spiritual contact. Most are misunderstood in the imagination. This class explains the reality underlying the legends to expose the actual para-psychological parameters of those Kabbalists well-trained enough to experience them.

What it means to experience Elijah the Prophet, and other ancient masters.

The true nature of human inspiration, and its relationship to "Divine" inspiration.

The experience of "cosmic/God" consciousness, and how it differs from experiencing spiritual insights through a mentally conceived form.

The internal power of integrated beliefs, devotion, and righteous behavior.

Also, the commonality of Torah-based experiences with those of various other religions, what we call the sparks of the exiled Torah.

Lesson 15 – Gate 6 – **The Levels of Extra Sensory Perception**
This lesson begins the concluding section of this course, and reviews the four worlds, and ten *sefirot*, and how they are to be viewed psychologically, with emphasis on practical embrace, and experience.

Numerous psychological examples are given to show how the Kabbalistic system actually works.

Emphasis on understanding the realms of the *Klipot*, and a discussion about one addressing one's personal sub-conscious emotional issues.

The ascent through the Palaces and the Gates, the meanings of archetypes, and how they are constructively used.

Again, this lesson makes regular reference to other spiritual traditions to emphasize the psychological reality underlying the Kabbalah of Spiritual Connection.

Lesson 16 – Gate 6 – **Ezekiel's Chariot & the Heavenly Palaces.**
A realistic overview of the ancient practice of *Hekhalot* ascent. All ascent is experienced psychologically, in what I refer to as a mental technology. Palaces,

guardians, and angels are all archetypal experiences, not limited to the individual imagination, although that is where each is visualized, and experienced.

Mental constructs are individualized, active imagination, prophetic vision unique to the individual.

An involved discussion about the realm of the *klipot*, the sub-conscious, and the importance of coming to peace with one's own internal emotional turmoil.

What is and is not an actual extraterrestrial encounter, and how these can be physical, mental or a combination of both.

Lesson 17 – Gate 6. **Kabbalistic Magic and Angelic Encounters.**

What is the actual nature of magic. What is the difference between the fantasy of magic, and its actual psychological, and para-psychological parameters. Discussion of herbology, magic wands, and other ancient forms.

Magical beliefs in society and politics, mention of the Nazi Thule, and the British Golden Dawn, (and of course, Harry Potter).

The levels of prophecy, and the unique nature of the experience of Moshe, who, in my opinion was genetically altered in his actual, and physical close encounter on Mt. Sinai. This is what differed in the nature of his prophetic experience from the later prophets. Explanation of what is means to prophecy through *Beriah* and *Yetzirah*. The world of Metatron, and the race of the Metatrons. What really happened to the four who entered the *Pardes*, and why such endeavors are psychologically dangerous.

What exactly is *Kabbalah Ma'asit*, and how it differs from prophetic meditation, and the usage of holy names, and the like.

The class concludes with an understanding of the nature of Earth spirits and why they are not be disturbed by human invocation soliciting their support, in contradiction to the nature of their missions.

Course Details
The cost of the course is $340.00.

To purchase this course: Log on to our KosherTorah School website. Click on any one of the links that say "support" or "donate". This will bring to you to our generic payment page. Make payment in the proper amount.

Upon checkout make sure that you note in the "comments box" which course you are purchasing. Write: **"for the _____ Course"**. Once your payment has been received you will receive in turn via email a PDF document that includes the class outlines, as well as the links to the online classes.

3. Sefer HaBahir
The book of Brilliance An Ancient Guide To Experiencing Spiritual Truths

A Fifteen (15) Lesson Audio Course Taught by Ariel Bar Tzadok

Course Outline

Class 1

Introduction into the book, its author(s) and its methods. Grecian methods of learning, and how they have become fully entrenched in Judaic literature. Two contradictory verses, with a third that comes to reconcile them. Thesis, antithesis and synthesis. This comes to teach us the Torah fundamental principle that all comes from God, be it good and evil, light and darkness, day and night. The importance of understanding contradictory realities. Quantum reality. The five elements of *Tohu* and *Bohu*.

Class 2

Sections 3 & 4. The meaning of blessing. It is never enough to understand Torah as religion, it must be understood as science. Relationship of the invisible to the visible, white fire to black fire, parallel universe to our universe, dark matter to seen matter. Torah is all around us, laws of Torah are the laws of nature. One does not see the King until one enters His house. One does not get to see YHWH before one enters *Elohim*. *Elohim* is the study of natural law, and science. Science/nature/*Elohim* is the path to YHWH. Zohar says that the gates of wisdom opened in the year 5600, this is technological advancement. This will assist us to bring about the messianic age.

Class 3

Sections 5 – 9. Torah Cosmology. How was the universe created. Biocentrism, readings from the book by Dr. Robert Lanza. Life before creation, not life from creation. Life's source is the unseen, our universe, the seen vessel for Life. How was it divided between the seen and the unseen. What is the relationship of these two, what is their future. First, there was creation, then 730 million years later, something else happened that revealed the Torah from its concealed state to its revealed state. This class will discuss literal cosmology in light of the Kabbalistic metaphorical worlds, of *Asiyah*, *Yetzirah* and *Beriah*.

Class 4

Sections 10 – 14. Cosmic Evolution and the Development of Consciousness.
Evolution occurs both within the cosmic universe and equally within the collective mind of humanity. The invisible (dark) part of our universe that surrounds us forms a unique relationship with the visible universe. This relationship is what the Bible referred to as *Bohu* and *Tohu*. These cosmic dimensions are the source of what we humans call good and evil. We define good as complete and evolved, whereas evil as defined as the incomplete and the evolving. More readings from Biocentrism, by Dr. Robert Lanza. We will also discuss the metaphor of the shapes of Hebrew letters.

Class 5

Sections 15-20. The Hebrew Letters, Poetic Metaphors for the Cosmos.
References from the Talmud *Sanhedrin*, and the *Sefer Baal Shem Tov*. A brief review of the different Hebrew scripts, Paleo-Hebrew, Assyrian script (modern block form), Rashi (*Sephardi*) and modern cursive (*Ashkenazi*). In which script was the Torah given to Moshe on Sinai. Primordial Torah prior to human events. The metaphorical meaning of the letters Alef, Bet and Gimel, and how they relate to the upper triad of *sefirot*, *Keter*, *Hokhma* and *Binah*. Using the symbols of the shapes of the letters to describe the development of the evolution of consciousness.

Class 6

Sections 21-25. The Creation of the Angels, the First Ones and the Second Ones. Relationship of the first evolved entities, the original collective of the Metatrons, the First Ones. Then as evolution progressed into forming this world other races evolved and became the Second Ones, creating a chain of command for the manifestation of the Singular Divine Will. Lessons about lower-case "g" gods, earth spirits, angels and archangels, what they are, and how they view us. Humanity's purpose, why our universe exists, and what purpose it serves.

Class 7

Sections 26-31. Evolution of Mind, the Universe, and Religious Thought.
Religious ideas develop and evolve over time. Secret meanings of the Hebrew word *Ish* (Man) and how this applies to God. This lesson shows the original forms of the teachings about the Small Face of God (*Zeir Anpin, ZA*). Three levels in creation, the higher realm (Hey), lower realm (lower Hey) and the bridge that connects the two (Vav). Many Zoharic and Lurianic lessons have their basis in these Bahiric teachings. Secrets of the Fallen Hey. Secrets of the Rectification

(Ascending Light, *Ohr Hozer*). Concluding lesson about the secrets of *Mashiah* in the Garden of Eden in Inner Earth.

Class 8

Sections 32-35. The Sacred Triad, God & the Invisible and Visible Universe. Not only are there the *"DU Partzufim"* of parallel worlds, there is also the third realm of the Divine that is separate and above them. This lesson introduces us to the idea of the triad, the sacred pyramid. We discuss its development and relationship to the universe in general, the mind of man in specific, and even reference how this idea was adopted into Christianity as the foundation of the concept of the Trinity. Brief mention is made between this idea and the concept of the *sefirot*. Also discussed is the relationship of the Divine source world to our visible universe, and we are designed to evolve and grow.

Class 9

Sections 36-39. Secrets of the Vowels. The vowels used in Hebrew prove that *Sefer Bahir* is a text of a much later period than either Temple or Talmudic times. The vowels are used to describe the relationship between the visible and invisible worlds referred to in later Kabbalah as the *Du Partzufim*. Earlier Torah based mysticism was based on actual experience and ascent into the invisible realm(s). As these practices were being replaced by the theoretical school of mysticism, called Kabbalah, the older experiences had to be explained, because most could no longer experience them. This lesson explains this relationship.

Class 10

Sections 40-46. Original Teachings of the Seven Lower *Sefirot*. Secrets of the Voice of God, the Great Fire and the Word of God. The *sefirotic* pattern is not a theoretical construct, rather it is an expression of the Universal Mind (God) as It manifests from concealed to revealed, and is received by that created in Its Image, that being the mind of man. At Sinai, the Voice above went forth, emanating through the Life Force (*Nefesh*/Chi) energy that permeates all matter, including the human mind/brain, and was there received and interpreted as Words. Thus the revelation of Sinai was telepathic in nature. This still occurs today in the form of the *Bat Kol*. This is also how communication was received via the Ark of the Covenant, through the High Priest's breastplate and the mysterious *Urim* and *Tumim*. All this is discussed in this lesson.

Class 11

Sections 47-50. The Partial Image of the Voice. A discussion about the different levels of Divine consciousness, the masks (*Partzufim*) of God. What actually happened at Mt. Sinai. Reading from Maimonides, Guide to the Perplexed, about the telepathic nature of Torah reception. Relationship of the Metatron class of angels to the Name of God, YHWH. The upper triad of *sefirot* and their relationship to the Heavenly Holy of Holies discussed in the ancient text, 2nd Enoch. *Hokhma*, *Binah*, and the nature of physical movement when the operations of reception (Kabbalah) are operational.

Class 12

Sections 51-55. Secrets of the Upper & Lower Waters, Gold & Silver. Referencing biblical metaphors to describe the nature and relationship of the physical/visible universe with the spiritual/invisible universe. How these universes are accessed. What is their place in the mind and in our experiences. A discussion about the ancient *Pesher* method of personalized biblical interpretations. Also discussed is how the Torah can either be an elixir of life or the elixir of death, all depending upon how one comes to approach it.

Class 13

Sections 63, 92-94. Secret of 32, the 72 Names of God and the Mechanics of Creation. The 32 is heart. This is a symbol for the mechanical operations of creation under the direction of various races of angels. The blue (*tekhelet*) in *tzitzit* represents the life force energy of biocentric consciousness (*nefesh*) that serves as the sign that God is the author and director of the system. This class explains the actual nature of the relationship between the dimensional planes, and how they actually operate in what I call a "mechanical" order. We discuss higher life forms, dimensional and planetary travel, and shape-shifting for the sake of intergalactic relocation (Enoch, Elijah).

Class 14

Sections 95-96, 98-99. Secrets of the Guardians of the Universe. The quantum universe operates in accordance to laws in three dimensions, space, time and consciousness. These are ruled over by three levels of "administrators" (angels). Human consciousness is a necessary component for discovering the proper "theory of everything". Light matter and dark matter. *Ophanim*, Dragons (*Teli*), *Hayot*, *Cherubim*. How other entities direct the universe, and direct human consciousness through direct (and indirect) telepathic contact. The heart, the purpose of Israel in the human race. The inner Garden of Eden.

Dangers of violating the laws of time, and space. Together with Class 13, these two lessons reveal a tremendous amount of secrets about things that are popularly questioned today.

Class 15

Sections 101-112. Secrets of the *Teli*. The secret identity of the Holy Servants of God in control of space, time and consciousness in a quantum universe. Their relationship to the *Merkava*, and Gavriel, Mikhael and Uriel. Their relationship to righteousness and the 36 righteous in each generation (the *Lamed-Vav*). The secret of the cosmic spiral where left and right turn and reverse, the secret of the Ouroboros. The secret of the Aharonic blessing, the three Names YHWH and the vowels to be used for its projection as a blessing. Secrets of projecting into the collective consciousness the powers of good and change, or evil and destruction, the warning of what goes around comes around. The secret Twelve Names of the Ascent through which one makes contact with the *Teli* and requests of them that which is to be requested. This class, along with classes 13 and 14 in the *Bahir* series form a triad which reveals secrets and meditative techniques that I have never previously discussed.

Course Details
The cost of the course is $300.00.

To purchase this course: Log on to our KosherTorah School website. Click on any one of the links that say "support" or "donate". This will bring to you to our generic payment page. Make payment in the proper amount.
Upon checkout make sure that you note in the "comments box" which course you are purchasing. Write: **"for the _____ Course".** Once your payment has been received you will receive in turn via email a PDF document that includes the class outlines, as well as the links to the online classes.

4. The Holy Names & their Usages
Jewish "Magic" a Ten-Hour Audio Course with R. Ariel B. Tzadok

Course Outline

Class 1 – **The 72 Triad Name of God, Lesson 1,** from *Pardes Rimmonim* of Rabbi Moshe Cordevero. The origins of the 72 triad name. The Zoharic explanation of its boustrophedon structure. The *sefirotic* relationships. Two different sets of vowels. Relationship of the *pasukim*, triads and letters. The meaning of the number 72. An overall explanation of how the name is understood in the theoretical school of Kabbalah, to distinguish this understanding from our following lessons showing the magical/prophetic properties of the name in Raziel, Abulafia, Vital and Zacuto.

Class 2 – **The 72 Triad Name of God, Lesson 2,** from the writings of R. Eliezer of Worms. *Sefer HaShem*, the book of the Name, and a special formula for using the Names in a ritual for healing. *Sefer Raziel HaMalakh*, the three orders of the Names and how in groups of 7 they are used for individual purposes, included are the Names, the invocations, and hints as to the proper hours and days when each is to be used. This lesson clearly shows the contrast between the theoretical school and the magical school.

Class 3 – **The 72 Triad Name, Lesson 3** from the writings of Avraham Abulafia and Hayim Vital. An overview and comparison from Rabbi Vital's *Shaarei Kedusha* and original insights from Rabbi Abulafia's works, *Hayei Olam HaBa* and *Sefer Heshek*. An overall usage of the 72 Name as a meditative tool, with the two Rabbis describing two differing forms for its usage. This class is an excellent review of the Abulafia techniques, which include active imagination and cultivating inner dialogue with one's higher self and spiritual guide.

Class 4 – **The 72 Triad Name, Lesson 4** from the book *Shoreshei HaShemot* of Rabbi Moshe Zacuto. Rabbi Zacuto was a secularly trained cosmopolitan Rabbi in the 17th century, living mostly in Amsterdam and Venice. Yet, as a Kabbalist, he authored this text which is unique as it serves as an encyclopedia for all holy names known at the time. In review of the 72 Name, Rabbi Zacuto references traditional material from Cordevero (covered in class 1), and some material from Vital (covered in class 3). The Rabbi then strikes out and adds outright magical material from sources not named. He includes various usages for each name, with angelic associations. He then proceeds to outline other forms of combining the three verses that construct the name and gives magical formulas for their usage. We conclude with looking at yet another name of 72 made up from three different verses from the first chapter of Ezekiel.

Class 5 – **Ana B'koah, the Name of 42, Lesson 1** from *Pardes Rimmonim*, *Sefer HaKana* and the *Shoreshei Shemot*. The similarities and differences between these three texts. This Name is unlike the 72. It is not mechanical, it is authentically alien. Like the 72, the 42 corresponds to angelic names, but unlike the 72, the 42 has two sets of names, one of which are familiar "*el*" names, and then another set of stranger, unfamiliar names. How these names are used, how the 42 is merged with YHW and not YHWH as is the 72. This is the name associated with creation, how this is so. The secret of the vessels, angels, *Elohim* that brought forth this universe.

Class 6 – ***Ana B'koah***, **Lesson 2,** magical uses of the individual names from *Sefer Shoreshei Shemot.*

Class 7 – **The 22 Letter Name** from *Birkat Kohanim* in *Pardes Rimonim*, the 12 letter Name from *Sefer Refuah vhayim mYerushalayim,* the name on the staff of Moshe. From Rabbi Nehuniah ben Hakana in *Pardes Rimonim*, the names of Heaven and Earth in the *Hekhalot* tradition, *Araritah* and *Ahoy.*

Class 8 – **Alphabetical List of Other Names,** including *Malakhim* from *Sefer Shoreshei Shemot.* The psychology of psychic projection that makes these types of activities actually work. The secret of the "prince of the cup". Gazing into a full cup to seek images that will communicate hidden knowledge. This was the practice of the magical cup ascribed to the biblical Yosef.

Class 9 – **The Alphabet of the Angels.** Selections of Names and Practices from *Shoreshei Shemot.* Select Names include Dikarnosa, Taftafya, Tzamarkad and others. Also covered is the pendulum meditation, in full details. Review of angelic letters, paleo-Hebrew and their relationship. Readings from *Sanhedrin* 21, with regards to what was the original script of the Torah. According to Rashi, it might have been angelic script. Using the *Mezuzah* as an amulet of protection.

Class 10 – **Laws of Using *Kabbalah Ma'asit*.** Readings from Rabbi Hayim Vital. *Sha'arei Kedusha*, Section 3, Chapter 6 defines for us what is *Kabbalah Ma'asit*, and thus also defines what it is not. We see that *Kabbalah Ma'asit* does not include the usages of Holy Names. *Sha'ar HaMitzvot, Shemot* also repeats the warnings of the *Sha'arei Kedusha*, but adds an important detail. One who meets a certain criteria as outlined in the Talmud, (*Avodah Zara* 35b) can and should use Holy Names. We review this Talmud for clear elucidation. We then proceed to review Rabbi Hayim's own use of *Kabbalah Ma'asit*. We learn how to call upon the dead to come to one in a dream (*Sefer Peulot*). We see the original "body of God" *Shiur Komah* in Rabbi Hayim's commentary to the magical text *Brit Menuha*, and we conclude with Rabbi Hayim's references to which angels perform which function, and how they are called upon. This is the final class in Semester 3.

Course Details
The cost of the course is $200.00.

To purchase this course: Log on to our KosherTorah School website. Click on any one of the links that say "support" or "donate". This will bring to you to our generic payment page. Make payment in the proper amount.
Upon checkout make sure that you note in the "comments box" which course you are purchasing. Write: **"for the _____ Course"**. Once your payment has been received you will receive in turn via email a PDF document that includes the class outlines, as well as the links to the online classes.

About Ariel Bar Tzadok & the KosherTorah School

Rabbi Ariel proudly welcomes to the KosherTorah School all peoples, of all backgrounds, who wish to learn about the authentic and original Biblical world outlook.

KosherTorah is not just about the Bible.

KosherTorah is not just about Judaism.

KosherTorah is not just about religion.

KosherTorah is not just about G-d.

KosherTorah is about us!

KosherTorah is about building bridges!

KosherTorah is about becoming a more decent human being!

KosherTorah is about common sense, simple living, righteous behavior, and liberty and respect for all.

For over thirty years, Rabbi Ariel has been a world renowned expert of the authentic, Biblical "Secrets of the Torah" teachings, that many today simply call "Kabbalah."

Rabbi Ariel teaches the sulam aliyah (ladder of ascent) school of Kabbalah, which consists of the Biblical teachings of the works of Ezekiel's chariot (Ma'aseh Merkava), and the prophetic meditative techniques passed down through the centuries.

The purpose of these teachings is to cultivate actual, authentic, and personal spiritual experiences, the likes of which are psychological, and transformational. The purpose of spirituality is to explore one's inner self, and to discover, and unleash one's inner, latent potentials. To this task is the KosherTorah School dedicated.

While knowledgeable of the theoretical/philosophical schools taught by others, Rabbi Ariel places special emphasis on teaching the "other schools" which most today are unaware of, or not qualified to teach. These specifically are the prophetic/meditative and so-called "magical" schools. Rabbi Ariel teaches others HOW-TO practice these ancient methods for each individual to acquire their own unique spiritual experiences.

The KosherTorah School focuses on teaching Biblical, and later mystical literature in a rational way to enable the student to extract their universal teachings from their numerous layers of myth and metaphor. The school proudly serves the educational needs of a global audience, and welcomes students from all walks of life.

Born and raised on Long Island, New York, Ariel Bar Tzadok studied abroad in Israel for a number of years. He studied in Jerusalem at the premier Sephardic institute, Yeshivat Porat Yosef (Old City), and later in Kollel Hekhal Pinhas. While studying for his rabbinic ordination, he was blessed to become the private student of the renowned Kabbalist, Rabbi Meir Levi, *obm*, the foremost student of the leading Kabbalist of Jerusalem, Rabbi Mordechai Sharabi *obm*.

In June 1983, Rabbi Ariel received his rabbinic ordination (Haredi/Orthodox) from Rabbi Ya'akov Peretz, Rosh Yeshiva (Dean) of Kollel Hekhal Pinhas, and Beit Midrash Sephardi in the Old City of Jerusalem.

Rabbi Ariel augmented his religious education with studies in the other religions of the world, esoteric studies and practices, philosophies and psychological systems, particularly studying Jungian psychology at the Jungian Center in New York.

In 1992, after teaching privately for many years, Rabbi Ariel officially established his school (with the original Hebrew name Yeshivat Benei N'vi'im) to address the growing concerns of spiritual misguidance, and misinformation that is pervasive in the Jewish community at large. Since then, while staying faithful to his Orthodox Torah origins, Rabbi Ariel has expanded the KosherTorah School to meet the needs of an ever widening audience.

Rabbi Ariel is a regular featured guest on the popular TV program Ancient Aliens. He also appears in other TV programs, speaks on radio talk shows, and is published in scholarly journals and newspaper articles. His YouTube page hosts hundreds of his videos and he regularly teaches live public classes on Facebook. He has spoken before religious congregations, university groups and lectures around the country.

Made in the USA
Las Vegas, NV
08 July 2024